complete kitchens

plan & build your dream kitchen

Better Homes and Gardens® Books
Des Moines, Iowa

Better Homes and Gardens® Books
An imprint of Meredith® Books

Complete Kitchens
Editor: Paula Marshall
Project Editor and Writer: Lisa Kingsley
Art Director: Mick Schnepf
Copy Chief: Terri Fredrickson
Copy and Production Editor: Victoria Forlini
Editorial Operations Manager: Karen Schirm
Managers, Book Production: Pam Kvitne, Marjorie J.
　Schenkelberg
Contributing Copy Editor: Kim Catanzarite
Contributing Proofreaders: Ellen Bingham, Sue Fetters,
　Willa Speiser
Contributing Photographers: n-haus photography
Contributing Illustrator: TheArt Factory
Indexer: Kathleen Poole
Electronic Production Coordinator: Paula Forest
Editorial and Design Assistants: Kaye Chabot, Karen
　McFadden, Mary Lee Gavin

Meredith® Books
Publisher and Editor in Chief: James D. Blume
Design Director: Matt Strelecki
Managing Editor: Gregory H. Kayko
Executive Editor, Home Decorating and Design: Denise L.
　Caringer

Director, Operations: George A. Susral
Director, Production: Douglas M. Johnston

Vice President and General Manager: Douglas J. Guendel

Better Homes and Gardens® **Magazine**
Editor in Chief: Karol DeWulf Nickell

Meredith Publishing Group
President, Publishing Group: Stephen M. Lacy
Vice President-Publishing Director: Bob Mate

Meredith Corporation
Chairman and Chief Executive Officer: William T. Kerr

Chairman of the Executive Committee: E. T. Meredith III

All of us at Better Homes and Gardens® Books are
dedicated to providing you with information and ideas to
enhance your home. We welcome your comments and
suggestions. Write to us at:
　Better Homes and Gardens Books
　Home Decorating and Design
　　Editorial Department
　1716 Locust St.
　Des Moines, IA 50309-3023

If you would like to purchase any of our home decorating
and design, cooking, crafts, gardening, or home
improvement books, check wherever quality books are sold.
Or visit us at: bhgbooks.com

contents

1

one room many ways

KITCHENS ARE THE HEART AND HEARTH OF THE HOME. They are multifunctional places for preparing and enjoying meals, working on projects, and simply spending time with family and friends. Some kitchens serve the needs of the serious cook, others the weekend cook. In this book, you'll find kitchens for those seeking simplicity and those wanting every up-to-date convenience. Many new kitchens come outfitted with professional-style appliances and a combination of work surfaces. If you love to cook and entertain, such options may appeal to you. Or perhaps your needs are simpler. Consider your current lifestyle and your kitchen requirements as well as those you'll have in the future. A kitchen that looks great and works efficiently enhances both your home and your life.

This renovated kitchen is modern in its efficiency while retaining the early 20th-century style of the house. Period lighting, cabinetry, and hardware are at home with a professional-style range that really cooks. The blackboard keeps every member of the household in touch and on top of appointments, schedules, and to-do lists.

Where there is food, people will follow. Or, in movie parlance, you might say: If you cook, they will come. The inviting smells emanating from the kitchen and the fun of hanging out with the cook—and whoever else shows up—draw family and friends to the kitchen.

The kitchen/family room combination has been around for centuries, only it used to be called the "keeping room." Now a gathering spot adjacent to and open to the kitchen is an indispensable component of many homes and at the top of many homeowners' wish lists.

A perfect time to renovate the family room or add a gathering place to your current kitchen is during a kitchen renovation. If you can't bump out a wall, consider annexing a portion of an adjacent room. Even a sliver of space can be transformed into a warm and cozy place to hang out. With all the use it will get, you won't regret carving out a corner for a sofa, a television, and a comfy chair or two.

The benefits of having a gathering place are many. Kids can be kept under surveillance while they watch television or work, surf, or play games on the computer; they can do homework, practice musical instruments, or pitch in by peeling vegetables while the cook makes dinner. The cook can catch up on world events while he or she whips up dinner, and when guests end up in the kitchen during parties and holiday gatherings—as they always seem to do—there will be a comfortable place to seat them.

A gathering place

This kitchen/family room combination, *opposite*, has it all: An efficient kitchen with an island that has plenty of counter space and a place for casual meals, a fireplace, and a desk for menu planning and bill paying. Although the room is large, it feels warm thanks to the earthy colors and relaxed style. Just how much a kitchen is open to a dining room or family room varies. The pass-through, *above*, allows food and dishes to move easily between kitchen and dining room without exposing kitchen clutter. The kitchen, *right*, is at the center of things in the primary living space of this house. On one end of the elongated "shotgun-style" room is dining space surrounded by windows; at the other is a comfortable family room. The hardworking kitchen component anchors and ties it all together, featuring lots of counter space and stylish storage.

Here's proof that everything old is new again: The unfitted kitchen is back. The unfitted kitchen resembles kitchens of 100 years ago, in which there was a pie safe here, a free-standing hutch there, and maybe a big pine table that served as both food-preparation and dining surface in the middle of the room. In a fitted kitchen, the perimeter of the room is ringed with floor-to-ceiling cabinets.

Fitted and unfitted kitchens both have their strong points: A fitted kitchen is much more efficient in its use of space; the look of an unfitted kitchen is homey and personal.

Fitted or unfitted?

The unfitted kitchen in this renovated older home, *opposite,* features a mix of painted and stained wood surfaces, free-standing furniture (including an antique buffet that holds a gleaming modern espresso machine), and open shelving. The whimsically hand-painted armoire, *below opposite,* well suits an unfitted kitchen. It serves not only as storage space for dishes, kitchen linens, and canned goods but also as decorative art. Unfitted kitchens work well in large spaces where appliances and cabinetry don't have to fit together seamlessly. In places where every inch counts, however, fitted kitchens—such as those at *right* and *below*—feature clean lines and offer maximum cabinet space, room for appliances, and the most storage bang for your remodeling buck.

The trophy kitchen

Identified by gleaming stainless-steel surfaces and professional-style appliances such as this range, the trophy, or gourmet, kitchen caters to serious cooks. This one is outfitted with warming drawers and a wine refrigerator.

In an age of celebrity chefs and TV cooks who hold viewers' rapt attention while they toast sesame seeds, the evolution toward trophy, or gourmet, kitchens has come about naturally. Professional-style ranges, gleaming stainless-steel refrigerators, warming drawers, and wine coolers are a few hallmarks of trophy kitchens. The promise that a top-end kitchen holds is inviting, but here's a caveat: Genuine commercial appliances are massive, poorly insulated energy hogs intended for restaurant use. To get the features and no-nonsense look of a trophy kitchen without the drawbacks, look for the new high-performance options created for the home. An array of hybrid "pro-style" appliances offer the brawn of cast iron, heavy-gauge stainless steel, and the wide range of Btus that allow professional cooks to sear a steak in a flash and melt chocolate without worry of scorching it. These appliances are also equipped with user-friendly features, such as electronic controls and insulated housings that allow for "zero-clearance" installation with standard cabinetry. Indulgent luxury or not, a gourmet kitchen suits the adventuresome cook.

The eat-in kitchen

In even the smallest kitchen, a space can be carved out for casual family meals, snacks, and quick breakfasts. A banquette tucked into a corner, *below*, is a space-saving way to incorporate dining space in the kitchen.

2

your home, your lifestyle

KNOWING WHAT KIND OF KITCHEN SUITS YOUR NEEDS is really about knowing yourself. When you move into anything but a new custom-built house, you inherit a kitchen that was built with someone else in mind. Remodeling gives you the opportunity to fashion a space suited to your lifestyle and to your personal style. Thinking about how you live and work in your current kitchen will help you make the vast number of decisions necessary in designing your new kitchen. Then there are those questions that deal directly with the renovation process, such as budget and time frame, that must be answered. Decide how much you expect to spend, how much you're willing to spend, and the amount you absolutely cannot exceed. By answering the questions raised in this chapter, you'll get a sense of your own situation, what your specific needs are, and what the project will involve. Then you can begin to create a design and a plan.

Communing with the great outdoors was a high priority in this kitchen's remodeling job, *opposite*. A wall of windows in the dining area creates the impression of alfresco dining all year long; sparkling mirrored backsplashes between base and upper cabinets enhance the feel by reflecting natural light and outdoor views.

Cooking in small spaces

Do you need a bigger kitchen or just a better one? Even the smallest spaces, such as this galley kitchen, *above*, can be efficient, beautiful places to work.

How is your kitchen used?

The most successful kitchen renovations fit the habits, preferences, plans, and needs of everyone in the household. To gather that information, many professional kitchen designers use a comprehensive questionnaire developed by the National Kitchen & Bath Association. You can do the same, using this sampling of the considerations covered in the questionnaire.

THE COOKS. Who is the primary cook? The secondary cook? Is the cook left-handed or right-handed? How tall is he or she? Does he or she have any physical limitations? Does anyone else in the household have any physical limitations? How many other household members cook? Do they have a cooking hobby, such as baking or grilling, or do they assist the primary cook with a specific task?

USE OF THE KITCHEN. At what time of the day is the kitchen used most frequently? What secondary activities, such as crafting, bill paying, or homework, take place there? Socializing? Computer use? Desk work? Laundry?

TABLE SPACE. Do you want counter seating? Table seating? How many seats will you need?

COOKING HABITS. Do you heat prepared foods or cook from scratch? Do you cook in large quantities? Do you do specialty cooking?

ENTERTAINING. Do you entertain frequently? Formally or informally? Do you need a wet bar? Buffet area? Where do you like your guests to be while dinner is being prepared?

PRODUCT STORAGE. Do you shop weekly or daily? Do you buy much fresh food? Canned or packaged goods?

KITCHEN ORGANIZERS. What specialized storage do you require? How do you plan to sort and store recyclables? What small electrical appliances do you use?

ADJOINING SPACES. How do you want the new kitchen to relate to the family room? Dining room? Home office? Laundry or mudroom?

Batterie de cuisine

If you're an enthusiastic cook, you may need more than the usual amount of storage space for pots and pans, such as in the kitchen, *above*.

The faces of a cooking space

You make your morning coffee and evening repast in the kitchen. But most kitchens have secondary roles too, as demonstrated by the photos, *above*. Kitchens act as impromptu garden sheds for potting plants or arranging flowers; as media rooms for catching up on the day's events while dinner cooks; and as spots to relax over a crossword puzzle and a cup of tea.

Assess your kitchen

Just as there is no such thing as a one-size-fits-all kitchen, no single formula transforms every beastly kitchen into a beautiful one. By considering the good and bad points of your current kitchen—and by conjuring up your dream kitchen—you can pick and choose the essential ingredients for a kitchen-planning recipe as individual as you are. On that note, ask yourself some questions about the kitchen you have now and about the kitchen you want.

HOW DO YOU USE your kitchen now? Simply as a way station for food storage and access, or as a versatile space to interact with others?

HOW DO SIMPLE TASKS, such as putting away groceries, finding cookware, storing dishes and tableware, or tossing garbage, reveal inconvenient features of the current layout? Trace your steps for a typical kitchen experience.

HOW OFTEN DO YOU use a stepladder or get down on your knees to get things you need?

WHEN YOU BRING ITEMS TO or from the table, is your route a "direct expressway" or a "multiple detour zone"?

WHEN YOUR ARMS are loaded with groceries, do you have a convenient place to set them before they can be organized and put away?

ARE YOU MASTER of the microwave oven or maestro of the eight-course meal?

DO YOU COOK SOLO, with a partner, or with helpers?

DO YOU WANT/NEED an eat-in kitchen?

DO YOU SPECIALIZE IN BAKING, candymaking, stir-frying, or other culinary adventures?

WILL YOUR NEW KITCHEN CATER to children or to teenagers? How many?

DO YOU WANT A self-contained kitchen or one that's open to a dining room or family room?

HOW MUCH CAN YOU DO yourself, and how much will be done by a professional?

IF YOU NEED TO EXPAND, can you borrow space from an adjacent room, or is it smarter to add square footage to the house?

HOW MUCH CAN YOU reasonably afford to spend? Where would you like to splurge? Where are you willing to compromise or economize?

DO YOU WANT A TUCKED-AWAY PLACE for everything and everything in its place, or is hands-on accessibility more important?

DO YOU NEED a bigger kitchen or just a better one? What matters most: tons of storage, generous work surfaces, top-of-the-line appliances, easy maintenance, a step-saving floor plan, or beautiful materials?

DO YOU ENTERTAIN on a large or small scale, and how often? Where do your guests seem to gather? Does your plan cater to special occasions or to everyday needs?

Your head is probably spinning from all these questions, but dealing with such issues up front helps you identify specific features to remove from your old kitchen or add to your new kitchen. When a solution is tailored, it will be one that fits the real you. Mull over the answers in your mind as you read on; the checklist later in the chapter will help organize your thoughts.

How much change?

A coat of paint does wonders in making your kitchen look new, but the room won't function any better because of it. Deciding on how much change is necessary is a crucial step in the planning process.

Think about what you like, or at least what you can live with, in your current kitchen. Maybe the layout you have is the only one that will work without moving windows and doors, and your budget won't allow that, but you can afford new floor-to-ceiling cabinetry, which will boost storage space. Perhaps enlarging just one window to let in more light will brighten the room's character. As you decide on the degree of change to make, consider these basic levels of remodeling and work your plan around them:

FRESHEN UP THE ROOM with new paint or wallpaper, new lighting and plumbing fixtures, new flooring and new furnishings. This may mean you keep your cabinets but either paint them or reface them and replace the hardware. You may or may not replace the countertop surface and backsplash. Major appliances remain in place.

INCREASE THE AMOUNT and efficiency of the storage space in your kitchen and upgrade electrical and plumbing services. In this scenario, you may buy new cabinets and rearrange the layout of your kitchen to make it better suit your needs. You may or may not purchase new major appliances.

REARRANGE EXISTING SPACE by adding or removing walls, windows, and doors. This is a complete renovation, including new cabinetry and new appliances.

CLAIM OR REWORK an adjacent space. Say there's a sunroom or a breakfast room or a mudroom that opens up into your tiny kitchen, and you've been longing for an eat-in area. This scenario would include annexing that space as part of your new kitchen and, obviously, knocking down walls.

BUILD AN ADDITION. Although it sounds major and expensive (and it can be), an addition can range from a simple bump-out on one wall to incorporate a banquette to an entire family room/kitchen space with a vaulted ceiling and attached greenhouse.

MOVE THE KITCHEN'S LOCATION in the floor plan of your home. This scenario means you are remaking another space in the house into the kitchen—one not likely outfitted with the proper plumbing and electrical systems to be a kitchen. You may not need new walls, but, like putting on an addition, relocating the footprint of your kitchen requires that you start from scratch with new cabinetry, plumbing and electrical systems, and appliances.

Small changes, big impact

Tearing downs walls isn't always the way to a new kitchen. The cabinets in the diminutive kitchen, *above*, got a buttery yellow coat of paint. The cabinets in the kitchen, *below*, were refaced and fitted with new hardware. With limited budget and effort, both kitchens got a major freshening up.

Know thyself

Doing much of the labor yourself can save you a bundle of money. Those improvements that are primarily aesthetic—paint, wallpaper, replacing light or plumbing fixtures—are easily accomplished by a homeowner who has modest experience. With the step-by-step instructions for redoing a kitchen from the ground up in Chapter 8 ("Building Blocks") and Chapter 9 ("Form and Function"), you can take hammer in hand with the necessary confidence to do small structural, plumbing, and electrical jobs. However, for the truly big jobs or those that require knowledge and expertise—such as moving load-bearing walls, running new drain or vent pipes, rewiring the whole house, or installing a solid-surface countertop—you'd be wise to call in a professional.

Be realistic about your own abilities, patience level, and commitment to doing it yourself. Consider your skill and confidence levels with the following scenarios. Trust yourself; you'll know when to tackle the project and when to hire a pro.

On removing a wall

WHEN TO HIRE A PRO: Have a professional builder check the wall to determine whether your wall supports an upper floor and whether it contains a lot of pipes and electrical wires.

IF YOU WANT TO GET A SNEAK PEEK or some initial idea on your own of what you're dealing with, knock a small hole in the ceiling. If the joists that support the floor above run parallel to the wall you want to remove, chances are the wall does not provide support to the upper floor. If the joists are perpendicular to the wall in question, it probably is a load-bearing wall.

On semiskilled jobs

WHEN TO HIRE A PRO: Let's say, for instance, that you have successfully cut and glued the tile to the backsplash, but you're having a hard time getting around to grouting the tiles. Hire a professional to apply the grout. If one part of a project is wearing you down—you either can't find the time or you don't have the desire—go for a pro. Having someone else take over for a time will be a relief.

On hiring an electrician

WHEN TO HIRE A PRO: Unless you're a licensed electrician, the only safe option is to use a professional to do major work on this system. With careful work, you can tackle smaller jobs, such as running a new electrical circuit (page 122) or installing light fixtures (pages 171–177).

More do-it-yourself advice

RESEARCH. Read home improvement magazines and books to get ideas and information. Ask salespeople questions before you buy to find out about costs, maintenance, ease of installation, and any other important information.

DON'T BE IN A BIG HURRY, or you'll pay for it straight out of your wallet. Take time in the design planning stage. Think it through. Take time selecting materials and doing the labor. When your kitchen remodeling project is complete, you'll savor the final masterpiece.

Calling Michelangelo

If your vision includes projects that require special skills and finely tuned artistic ability not in your repertoire, such as this fair fowl floor, *below*, call in a professional.

Kitchen Wish List

Planning for the kitchen you want requires understanding the kitchen you have, then imagining what you'd like to change and how you'd change it. This wish list will help you identify what kind of kitchen you're living with now, what its drawbacks are, and what your needs are. Don't worry if you can't answer every question immediately. Chapters 1–4 of this book are designed to help you make decisions. Fill out what you can now, then complete the rest of the form as you find out more about the design and product choices available to you. If you decide to work with a design professional, take this wish list with you, along with the dimensions of your kitchen. You'll have a solid start.

KITCHEN TYPE

	The Kitchen I Have	The Kitchen I Want	What Do I Love?	What Do I Hate?
Galley	☐	☐	_____	_____
L-shape	☐	☐	_____	_____
U-shape	☐	☐	_____	_____
Island	☐	☐	_____	_____
Dual workstation	☐	☐	_____	_____
____ Age of existing kitchen			_____	_____
____ Number of people using the kitchen (or projected number if family is growing)			_____	

KITCHEN USES

	My Current Kitchen	My New Kitchen
Light cooking (fast-food prep or cooking for one or two)	☐	☐
Family cooking (large meals for families or planned leftovers)	☐	☐
Gourmet cooking (specialty baking, international cuisine, party food)	☐	☐
Entertaining (dinner parties or cooking sessions with friends)	☐	☐
Informal dining (eat-in breakfast or snack bar)	☐	☐
Formal dining (table for six or more)	☐	☐
Adults' work space (home office, crafts, sewing)	☐	☐
Children's work space (homework or games)	☐	☐
TV viewing (either in kitchen or in adjoining family room)	☐	☐
Computing (either in kitchen or in adjoining family room)	☐	☐
Laundry (sorting, washing/drying, ironing, mending)	☐	☐

AMENITIES

	My Current Kitchen	My New Kitchen
Efficient food storage (lazy Susans, spice drawers, pullout pantries)	☐	☐
Standard dish storage (pots and pans drawers, platter slots)	☐	☐
Specialty dish storage (punch bowl, soup tureen, etc.)	☐	☐
Small appliances storage (bread machine, rice cooker, etc.)	☐	☐
Utensils storage (separate drawers for knives, flatware, utensils)	☐	☐
Linens storage (napkins, dish towels, tablecloths)	☐	☐
Cleaning products storage (cleaners, paper towels, plastic bags)	☐	☐
Pet storage and eating area	☐	☐
Shelves for cookbooks and decorative items	☐	☐
Cooking space (around cooktop)	☐	☐
Prep-work space (near sink and refrigerator for preparing food)	☐	☐
Cleanup space (for dirty dishes to gather)	☐	☐
Casual eating area (snack bar)	☐	☐
Garden area (potting sink or greenhouse window)	☐	☐
Recycling area (containers for paper, aluminum, plastic, glass)	☐	☐

ACCOUTREMENTS AND CONDITIONS

In the far-left column, check off each appliance you own; at right, indicate whether its condition warrants reusing as is, refurbishing through paint or repair, or replacing because of age or function. Then use the column to the far right to check any additional appliances you would like to install during your kitchen remodeling.

Appliances	Good (reuse)	Fair (refurbish)	Poor (replace)	New Purchase
☐ Convection oven	☐	☐	☐	☐
☐ Conventional oven	☐	☐	☐	☐
☐ Microwave oven	☐	☐	☐	☐
☐ Cooktop	☐	☐	☐	☐
☐ Freestanding range	☐	☐	☐	☐
☐ Warming drawers	☐	☐	☐	☐
☐ Overhead vent	☐	☐	☐	☐
☐ Downdraft vent	☐	☐	☐	☐
☐ Refrigerator	☐	☐	☐	☐
☐ Refrigerator drawers	☐	☐	☐	☐
☐ Wine cooler	☐	☐	☐	☐
☐ Freezer	☐	☐	☐	☐
☐ Dishwasher	☐	☐	☐	☐
☐ Second dishwasher	☐	☐	☐	☐
☐ Disposal	☐	☐	☐	☐
☐ Single-bowl sink	☐	☐	☐	☐
☐ Double-bowl sink	☐	☐	☐	☐
☐ Triple-bowl sink	☐	☐	☐	☐
☐ Secondary prep sink	☐	☐	☐	☐
☐ Trash compactor	☐	☐	☐	☐
☐ Water purifier	☐	☐	☐	☐
☐ Washer/dryer	☐	☐	☐	☐
☐ Other	☐	☐	☐	☐

In the sections below, if you check Poor (replace), indicate the material you would like to install in place of the existing material.

CABINETS
- ☐ Good (reuse) ☐ Fair (refurbish) ☐ Poor (replace)
- ☐ Cherry ☐ Hickory ☐ Maple ☐ Melamine ☐ Metal
- ☐ Oak ☐ Pine ☐ Thermofoil ☐ Other

COUNTERTOPS
- ☐ Good (reuse) ☐ Fair (refurbish) ☐ Poor (replace)
- ☐ Ceramic tile ☐ Laminate ☐ Solid-surfacing ☐ Stainless steel ☐ Stone
- ☐ Wood ☐ Other

FLOOR
- ☐ Good (reuse) ☐ Fair (refurbish) ☐ Poor (replace)
- ☐ Ceramic tile ☐ Concrete ☐ Laminate ☐ Linoleum ☐ Stone
- ☐ Vinyl ☐ Wood ☐ Other

If you own or plan to own several small appliances, fill out the following section so you can accommodate their space needs when you remodel your kitchen. Check the ones you own as well as the ones you plan to purchase.

Small Appliances	New Purchase
☐ Blender	☐
☐ Deep fat fryer	☐
☐ Electric can opener	☐
☐ Electric crockery cooker	☐
☐ Electric dehydrator	☐
☐ Electric juicer	☐
☐ Electric knife sharpener	☐
☐ Electric wok	☐
☐ Flour/grain mill	☐
☐ Food processor	☐
☐ Griddle/grill	☐
☐ Hand mixer	☐
☐ Meat grinder	☐
☐ Secondary microwave	☐
☐ Stand mixer	☐
☐ Toaster	☐
☐ Toaster oven	☐
☐ Baby food maker	☐
☐ Bread machine	☐
☐ Cappuccino maker	☐
☐ Coffeemaker	☐
☐ Espresso maker	☐
☐ Ice cream maker	☐
☐ Pasta machine	☐
☐ Popcorn popper	☐
☐ Rice cooker	☐
☐ Yogurt maker	☐
☐ Other_____	☐
☐ Other_____	☐

BUDGET

$_____ The total I hope to spend.

$_____ The realistic total I think I'll spend.

$_____ The total I could spend if I have to.

$_____ The total I absolutely, positively cannot go over.

Let the sunshine in

What was a dark, cramped room before the renovation is now an uplifting, light-filled haven that looks out onto a southern garden. The wall that once housed the refrigerator was knocked out and replaced with glass windows and a set of patio doors. The change required the costly job of moving the electrical box, but it was well worth it.

saving face

Marie Archuleta took a thoughtful approach to the renovation of her 1950s ranch house kitchen in Houston. She loved the look of the original knotty pine cabinetry because of a fond family association: It reminded her of her aunt's ranch house in New Mexico. The rest of the kitchen, however, was a real eyesore.

The house was built in 1953. If the kitchen had ever been updated, Marie surmises that it was done in the late 1960s or early 1970s—and it looked like it. The vinyl terrazzo flooring had long since lost its texture from wear, the laminate countertop had warped from water damage, and the lighting consisted of whatever glow emanated from a ceiling-fan light and a fluorescent tube over the sink.

The task of figuring out how to save the rustic look of the knotty pine cabinets while rearranging the entire kitchen and outfitting it with brand-new appliances fell to a team of five: Marie and her husband, photographer Hal Lott, who did all of the demolition work himself; an architect who did preliminary drawings; interior designer Joetta Moulden; and carpenter Mike Little.

During the four-month renovation, they gutted the kitchen down to the studs and moved or updated every component. The gas line for the range was moved across the room, the electrical box was relocated, the plumbing was upgraded, and a significant amount of storage space added.

The new kitchen features a seamless blend of the original and new custom-made knotty pine cabinets. After having years of kitchen grime cleaned off them, the old kitchen cabinets looked brand new.

The carpenter was able to retrofit much of the old cabinetry into the new kitchen, and where it didn't work, he built new cabinets from new knotty pine. Where there were stationary shelves in the old cabinets, he built roll-out shelving for easy access to storage. Rolling bins around the base cabinets hold up to 200 pounds each. The new kitchen offers so much storage space Marie can't use it all.

The other major issue in the old kitchen was a lack of natural light. Marie, an avid gardener, wanted to knock out the wall that faced her backyard garden and patio, but placement of the new refrigerator became problematic. Access to the mechanical room, which contained the home's

Doors and more

A panel behind the rolling refrigerator, *above*, opens to the home's mechanical room, which gives access to the hot-water heater and furnace. A custom-built Dutch door, *below*, keeps out the food-thieving family dog while allowing the cook to keep in touch with the family.

house had to be moved. That alone cost $5,000, but it was absolutely necessary. Next, the home's aging electrical system required upgrading to handle a new professional-style Viking range and its accompanying high-power ventilation system.

The mechanical room is well hidden. The new stainless-steel side-by-side refrigerator, which sits on wheels and extends just 2 inches into the room from a recessed area, can be pulled away from the wall to reveal an access panel. The mechanical room is behind the panel, making getting to the major systems in the home a no-hassle proposition—and granting Marie's wish for a garden view.

With all the natural light that would come streaming through the patio doors, Marie felt she could downsize one window to free more room for counter space. Marie stuck to her top aesthetic priority of preserving the rustic ranch house look by keeping the knotty pine cabinetry, but everything else could go. So the old window was removed to open up the necessary space to extend the countertop on that wall. There is no loss of view from the window resizing, Marie says, because it faces a neighbor's house and fence.

The new kitchen is outfitted with a countertop made of a highly durable manufactured solid-surfacing material. A new 42-inch apron-front sink makes it possible for Marie to scrub big pots and pans easily without splashing most of the water outside. The backsplash is tumbled Italian marble, and the floor is made of 14-inch green slate tiles, which add a nostalgic component: On a trip to Glacier National Monument, Marie and Hal fell in love with the beautiful green slate in the Montana mountains. When they returned and began remodeling their kitchen, they found tiles that closely resemble the beautiful green hue they remember from their mountain vacation.

The way the kitchen flows into the rest of the house changed slightly, too. Where a set of swinging cafeteria-style doors once led from the kitchen to the casual dining/family room area, a handmade Dutch door of knotty pine serves both an aesthetic and practical purpose.

Over the years, Marie and Hal's big dog had become quite adept at stealing food, ready-to-serve meals as well as food set out to be prepared. The Dutch door allows them to keep the furry thief out of the kitchen but doesn't close off the

hot water heater and furnace, had to be maintained—and it was on that wall. The solution was clever—and expensive. First, the location of the electrical box that served the whole

cook from the goings-on in the family room. It also accentuates the ranch house look Marie loves so much.

Marie and Hal used to spend as little time as possible in the old, dark kitchen; they'd cook their meals and get out, retreating to the more pleasant family room area. After the renovation, however, they find themselves spending most of their morning time in this sunny part of the house—and many dinners, too, eating at the antique butcher block table while perched atop old pub stools they re-covered in black and white cowhide.

Marie's favorite thing to do in the kitchen is to simply sit and drink coffee in the morning and gaze at her garden. When guests come over, they end up hanging out in the kitchen, which has become the primary gathering spot in the house.

The rest of the house, Marie and Hal say, is just a nice little ranch house, but nothing special. They no longer can say that about the kitchen.

Before and after

An antique butcher's block, *above*, serves as a spot for food preparation and casual meals. The homeowners loved the look of the knotty pine cabinets, *below*, in their 1950s ranch but hated everything else about the old kitchen. The worn terrazzo floor was the first thing they ripped out.

right layout

wrong style

Like a well-worn coat, the kitchen in Jamie and Kay Martin's 28-year-old home had done its job well, but it was getting too threadbare to continue.

With the help of kitchen designer Victoria DeGrette, the Martins transformed a 1970s-era kitchen into a state-of-the-art facility infused with old-world warmth and charm.

After nearly three decades of treading its floors, the Martins knew that the floor plan of the kitchen worked well; they wanted the new kitchen to work the way the old kitchen did, only better. Thanks to the addition of several new appliances and amenities, it does just that. The only real layout changes the Martins made consisted of moving the cooktop to the center of the south wall and transposing the locations of the refrigerator and desk area.

What truly changed in this kitchen was its function. With the Martins' children grown and moved out, most meals are made for two. But holidays bring the family back together for big dinners, and throughout the year grandchildren often

New and improved

Although the basic layout of the new kitchen, *right*, didn't change much from the old kitchen, *below*, the fresh look and higher function of the renovated kitchen better suits the homeowners' tastes and needs. The addition of a window brings in more light and beautiful views.

Cooking central

A separate cooktop and oven, *above*, gently jut into the room, emphasizing their prominence, *above,* and allowing for a spice-and-oil niche behind the cooktop. A granite countertop is beautiful, easy to clean, and stands up to hot pots and roasting pans placed on its surface.

Seconds, please

Whether the Martins feed a crowd or eat in shifts, a new warming drawer, *left,* situated in the peninsula, is a much-loved feature of their new kitchen. While freeing the cooktop and oven for subsequent rounds of cooking and baking, it keeps big family meals piping hot and as fresh as a just-made meal.

stay for a day or more. The kitchen that once handled a consistent number of meals and family members now works just right for meals for one, two, three, on up to more than a dozen people. A new convection oven large enough to make big meals fast has a warming drawer that ensures everything gets to the table at the right temperature and that seconds taste as hot and fresh as firsts. An extra-deep sink handles big pots and pans as easily as it does a few plates. And an ultra-quiet dishwasher muffles swishing noises in the kitchen, which is located just 10 steps from the living room.

Along with outdated appliances, the Martins also banished outdated style. Where a soffit once stood, custom cherry cabinets rise to the ceiling. Upper corner cabinets on the diagonal maximize the use of space and soften the turn, visually expanding the room. A tumbled-marble tile backsplash exudes warmth, and a polished granite countertop adds a sophisticated touch.

Gentle steps up and back in the upper cabinet facades give the kitchen a touch of unfitted flair. Below, the cooktop and oven sit forward 6 inches, allowing space for a spice-and-oil niche behind the cooking center. A pair of classic rich cherry columns flank the projecting corners, lending a furnished look to a high-function area.

Though the hardworking peninsula functions much as it did before, it now houses generous storage space, the trash compactor, and a new warming drawer.

The facade of the cabinets changed dramatically, but what was inside did too. The previous pantry was simply a stack of deep shelves that required a lot of stretching to reach items in the back. The new pantry, composed of rows of roll-out shelves for accessible food storage below, boasts two large stationary shelves above, which hold seldom-used big bowls and platters.

The old desk, once simply a stopping place for mail and keys, has been refashioned into a high-tech communication hub. The telephone acts as the base unit for several phones throughout the house. Its half-mile range, multiple lines, and intercom features allow the Martins to keep in touch with each other no matter where they may roam on their two-acre lot.

It's also the place where Kay keeps in touch with her real

Create your niche

A niche behind the cooking center, *above*, provides a handy place for storing often-used cooking oils and spices while imparting a touch of old-world charm.

estate business and her children, via e-mail, the Internet, and a multifunction phone. Grandson Ross has dibs on the sleek new computer for his favorite games. The computer's high-powered works are tucked in a thin space behind the flat LCD screen. Bookshelves above the desk display mementos and keep cookbooks organized.

Although the aesthetics of the kitchen changed dramatically, the beauty of the Martins' country setting did not. Saving the southern view was a must. Two tall windows sit at countertop height and flank the stove, bringing in southern sunlight and a view of who is coming up the drive.

They trimmed the double-hung windows over the sink in wood. Though there was no need to replace them, the look certainly didn't blend well with the new frameless casements on the south wall. The painter wisely recommended painting the framework to make the contrast less apparent.

Walking the work triangle in the Martins' new kitchen has become a familiar path, but their steps are now lighter.

3

elements of kitchen design

HOW DO YOU DREAM ABOUT YOUR NEW KITCHEN? You may stand in the kitchen you have now and imagine the refrigerator on one wall, a commercial-style range on another, bright windows over the sink, and a warm, cozy spot for eating. Or you may spend hours sketching your ideal kitchen on paper. Maybe you do both. Either way, it's all about visualizing the possibilities for your space; and while there are no limits on dreams, long-established design tenets and guidelines can give your dreams a solid foundation. Good design boosts both the efficiency and the aesthetic quality of a space. Here's everything you need to know about how to design a kitchen that works beautifully and looks that way too.

Designing your kitchen with a series of interrelated work centers adds up to a functional and well-organized space that is a pleasure to work in. This kitchen's cooking center, *opposite*, includes a cooktop, double ovens, and a microwave oven. Other essential kitchen work centers include a food-preparation center, cleanup center, and serving center. Where space allows, an eat-in area creates a gathering place.

the
work triangle

The work triangle, present in virtually every kitchen, is made up of the walking path formed by the refrigerator, the sink, and the cooktop or range. If you keep the triangle as compact and unobstructed as possible, you'll reduce your travel time between these key appliances and make your kitchen more enjoyable overall. When planning, be sure the triangle does not interfere with traffic flow.

Draw a line from the center of the sink to the center of the refrigerator to the center of the cooktop, then back to the sink's center. It should make a triangle that measures a total of no more than 26 feet. Active cooks may prefer a triangle of 22 feet or less. Either way, each side of the triangle should measure at least 4 feet but no more than 9 feet.

Triangle trends

The classic work triangle of sink, cooktop, and refrigerator has been a guide for planning an efficient kitchen for more than half a decade, and it still is. Keeping those elements relatively close together not only makes work in the kitchen convenient but is a matter of common sense. Adaptations of the formula have become common due to bigger kitchens with more elements— dishwashers, secondary chef's sinks, wine coolers, refrigerator drawers, and warming drawers, to name a few.

Designers today think in terms of overlapping triangles or multiple zones, each with a work triangle of its own, where two or more cooks can work simultaneously without getting in each other's way. Still, no single formula applies to every kitchen. Instead, consider how you cook and how your family utilizes the kitchen, and adapt accordingly.

Do U like to cook?

The U-shape kitchen, such as the one *below,* is perhaps the most efficient design (see pages 32 and 33 for a look at basic kitchen layouts). Each of the workstations— sink, refrigerator, and cooktop—sits on one wall. A U-shape requires a minimum of an 8×8-foot space.

Just like people, kitchens come in all shapes and sizes. Some kitchens are square, some are rectangular, some have curves or angles. Some are large and some are small. The kitchen layout that will be most efficient and aesthetically pleasing to you—and most feasible in the space you have to work with—depends on the dimensions of your kitchen and the basic shape the walls make.

Each layout has its strong and weak points. Consider these shapes a place to start. You can put two of these layouts together, crank out a 90-degree corner for an angled stretch of countertop, or incorporate whatever suits your fancy.

THE ONE-WALL KITCHEN: This layout is made for smaller open spaces but is the least efficient shape for the cook because it requires walking up and down the stretch of the entire wall to reach the range, refrigerator, sink, and storage. One-wall kitchens work best with the sink in the center, flanked by the refrigerator and cooktop with 4 feet of counterspace between them. Locate doors away from the busy work wall to avoid foot-traffic hassles.

THE GALLEY KITCHEN: Many older homes have this type of long, narrow kitchen built between parallel walls. Contrary to popular belief, galley kitchens are efficient because they allow the cook to move easily from one work area to another. Plan for at least 4 feet of space between opposite counters. It's best to put the sink and refrigerator on one wall, with the cooktop centered between them on the opposite wall. Unfortunately, a galley kitchen doesn't allow for much dining space; if there are doorways at each end of the galley, foot traffic crosses the work triangle, resulting in collisions.

THE L-SHAPE KITCHEN: This layout requires two adjacent walls and is particularly efficient when work areas are kept close to the crook of the L. You can save additional steps by planning the work flow to go from refrigerator to sink to the cooktop and serving areas. Because the work core tucks into the crook of the L, foot traffic is rarely a problem.

THE L-SHAPE WITH ISLAND KITCHEN: Adding an island to the L-shape kitchen makes room for more than one cook, more counter space, a place for a snack bar, and increased space for storage and dining. The island also works as a room divider, shielding some of the kitchen clutter from any adjacent space, such as a family room.

THE U-SHAPE KITCHEN: The cozy U-shape kitchen works best when it places one workstation—the sink, cooktop, and refrigerator—on each of three walls. The U-shape kitchen is highly efficient for one cook and allows for many design possibilities, but you need at least an 8×8-foot kitchen space. If there are multiple cooks in your family who prefer working together, small U-shapes can make it

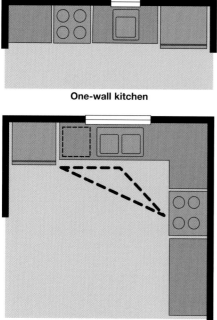

One-wall kitchen

L-shape kitchen

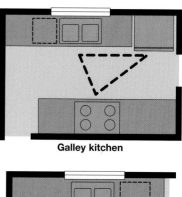

Galley kitchen

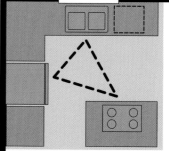

L-shape with island kitchen

difficult for everyone to maneuver within the space.

THE U-SHAPE WITH ISLAND KITCHEN: If you're not sure about how to make your large kitchen work efficiently, this layout may be your answer. A sink or cooktop may be placed in the island—consider a special-function countertop such as butcher block for chopping or marble for rolling out pastry. Allow 42 inches of aisle space on all sides of the island; if yours is a kitchen for two cooks to share, 48 inches is better.

THE G-SHAPE KITCHEN: This layout provides room for an audience. The G-shape kitchen features a peninsula anchored to a line of cabinets. The peninsula can be outfitted with a cooktop or sink, or it can function as a dining bar or buffet. It also serves as a room divider, allowing family and friends to hang out with the cook without crossing paths.

THE TWO-COOKS KITCHEN: If your kitchen regularly gets a workout from two cooks, this plan may be for you. The two-cooks kitchen incorporates work zones or triangles that allow both cooks to work efficiently without bumping into each other. The layout calls for two triangles that share a leg, often anchored at the refrigerator—generally the least-used leg of the triangle. Two-cooks kitchens can, but don't have to, include a second smaller prep sink, a stretch of counterop, or a small second refrigerator.

Island life

A kitchen island provides space for a cooktop or a secondary sink for washing and preparing fruits and vegetables—or a casual eating place for quick meals and coffee breaks.

An island should enhance—not interrupt—the flow of work between the stove, refrigerator, and sink (for more information on the classic kitchen work triangle, see pages 30–31).

If you tuck away a dishwasher or install an under-the-counter refrigerator in an island, make sure all appliance doors open comfortably and won't hinder traffic. If you equip the island with a cooktop, allow at least 12-inch-wide runs of countertop on either end and install a downdraft vent or overhead hood. All around the island, plan for aisles at least 42 inches wide. If two cooks use the space regularly, opt for 48 inches. For seating, allot 2 feet of running counter space per person and position the area outside the work flow. If you can't meet these criteria, reconsider installing an island.

See pages 148–149 for instructions on how to build a simple, attractive, and functional island from two stock base cabinets, side panels, and a veneered plywood back panel.

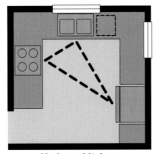

U-shape kitchen

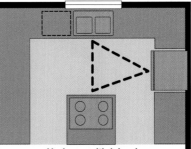

U-shape with island

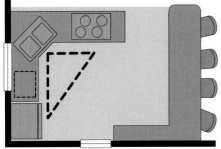

G-shape kitchen

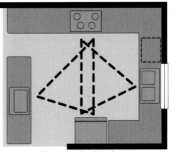

Two-cooks kitchen

kitchen work centers

Interrelated work centers make your kitchen more efficient and comfortable. Just as the kitchen work triangle simplifies life by putting the refrigerator, sink, and cooktop within comfortable reach, work centers with specific functions make planning, preparing, cooking, serving, and cleaning up after a meal quick and easy. Here's how to devise a plan that includes work centers that suit your space and needs.

The planning center

Having a space in the kitchen to plan meals, leave and collect messages, pay bills, and use a computer is a growing necessity for many homeowners.

Locate the planning center well outside any work triangles. Be sure the desk itself or someone sitting at it won't interfere with traffic or cabinet and appliance doors.

Include plenty of storage for books and files, as well as computer and electronic equipment. Having a computer in the kitchen is great for tasks such as correspondence, paying bills, and planning meals. A set of mailboxes or baskets gives each family member a place for paperwork, and a big calendar keeps track of everyone's schedule.

Be sure to locate your planning center in a place where the computer won't be disturbed by normal kitchen traffic, food preparation, and cleanup.

Command central

A drawer in the center of this kitchen desk, *above*, neatly stores a laptop computer when it's not in use. Generously sized file drawers on both sides of the chair help keep children's homework, bills and correspondence, or all kinds of paperwork organized and at hand. This planning center is an integral part of the kitchen though it remains out of the major flow of food preparation and people.

High function in a small space

This diminutive planning center, *left*, proves that you don't have to have a huge kitchen or tie up a major chunk of floor space to incorporate a basic telephone and writing desk. Three small drawers keep mail organized, and a shelf for storing cookbooks makes meal planning a breeze. Desktop space for a telephone and address book—as well as a place to jot down notes—makes keeping in touch with friends, family, and business associates as easy as turning a page and dialing a number. Although this planning center sits a step away from the food-preparation center, it obstructs nothing. When the stool is not being used, it simply tucks under the desk, where it stays out of the kitchen's normal traffic flow.

Planning-center considerations

WIRE A SEPARATE CIRCUIT for the computer, so surges and pulls from major appliances don't cause the computer to crash. You may want to hire an electrician to do this.

KEEP YOUR COMPUTER away from the cooktop, wall ovens, dishwasher, and other heat- and moisture-producing appliances. Grease, heat, and moisture can wreak havoc with sensitive computer circuitry.

DESK SPACE should be at least 30 inches wide and 24 inches deep to accommodate a desktop computer. Upper cabinets should allow enough clearance for the monitor.

PLAN EXTRA SHELF SPACE or counter space for a printer, fax machine, or other peripherals.

THE COMFORTABLE HEIGHT for using a keyboard is approximately 26 inches above the floor, which is 2 to 4 inches below standard desk height. To avoid undue stress on your wrists, neck, and back, modify a section of the desktop or mount an undercounter bracket for the keyboard.

THE DISTANCE from your eye to the computer monitor should be 14 to 20 inches.

TO AVOID EYESTRAIN and screen glare, design planning center lighting that is separate from other kitchen illumination.

FIND A COMFORTABLE CHAIR that offers good back support. Consider an adjustable chair if several family members use the computer.

The cleanup center

More than just the star of the cleanup center, the sink also plays a supporting role in a kitchen's food-preparation and cooking centers. This is where fresh vegetables get clean and where soup and pasta pots fill with water. Because of all the use it gets, the sink saves the most steps when it is placed at the center of the work triangle, between the range and refrigerator. Other necessary components of the cleanup center are the garbage disposal and dishwasher, so dirty plates can be scraped and loaded into the dishwasher without exerting extra steps. The dishwasher works well on either side of the sink. Decide which location suits you best. Or, if you entertain frequently, you may need two dishwashers. Put one on each side of the sink or locate one in the island near a second sink. Storing everyday glasses, dishes, and utensils near the dishwasher makes sense, but you may decide to move some of those items to more convenient locations near the table or in the snack area of the food-preparation center. Consider

A beautiful kitchen times two

This sunny kitchen, *above*, features a model cleanup center. From a practical standpoint, the sink, dishwasher, and drying rack are all closely aligned—and are in close proximity to the cupboards that hold the primary dishware. From an aesthetic standpoint, gazing out of the big, bright windows that serve as a backdrop to the sink makes doing dishes a more pleasant task.

raising the dishwasher several inches off the floor to ease the loading and unloading of dishes. Many designers consider a raised dishwasher more attractive when it's located at the end of a run of countertop. If you plan to use a trash compactor, install it on one side of the sink, with the dishwasher on the other side. This saves you steps and makes the most effective use of the sink-area countertops. Design your cleanup center with space to store dish towels, cleaning products, and a trash container or recycling bin. Every year, more cities and

towns require that garbage and recyclables be sorted prior to pickup. To organize this task, install a recycling drawer with room for three or four plastic containers, each large enough to hold a standard paper bag for sorting and carrying glass, paper, plastic, or cans. (Many cabinet companies sell ready-made recycling drawers.) If possible, designate recycling space near your sink so you can rinse cans and bottles before tossing them into the sorters. You can also turn a base cupboard into a recycling center by using stackable plastic bins.

Cleanup 1-2-3

Everything a cook needs to clean up efficiently is at hand in this kitchen, *far left.* The trash compactor and dishwasher flank the sink, and getting at the garbage can and recycling bins is as easy as opening the undersink curtain, which also serves to brighten and soften the space.

A sink to suit all pots

One of the most important elements of the cleanup center, of course, is the sink. This extra-deep apron-front sink, *left,* takes the struggle out of both scrubbing big pots and filling them with water for cooking pasta or vegetables. It also easily hides a stack of dirty dishes until you can get to it.

Guidelines for creating an efficient cleanup center

IF POSSIBLE, allow 30 to 36 inches of counter space on each side of the sink. If space is tight, you can have a minimum of 24 inches on the dishwasher side and 18 inches on the other.

IF A SECOND SINK is part of your plan, allow at least 3 inches of counter space on one side and 18 inches on the other side.

THERE SHOULD BE 2 inches of space between the sink's front edge and the edge of the counter.

LEAVE 22 INCHES of clearance between the sink rim and an overhead cabinet.

KEEP AT LEAST 14 inches of space between the center of the sink bowl and a turn of a counter.

ALLOW 21 INCHES of standing room between the dishwasher and adjacent counters, other appliances, and cabinets.

THE DISHWASHER should be located within 36 inches of the sink for maximum efficiency and to combine waste lines.

The preparation center

The food-preparation center commonly stores the canned and dry goods, mixing bowls, casserole dishes, cookbooks, storage containers, and small appliances. Because big meals no longer are nightly affairs for most families, a snack center joins the refrigerator and pantry in today's well-planned preparation center. The area might include a microwave oven, a wrapping station for lunches or leftovers, and even a second sink. This space is especially handy for those on-your-own weeknight meals.

In addition to being efficiently configured for making a quick bite to eat, however, the preparation center also must cater to weekend cooks who enjoy making a big meal or baking. Think carefully about the kinds of cooking you do. If you do a lot of soup-making, salad-tossing, or baking, for instance, think about grouping the items required for those activities to maximize the ease of preparation.

The most sensible cabinets for keeping foods are those attached to cool outside walls, near shaded or north-facing windows. Cabinets located near heat sources—the dishwasher, oven, refrigerator, and southern exterior walls—are not the best choices for storing food. The handle side of the refrigerator should face into the work triangle and the door should open completely so bins can be pulled out with ease. The refrigerator door should not swing into a doorway.

Consider making one section of countertop in the preparation center a few inches lower than the rest, so it's easy for kids to grab their own snacks or to help with meal prep. The lowered countertop will also be at a handy height for weekend bakers—it's easier to knead dough on a lower surface.

Guidelines for the preparation center

PLAN FOR 36 TO 42 INCHES of running counter space close to a water source.

IF THIS WORK CENTER stretches into a corner, install 36-inch base cabinets along both walls for a lazy Susan-style pantry.

LEAVE AT LEAST 15 INCHES of counter space next to the handle of the refrigerator. Locate at least a 15-inch landing space within 48 inches across from the refrigerator. You can unload groceries more easily when you have space to set down items as you make room on refrigerator shelves.

TO INCREASE FLOOR SPACE, consider a refrigerator that is only 24 inches deep instead of the standard 30 or 33 inches.

A STANDARD REFRIGERATOR with a freezer on top or at the bottom is 28 to 30 inches wide. Side-by-side models are generally 30 to 36 inches wide.

Knife, please

Everything a cook could need for peeling, chopping, or slicing is within arm's reach in this food preparation center, *left*. Because it's located in an island surrounded by wide aisles, it doesn't interfere with helpers who volunteer to empty the dishwasher or scrub the pots and pans.

Cooking and catching up

Avid bakers and newshounds couldn't help but feel right at home working in this kitchen, *bottom left*. A stand mixer and set of mixing bowls are handily stored in an appliance garage in the corner, a sometimes difficult-to-use space. The TV is tucked behind sliding pocket doors when it's not in use.

Spread out

The generous expanse of granite countertop on the island, *below*, provides a clean, uncluttered space for preparing vegetables for soup on top of a cutting board, mixing up a batch of brownies, or rolling out dough. A row of comfortable chairs that fit under the island's overhang allows family and friends to sit down and have a chat with the cook while he or she works.

Olive, sesame, or canola?

This kitchen's cooking center integrates not only the hardware used in meal preparation—pots, pans, and utensils—but also frequently used ingredients such as oils, vinegars, and spices.

The cooking center

This part of the kitchen is a busy place. If cooking is a communal activity, an efficient layout is even more vital. The main ingredients of the cooking center are the cooktop or range and the microwave oven.

A conventional oven separate from the cooktop is likely to be your least-used appliance and, as such, can be placed outside the work triangle. The cooktop is most labor-efficient, and safest to use, with at least 18 inches of counter space on each side. This enables you to turn handles away from the front of the cooktop and provides room for setting pots after removing them from the cooking surface. However, if space is at a premium, a range that includes a cooktop and oven is the most space-efficient.

Consider installing a heat-resistant countertop surface adjacent to the range so you'll have a place to set hot pans or baking sheets. Also, for safety's sake, don't install the microwave oven above the cooktop. Loose clothing could come in contact with a hot burner when you're reaching toward and into the microwave oven.

Another important component of the cooking center is a ventilation system. There are many options in ventilation, including range hoods that match cabinetry, downdraft systems, and units that pull out from under cabinets when needed. The system you choose should have a fan rated at a minimum of 150 cubic feet per minute. (See page 66 for more information on ventilation systems.)

A cooking center also requires ample storage for pots and pans, utensils, hot pads, spices and seasonings, and food products that go directly from storage container to simmering pot. Some cooks prefer to keep often-used paraphernalia at hand. Attractive wire-grid systems provide a place to hang these items within easy reach. Baskets brimming with whisks and wooden spoons can gather near the stove. If you prefer a clutter-free look, you'll need to plan behind-doors storage space for all of these essential cooking accoutrements.

Dimensions for designing the ideal cooking center

LEAVE 15 TO 18 INCHES of open counter space near the microwave oven for setting hot dishes.

PLACE A SHELF for the microwave oven between 2 inches below the cook's elbow and 10 inches above.

LEAVE 18 TO 24 INCHES of counter space on each side of the cooktop. If the cooktop is an island, leave at least 12 inches on each side.

Ready, set, cook

1: A slim, handy pullout drawer containing cooking sprays, oils, and spices is just a finger pull away from whatever's on the stove. 2: You can store dried herbs and spices (and easily find any one of them) in a drawer outfitted with a spice rack such as this one. If you really want to be organized, alphabetize them. 3: Forget digging around in the utensil drawer and shredding your knuckles on the grater; attractive stainless-steel racks, such as this one, keep cooking utensils in plain sight.
4: No lugging here: A hot-water faucet installed on the wall behind the cooktop makes pot filling easy.

LEAVE 27 TO 36 INCHES of clearance between a range or cooktop and an overhead cabinet.

LEAVE 16 INCHES of clearance between the center of the front burner and a wall or cabinet. Leave 14 inches of clearance between the center of the front burner and a turn in the countertop.

DON'T PUT A COOKING SURFACE below an operative window unless the window is more than 3 inches behind the cooking unit and 24 inches above it.

TO DETERMINE the ideal height for a wall oven, find the spot where the open door would be between 5 and 7 inches below the cook's elbow.

Gather 'round

The dining area of this graceful, granite-topped island, *above,* provides ample elbow and leg room. Lowering the island height to standard table height (30 inches) allows the use of regular dining chairs. The island also makes a perfect spot for laying out a buffet. The banquette, *opposite,* although physically removed from the rest of the kitchen, remains part of it thanks to a pass-through that allows for easy movement of food and dishes.

The serving/dining center

Cozy in-kitchen seating areas offer intimate dining within limited dimensions. By rearranging the room you have, you may be able to carve out space for your own eating place. If expansion is in the cards, a bump-out may provide all the room you need.

The ideal kitchen dining area enjoys proximity to the work core as well as plenty of natural light. Even in a small kitchen, this airy atmosphere will encourage guests to linger. In larger kitchens, the simplest way to gain dining space is to move all appliances to a corridor or L-shape layout, leaving one wall or corner for a freestanding table and chairs or a built-in banquette. Popular open-plan kitchens feature an island or peninsula of cabinets or a countertop, with stools to allow socializing while screening cooking activity. Chairs or stools make the island or peninsula a handy spot for breakfast and casual meals; remove the chairs or stools and the island turns into a convenient buffet for parties.

Another option is to cantilever an island or peninsula work surface to create a diner-style eating counter. Of all the dining-center options, the eating counter requires the least floor space. A counter can be any shape, and there's no need to surface it with the same material as other countertops; a contrasting material may add a design impact.

Keep in mind that most islands do not allow the luxury of full seating around their perimeter. Many house a cooktop, sink, or other appliances, such as a warming drawer or a trash compactor, which can't be blocked with seating.

Booths and banquettes provide more intimacy than counters and require less area than a freestanding table and chairs. In addition, they provide hidden storage space for seasonal or rarely used kitchen equipment. They are, however, less convenient for serving and eating and can be difficult to get in and out of if a person's mobility is limited.

Guidelines for the serving/dining center

PLAN A MINIMUM OF 21 INCHES of counter width for each person. If your eating surface is standard counter height (36 inches), you'll need stools 24 inches high. If you choose to make your counter higher—standard bar height is 42 inches—barstools that are 30 to 32 inches high will fit best.

IF YOU LOWER YOUR EATING COUNTER to dining table height (30 inches), standard dining chairs offer you the most versatility. Allow a minimum depth of 15 inches for legroom; 20 inches is recommended.

TO DETERMINE THE DIMENSIONS of a booth or banquette's surface, figure 21 inches of table width and at least 15 inches of depth for each person. Using these guidelines, a family of four would require a 30×42-inch surface.

WITH THE BANQUETTE'S EATING SURFACE at the standard 30-inch height, the banquette seat should be 18 inches deep and 18 inches above the floor. The bench should be as long as the table surface.

PLAN TO HAVE the table's edge overlap the front of the banquette's seat by 3 to 4 inches.

Specialty work centers

If you have the space and inclination, you might consider what kinds of additional household activities or special culinary activities take place in your kitchen. If you're an avid baker, you might consider creating a baking center, with all your mixing bowls, baking pans, small appliances, oven mitts, and ingredients, such as flour, sugar, flavorings, and leavenings placed near the oven.

Other specialized work centers might include a beverage or coffee center, a juicing center, an ironing center, or an entertainment center (not the kind that occupies the family room). If you throw a lot of dinner parties, this center might be outfitted with a second sink, small refrigerator to chill beverages, wine cooler, ice maker, large-capacity dishwasher, and space to store tabletop appliances such as an indoor grill, fondue pot, or espresso/cappuccino machine. This would keep guests happy—and out of the main work triangle.

2

1

Getting it done in the kitchen

Your kitchen can incorporate work centers that serve tasks best done in the kitchen or that provide for any special interest you might have—culinary or otherwise. 1: Making perfect pastry is no problem in this baking center, which features a cool marble surface that's just right for rolling out dough, and ample and clever storage for appliances, ingredients, and pans. 2: Don't run to the basement or garage every time you empty a milk container or soup can. Pullouts such as these make the task of sorting recyclables painless. 3: If you're tired of tripping over Fido's food and water bowls, consider tucking a pet-feeding station into a lower drawer. 4: Ironing becomes a more pleasant task in a bright kitchen rather than in a dark basement laundry room. 5: The kitchen always seems to be the first place kids rush to when they come in the door. Keep things neat with a built-in "mudroom" where they can park their shoes, coats, and sports equipment. 6: A menu-planning center with space for a message board, computer, and cookbooks keeps trips to the grocery store to an efficient minimum.

Eggs
Milk
Coffee
Lettuce
Cat food

Guidelines for good design

The National Kitchen & Bath Association has a set of design guidelines that are updated periodically to reflect kitchen trends and products. Review these recommendations and incorporate them into your kitchen layout. They will help make your new kitchen as efficient, comfortable, and aesthetically pleasing as possible.

Traffic and work flow

Easy movement is essential to kitchen efficiency. These tips will help avoid traffic jams.

■ Make sure doorways are a minimum of 32 inches wide and no more than 24 inches deep. When two counters flank a doorway, the minimum 32-inch-wide clearance should be measured from the edge of one counter to the edge of the counter on the opposite side.

■ Walkways (passages between vertical objects greater than 24 inches deep where not more than one is a work counter or appliance) should be 36 inches wide.

■ Work aisles (passages between vertical objects, both of which are work counters or appliances) should be at least 42 inches wide in one-cook kitchens and at least 48 inches wide in multiple-cooks kitchens.

■ The work triangle (the shortest walking distance between the refrigerator, sink, and primary cooking surface) should be no more than 26 feet, with no single leg of the work triangle shorter than 4 feet or longer than 9 feet. The work triangle should not intersect an island or peninsula by any more than 12 inches.

■ If two or more people cook at the same time, a work triangle should be placed for each cook. One leg of the primary and secondary triangles may be shared, but the two triangles should not cross one another. Appliances may be shared or separate.

■ Don't allow major traffic patterns to cross through the work triangle.

■ No entry door, appliance door, or cabinet door should interfere with another.

■ In a kitchen seating area, 36 inches of clearance should be allowed from the counter or table edge to any wall or obstruction behind the seating area if no traffic will pass behind a seated diner. If there is a walkway behind the seating area, allow 65 inches of total clearance, including the walkway, between the counter or table edge and any wall or other obstruction.

Cabinets and storage

Wall cabinet frontage recommendations vary according to the size of the room. For small kitchens (less than 150 square feet), allow at least 144 inches of wall cabinet frontage, with cabinets that are at least 12 inches deep and a minimum of 30 inches high and that feature adjustable shelving. Difficult-to-reach cabinets above the range hood, oven, or refrigerator do not count unless devices are installed within the cabinet to improve accessibility. For large kitchens (more than 150 square feet), allow at least 186 inches of wall cabinet frontage, with cabinets at least 12 inches deep, and a minimum of 30 inches high, with adjustable shelving. Difficult-to-reach cabinets above the range hood, oven, or refrigerator are not included in this figure unless devices are installed within the cabinet case to improve accessibility.

The following list provides additional storage guidelines.

■ In either small or large kitchens, diagonal or pie-cut cabinets count as a total of 24 inches.

■ Cabinets 72 inches or taller can count as either base cabinets or wall cabinets but not both. The calculations follow:

■ 12-inch-deep, tall units=1× the base lineal footage or 2× the wall lineal footage.

■ 18-inch-deep, tall units=1.5× the base lineal footage or 3× the wall lineal footage.

■ 21- to 24-inch-deep, tall units=2× the base lineal footage or 4× the wall lineal footage.

■ Include at least 60 inches of wall cabinet frontage, with cabinets at least 12 inches deep and a minimum of 30 inches high, within 72 inches of the primary sink centerline.

■ Base cabinet frontage is determined by room size. For small kitchens (less than 150 square feet), allow at least 156 inches of base cabinet frontage, with cabinets at least 21 inches deep. For large kitchens (more than 150 square feet), allow at least 192 inches of base cabinet frontage, with cabinets at least 21 inches deep.

■ In either small or large kitchens, pie-cut or lazy-Susan

Pull up a chair

The National Kitchen & Bath Association recommends that a 36-inch high eating counter allow for 15 inches of knee space; a 42-inch high counter should provide for 12 inches.

base cabinets count as a total of 30 inches.

Drawer or roll-out shelf frontage is determined by room dimensions. For small kitchens, allow at least 120 inches of drawer or roll-out shelf frontage. For large kitchens, allow at least 165 inches of frontage. Here's more information:

■ Multiply cabinet width by the number of drawers and roll-outs to determine frontage. Drawers or roll-out cabinets must be at least 15 inches wide and 21 inches deep to count.

■ At least five storage or organizing components, located between 15 and 48 inches above the finished floor (or extending into that area) should be included in the kitchen to improve functionality and accessibility. These items may include but are not limited to lowered wall cabinets, raised base cabinets, tall cabinets, appliance garages, bins and racks/swing-out pantries, interior vertical dividers, and specialized drawers and shelves. Full-extension drawers and roll-out shelves greater than the 120-inch minimum for small

kitchens or the 165-inch minimum for large kitchens may also be included in the plan.

■ For kitchens with usable corner areas, at least one functional corner storage unit should be included.

■ The top edge of a waste receptacle should be no higher than 36 inches. The receptacle should be easily accessible and should be removable without raising the receptacle bottom higher than the unit's physical height. Lateral removal of the receptacle that does not require lifting is preferred.

Counter surface and landing space

At least two work-counter heights should be installed in the kitchen for different uses and functions, with one between 28 and 36 inches above the finished floor and the other 36 to 45 inches above the finished floor.

■ For small kitchens (less than 150 square feet), allow at least 132 inches of usable countertop frontage. For large kitchens (more than 150 square feet), allow at least 198 inches of usable countertop frontage.

■ Counters must be a minimum of 16 inches deep, and wall cabinets must be at least 15 inches above the counter's surface for it to be included in the frontage measurement. Do not count corner space.

■ If an appliance garage or storage cabinet extends to the counter, there must be 16 inches of clear space in front of the cabinet for the area to be counted as usable countertop.

■ There should be at least 24 inches of countertop frontage on one side of the primary sink and 18 inches on the other side (including corner sink applications), with the 24-inch counter frontage at the same counter height as the sink. Countertop frontage may be a continuous surface or the total of two angled countertop sections. Measure only countertop frontage; do not count corner space.

■ The minimum allowable space from a corner to the edge of the primary sink is 3 inches; it should also be a minimum of 15 inches from that corner to the sink centerline.

■ If there is anything less than 18 inches of frontage from the edge of the primary sink to a corner, 21 inches of clear counter (measure frontage) should be allowed on the return.

■ A minimum of 3 inches of countertop frontage should be

provided on one side of a secondary sink and 18 inches on the other side (including corner sink applications), with the 18-inch frontage at the same counter height as the sink. The countertop frontage may be a continuous surface or the total of two angled countertop sections. Measure only countertop frontage; do not count corner space.

■ At least 15 inches of landing space, a minimum of 16 inches deep, should be planned above, below, or adjacent to a microwave oven.

■ In an open-ended kitchen configuration, at least 9 inches of counter space should be allowed on one side of the cooking surface and 15 inches on the other, at the same counter height as the appliance. For an enclosed configuration, at least 3 inches of clearance space should be planned at an end wall protected by flame-retardant surfacing material and 15 inches should be allowed on the other side of the appliance, at the same counter height as the appliance.

■ For safety, the countertop should also extend a minimum of 9 inches behind the cooking surface, at the same counter height as the appliance, in any instance where there is not an abutting wall or backsplash.

■ In an outside-angle installation of cooking surfaces, there should be at least 9 inches of straight counter space on one side and 15 inches of straight counter space on the other side, at the same counter height as the appliance.

■ Allow for at least 15 inches of counter space on the latch side of the refrigerator or on both sides of a side-by-side refrigerator, or at least 15 inches of landing space that is no more than 48 inches across from the refrigerator.

■ Although it is not ideal, it is acceptable to place an oven adjacent to a refrigerator. For convenience, locate the refrigerator next to the available countertop. If there is no safe landing area across from the oven, this arrangement can be reversed.

■ Allow for at least 15 inches of landing space that is at least 16 inches deep next to or above the oven if the appliance door opens into a primary traffic pattern. At least 15×16 inches of landing space that is no more than 48 inches across from the oven is acceptable if the appliance does not open into a traffic area.

■ Plan for at least 36 inches of continuous countertop that is at least 16 inches deep for the preparation center. The preparation center should be adjacent to a water source.

■ The preparation center can be placed between the main sink and the cooking surface, between the refrigerator and the primary sink, or adjacent to a secondary sink on an island or other cabinet section.

■ No two primary work centers (the main sink, refrigerator, preparation or cooktop/range center) should be separated by a full-height, full-depth tall tower, such as an oven cabinet, pantry cabinet, or refrigerator.

■ Countertop corners should be clipped or curved; counter edges should be beveled or rounded to eliminate sharp corners.

Appliance placement and use/clearance space

■ Knee space, which may be open or adaptable, should be planned below or adjacent to sinks, cooktops, ranges, and ovens whenever possible. Knee space should be a minimum of 27 inches high × 30 inches wide × 19 inches deep under

Room to move
The aisles between work spaces such as this island and sink should be a minimum of 42 inches wide in a one-cook kitchen and at least 48 inches in two-cook kitchens.

the counter. The 27-inch height may decrease progressively as depth increases. Surfaces in the knee space area should be finished for safety and aesthetic reasons.

■ Allow for a clear floor space of 30×48 inches at the sink, dishwasher, cooktop, oven, and refrigerator. These spaces may overlap, and up to 19 inches of knee space beneath an appliance or counter cabinet may be part of the total 30-inch and/or 48-inch dimension.

■ Allow for a minimum of 21 inches of clear floor space between the edge of the dishwasher and counters, appliances, and/or cabinets that are placed at a right angle to the dishwasher.

■ The edge of the primary dishwasher should be within 36 inches of the edge of one sink. The dishwasher should be accessible to more than one person at a time to accommodate other cooks, kitchen cleanup helpers, and/or other family members.

■ If the kitchen has only one sink, it should be located between or across from the cooking surface, preparation area, or refrigerator.

■ Allow at least 24 inches of clearance between the cooking surface and a protected surface above, or at least 30 inches of clearance between the cooking surface and an unprotected surface above. If the protected surface is a microwave hood combination, manufacturer's specifications may dictate a smaller clearance.

■ All major appliances used for surface cooking should have a ventilation system, with a fan rated at a minimum of 150 cubic feet of air per minute.

■ Do not place the cooking surface below an operable window unless the window is 3 inches or more behind the appliance and more than 24 inches above it. Windows, operable or inoperable, above a cooking surface should not be dressed with flammable window treatments.

■ Place the microwave oven so that the bottom of the appliance is between 24 inches and 48 inches above the floor.

Guidelines for eat-in kitchens

There are different per-diner space recommendations for kitchen eating areas, depending on the height of your table

A spot for a hot pot
The countertop flanking this range meets recommendations for landing space: at least 9 inches on one side of the cooking surface and at least 15 inches on the other side.

and/or eating counter. Recommendations are as follows.
For 30-inch-high tables and counters:

■ Allow a 30-inch-wide × 19-inch-deep counter or table space for each seated diner, and at least 19 inches of clear knee space.

For 36-inch-high counters:

■ Allow a 24-inch-wide × 15-inch-deep counter space for each seated diner, and at least 15 inches of clear knee space.

For 42-inch-high counters:

■ Allow for a 24-inch-wide × 12-inch-deep counter space for each seated diner, and at least 12 inches of clear knee space.

Utility requirements

If you have an older home whose mechanicals haven't been updated recently—or if you plan on moving the kitchen sink or purchasing heavy-duty appliances—you need to be sure your kitchen is sufficiently wired and plumbed to handle your new utility requirements. If not, bringing your kitchen up to speed is a necessary step in your kitchen project.

Electrical requirements

You'll need to check your local building codes for the specifics of what your area requires, but in general, an electrically well-equipped kitchen requires up to seven individual circuits.

Major appliances other than the refrigerator—such as an electric range, dishwasher, and microwave—all need their own designated circuits. You need a 120/240-volt circuit for the range (the clock and timer require 120 volts and the heating elements require 240 volts), and two 120-volt circuits, one each for the dishwasher and microwave. If you install a garbage disposal in your kitchen, it's a good idea to put it on its own 120-volt circuit too.

To power small appliances, such as toasters, coffeemakers, and blenders, you'll need at least two 120-volt, 20-amp GFCI (ground fault circuit interrupter, a safety device that senses shock hazard and shuts down a circuit or receptacle) countertop receptacles. Countertop receptacles are placed no more than 4 feet apart so that no spot on the countertop is more than 24 inches from a power source when measuring horizontally. Your kitchen also needs one general lighting circuit to power all the room's lighting with electricity.

If you are adding circuits, you must be sure your electrical panel can handle the number of circuits you plan to add. To run a test, figure out how many circuits you need in your kitchen. Turn on all the fixtures and appliances in the room, then either flip the breakers or pull fuses at the electrical panel to figure out how many you already have.

When you know how many you have to add, count how many slots are open in your electrical panel (remember that a 240-volt circuit requires two slots). If you have enough and are competent to do so, you can run them yourself. If not, you'll need to call an electrician to install a new panel—which requires an electrical permit. Let your electric company know when the new panel is installed. An inspector will check to be sure the incoming cable is large enough to handle the load from the power line.

Plumbing requirements

Your home's plumbing system may have several faucets, but it has two main facets: The supply side brings water to a fixture, whether it's a tub, toilet, or sink. The drain, vent, and waste (commonly called DVW) system takes wastewater away and vents sewer gases to the outside.

If your new kitchen design doesn't require that you move your sink, the plumbing part of your project might be something you could do. Moving plumbing is a tricky proposition. You have to worry about the slope of drainpipes (¼ inch per foot from the fixture drain to the vertical stack), making sure the sink doesn't stray too far from the main stack, pipe

How much wattage?

There's a simple way to figure out how many circuits your kitchen will require. The wattage that any one circuit can handle is equal to the amperage of the breaker times 120. For example, a 20-amp breaker (20×120) can handle a draw of 2,400 watts. It's a good idea, though, to use a circuit at a maximum of only 80 percent of its capacity—in this case, that would be 1,920 watts.

The chart below lists some common wattage ratings for kitchen appliances. Appliances both large and small generally have their wattage rating printed on the back or bottom of the appliance. Add up the wattage of the appliances you plan to plug into each circuit. If you have a microwave and a toaster on the same circuit, for instance, you're going to have a lot of breakfasts interrupted by a blown fuse. Keep these numbers in mind when you plan your circuits.

APPLIANCE	WATTAGE
Blender	200–500
Coffeemaker	600–1,000
Food processor	300–500
Microwave oven	500–1,200
Toaster	800–1,200
Toaster oven	1,500

A kitchen for everyone

Universal design is for everyone, despite physical limitations. Here are ideas for making your kitchen user-friendly. 1: A seated cook can easily slide a heavy pot across a smooth cooktop. 2: Raising the dishwasher makes unloading easier on the back. 3: There's no reaching for the microwave when it sits low. 4: A side-hinged door gives a seated cook easy access to the oven.

size, fittings, and local code requirements. Consider calling a professional for any major plumbing job.

Here are some general plumbing considerations to keep in mind when designing your kitchen:

■If pipes will be moved to exterior walls, they will have to be protected from freezing.

■To maintain the structural integrity of your floor, no joists should be cut to route pipes to the vertical stack.

■If the sink will be moved to a load-bearing wall, the structural integrity of the framing will have to be maintained when routing pipes.

■Code requires that a sink trap must be located within a

specific distance of the vertical stack. Sinks must also be situated a specific distance from side walls and must have a designated amount of clear floor space in front of them. You or your plumber will have to install the sink in compliance with local code.

■There are two basic types of pipe: copper and plastic. Copper is best for supply pipes because it can withstand the water pressure inherent in the supply system. Plastic pipe is generally best for drain systems because it doesn't rust. To meet code, be sure you get polyvinyl chloride (PVC) pipe. If you are connecting to an existing metal drain system (common in older homes), you'll need a transition fitting.

4

materials

THERE ARE MULTIPLE COOKING STYLES AND APPROACHES. Whether you are a gourmet chef or a pragmatic family cook who feeds and cleans up after small children and multiple pets every day may influence whether you put your money on high-end appliances or on virtually indestructible countertop and flooring materials. If you have any special culinary interests, they too will determine some of the features of your new kitchen. Your family life also will dictate certain requirements, whether you have babies and toddlers, teenagers, or grandchildren, or are empty nesters. These are the lifestyle questions that are crucial in designing the kitchen that will provide you with the most efficient and pleasant work space for your daily and special-occasion needs and will give you a place where you're happy to spend time. Achieving your kitchen goals requires an understanding of the vast options available as you select the cabinetry, work surfaces, flooring, lighting, appliances, and finishing details that make your kitchen work for you, before you need to make purchasing decisions. Only then can you make informed choices when buying or working with a professional designer or building contractor on your remodeling project.

A blend of hardworking, durable surface materials—steel, copper, wrought iron, unglazed tile, and wood—combine in this kitchen for a look that's both serious and warm. The elements are united by their tones and repetition. Steel and copper in the range hood, for example, are repeated in the owner's pots and pans. Steel cabinet fronts are edged with wood, as is the tile island top.

all about cabinetry

Few things feel quite as permanent as the new cabinets you choose for your kitchen. For such a big purchase (cabinetry accounts for 40 percent of the price tag of a typical kitchen remodeling project), it's important to focus on the essentials: how your new cabinets will look and work.

Because of its price tag and longevity, cabinetry may be one of the kitchen components least subjected to fads and fashion, but a look at some broad trends over recent years will help you zero in on the features you'll love now, and still love down the road.

The finish line

High-quality finishes help transform a cabinet from a piece of wood to a work of art. Distressed finishes add premature age, but today's look leans more toward worn than crackled. To create the effect, painted finishes are rubbed away in areas to reveal the natural wood underneath, then finished with a glaze that darkens any grooves or embellishments. Similarly, multiple layers created with any combination of paint, stain, and glaze bring depth and richness to natural wood surfaces.

Mighty maple

A range of colors achieved through various finishing techniques has made it appear that new and unusual species of wood are taking root in today's kitchens, but in reality, maple is the No. 1 choice for cabinetry, according to the National Kitchen & Bath Association.

In its natural hue, maple provides a lighter touch than the darker oak and walnut versions used over the years. But it's also just as likely to be stained—wood-tone or colored—and appreciated for its grain and hardness. The chameleon qualities of maple have also helped establish its reputation as timeless. Dressed up with stainless-steel appliances and dark stone countertops, or made comfortably casual with white appliances and matching laminate or solid-surfacing countertops, maple cabinetry makes itself at home in virtually any kind of kitchen.

Details, details

Gone are the days when cabinets were unembellished boxes. Today's most interesting styles take their finishing touches from furniture and architecture. Add-ons, such as fretwork, light valances, undercounter corbels, and mullioned doors, give a standard setup custom appeal. Islands with fancy feet, commanding pilasters, and arched openings achieve a focal-point status that's more a result of style than of location. Carvings, cutouts, and moldings all add emphasis to a cabinet's decorative aspects, creating the inclination to evaluate cabinetry quality using furniture standards.

Surprises inside

It used to be that a kitchen was well-equipped if it included a lazy Susan and a built-in spice rack. Now storage options are plentiful, ranging from wine racks and roll-out trays to bread boxes and appliance garages. What's most interesting about the concealed features, though, is where and how they're hidden. Where you'd expect to find swinging doors opening to reveal storage inserts, there are pullout doors attached to shelves for pots and pans, holders for recycling and garbage bins, and racks for canned and dry goods. Equipped with glides similar to those used for drawers, these pullout units speak to efficiency: no wasted movements opening doors and then pulling out racks, and no struggling with hard-to-reach items in the back of the cabinet.

On their own

Call it the European influence or a return to this country's early 19th-century notions: Many of today's kitchens assign furniture duties to cabinetry. Some pieces—such as base cabinets on legs or casters doing time as islands—are freestanding. But others simply appear to be freestanding china hutches, pie safes, and buffets. Moldings finish upper cabinets, backsplashes complement upper and base cabinets. And because they're physically separated from the rest of the built-in units, these freestanding look-alikes are proving so versatile that they make it easy to carry your kitchen style into a breakfast room or dining room, where storage and display space is always welcome.

Mix it up

Accent pieces—in any color or wood other than the rest of the kitchen—fit a cabinetry plan much like a patterned scarf

or tie with a solid-black suit. A cabinetry section or unit that breaks up the monotony can be a pivotal design piece. A popular example is a colored island surrounded by wood-tone or white cabinets. It's not uncommon to find a hutch or one section of cabinetry treated in the same manner. This mix of finishes is most effective when the two hues are used in unequal portions and when the lesser-used finish is repeated in some other way. A breakfast table that matches the kitchen island links the kitchen and the breakfast room.

Defining your options

Shopping for kitchen cabinets is like assembling a wardrobe. You can buy everything off the rack, invest strictly in tailored clothes, or work with a combination of both. Though the distinctions among the types of cabinetry—stock, semi-custom, and custom—are not always clear-cut, there are some differences that may help you zero in on your options.

Stock cabinets

Mass-produced, readily available units built to standard sizes are known as stock, or standard, cabinets. You can generally buy them through a home center and take them home immediately or have them delivered in a matter of days.

Furniture for your kitchen

Storage space is plentiful in this warmly lit cherry kitchen, *above.* Pots, pans, small appliances, and staples stow away behind solid cabinet doors, and glass-front doors display a collection of colorful Fiestaware with flair. Fashioned from reclaimed pieces of antique pine, this beautiful larder, *below,* offers convenient and accessible storage for dishes, staples, and baking items.

Though stock cabinetry is considered the most affordable option, this is not a reflection of quality as much as it is of selection: You're limited to the sizes and styles manufacturers produce in volume. Stock units are manufactured in 3-inch-width increments. If that doesn't work out nicely with your kitchen's dimensions, you'll need to add matching wood pieces, called filler strips, to close gaps between cabinets.

The finishes for stock cabinets tend to be the most popular wood species, and the choice of door styles usually is limited. Storage features also are relatively basic: You're most likely to find lazy Susans, spice racks, microwave oven shelves, appliance garages, and pullout trays, but the options are improving all the time, and some lines feature amenities once limited to the custom and semicustom realms.

Stock cabinetry is a good choice for those willing to choose from a smaller range of options in order to devote more of their kitchen budget to other elements.

What you don't see

Manufactured wood products called substrates are hidden behind laminate, vinyl film, and wood veneers. Here are the types of substrates you'll find:

PARTICLEBOARD is made from wood particles mixed with resin and bonded under pressure. It serves as the base for most cabinetry covered with laminate and vinyl film. New technology and improved resins are making particleboard a strong, reliable building material. In poor grades, though, hinges and other fasteners tend to fall out. Particleboard that's too thin will buckle or warp under the weight of kitchen gear.

MEDIUM-DENSITY FIBERBOARD, called MDF, is a high-quality substrate material made from finer fibers than particleboard. It offers superior screw-holding power, clean edges, and an extremely smooth surface. In addition, its edges can be shaped and painted.

PLYWOOD is made by laminating thin layers of wood to each other, with the grain at right angles in alternate plies. Varying the direction of the grain gives plywood equal strength in all directions. The layers are bonded with glue under heat and pressure. Thin plywood is typically used on cabinet backs; thick plywood forms the sides. Plywood is also noted for its strength and ability to hold screws.

Semicustom cabinets

Stepping up to semicustom cabinetry allows you more choices and greater design flexibility than stock cabinets while keeping costs reasonable. Semicustom options feature a hybrid of stock and custom work that offer a custom look.

The units are factory-made but not until you place an order based on your kitchen's specifications. You're still generally limited to 3-inch width increments, but you'll find more height and width options than in stock units.

You have some freedom to outfit units for specific needs. For example, you may want to include a roll-out trash bin in one of the base cabinets, or glass inserts in some of the upper cabinet doors. Semicustom cabinetry brings these amenities and others—wine and plate racks, apothecary-style drawers, phone desks, mini pantries—into play. Choosing semicustom cabinetry generally requires that you visit a showroom and discuss your requirements with a manufacturer's sales representative. You decide on wood species, finish, door and drawer styles, and any special features. The manufacturer customizes existing designs to suit your needs. It's like buying a garment off the rack and then having it altered to your specific measurements.

Custom cabinets

Cabinetry built in the material of your choice and to your kitchen's exact specifications, regardless of standard widths, heights, depths, or shapes, is known as custom. Considered top of the line and the most versatile, you can expect custom cabinets to cost twice as much as stock goods. Yet a custom job can be comparable to or even less expensive than semicustom, depending on the special features you choose.

What you're buying is design freedom and a look tailored to your lifestyle. You can have cabinets that follow curves, sit at odd angles, or support raised or lowered countertops, or whose interiors are extra tall, wide, or deep. Drawers, racks, and shelves may be shaped to hold specific items or collections; you might want the wood species, finish, and hardware to be consistent with a particular style or faithful to a certain historical era.

With so much freedom—and such a large investment at stake—it's wise to hire a kitchen designer, architect, or other

Style and substance

The cherry armoire contains a pantry and a refrigerator. The hutchlike cherry unit contains a concealed microwave oven and a ceramic glass cooktop.

professional to assist you with your complete kitchen design. A design professional helps you convey your wishes to the custom cabinetmaker, whether you choose to have the units built by a woodworking friend or relative, a local cabinet shop, or a nationally known manufacturer.

Below the surface

The material your cabinets are made of determines how they look and how they'll stand up to daily use. To help you strike a balance between style and structural support, here's a look at the most common cabinetry materials.

SOLID WOOD AND VENEER: Most cabinets are made from hardwoods, but to reduce costs, these hardwoods are often applied as veneers over a substrate, such as plywood. Veneered cabinets are more stable than solid lumber is in high-humidity areas, and the grain matching may be better.

Before you select the wood for your cabinets, consider whether you like the wood grain or the natural color of the wood (see examples, page 58). You're not necessarily wedded to a wood's natural color. Stain can replicate the color of maple on a birch base, for example.

Wood warps easily as its moisture content changes. That's why it's important that the wood be finished on all sides before it leaves the factory. Unfinished cabinetry should be finished on-site as soon as possible to prevent warping.

LAMINATE AND THERMOFOIL: Cabinetry that is not made of solid wood or wood veneer is generally laminate or Thermofoil, both of which are applied to substrates (see "What You Don't See," opposite). Laminate and Thermofoil come in a range of colors and patterns, including some that mimic wood. Though they are typically used on flat doors, both processes can accommodate the curves of raised-panel doors as well.

Laminates are made of three resin-saturated layers: a base layer of paper, a printed and colored layer (which may look like wood), and a protective transparent layer. Heat and pressure fuse a laminate to a substrate. The weight of the substrate makes laminate cabinets surprisingly heavier than those made of solid wood. Laminate is used to cover exterior cabinetry surfaces, the fronts and backs of doors, and some interior surfaces.

High-pressure laminates give the best performance of any laminate, but they are relatively expensive. Difficult to damage (but also to repair), this strong material provides vertical surfaces with the same durability as countertops. Low-pressure laminates, also called melamine, work well for most vertical surfaces. They are less impact resistant than are high-pressure laminates and have a tendency to crack and chip. The use of better substrates reduces these problems.

Thermofoil is a vinyl film applied to a substrate with heat and pressure. The application process makes it possible for Thermofoil to more closely resemble wood detailing than

Types of wood

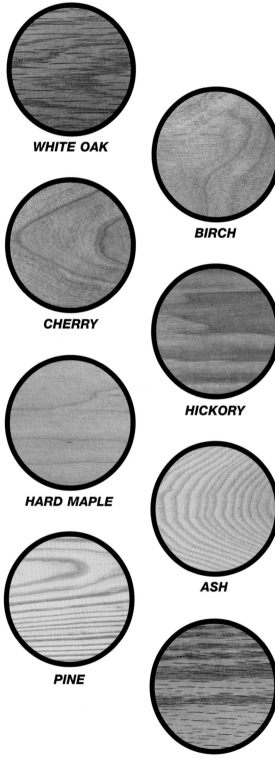

WHITE OAK

BIRCH

CHERRY

HICKORY

HARD MAPLE

ASH

PINE

RED OAK

laminate can. Most often available in white or almond, Thermofoil cabinets are easy to care for and are much less likely to chip than painted cabinets are.

Wood varieties

RED OAK is strong and durable and relatively inexpensive. Available in a wide range of styles and finishes, it features pronounced grain patterns and is most often used for traditional cabinet styles. This wood is an option for stock and semicustom cabinets as well as more costly selections.

WHITE OAK is as durable and a bit stronger than its red counterpart. With more golden tones, white oak offers a more subtle hue and is often quarter-sawn for custom cabinetry—especially for an Arts and Crafts or period look. Generally, white oak is available only as a custom option.

HARD MAPLE is a fine-grain, light-color wood that's slightly more expensive than oak but less dense. This is a popular choice among those shopping for semicustom and custom cabinets. Maple can be stained but more often has a clear or natural finish to achieve a light, contemporary look.

HICKORY is lighter in color than oak but similar in grain pattern and strength. This creamy, pale-yellow wood can be stained; however, like maple, its blond tones are most often complemented with a clear or natural finish. Lending itself to a rustic style, hickory is a rare choice, usually for custom and semicustom cabinetry.

CHERRY is elegant and formal when used for certain traditional cabinetry styles but is hard enough to withstand everyday knocks and marring. Cherry's design versatility can also give a kitchen a contemporary personality. This smooth, fine-grain red to reddish-brown wood darkens with age so it often is stained to ensure uniformity of color.

BIRCH is a durable, fine-grain wood that is slightly darker than maple. It takes finishes well and easily masquerades as a more expensive wood. When stained, it can achieve a good faux cherry or maple look. Prone to some irregular coloring, birch is a relatively inexpensive wood available in both stock and semicustom lines.

ASH is similar in strength and durability to oak but has a light color and a more pronounced figure. This straight-grain lumber takes on a contemporary character when it's

given a clear or natural finish. It's most often seen in custom work but has limited availability in some semicustom lines. **PINE** is the only softwood species commonly used for cabinetry, but it dents more easily than hardwoods. This pale-yellow wood can be stained and often features knots used to underscore traditional and country styles. Eastern white pine and Western white pine are found in select semicustom lines.

Building boxes

Why should you worry about how cabinetry is designed and constructed when you want to buy new cabinets, not build them? Because when your home center salesperson asks, "What kind of cabinets would you like for your new kitchen?" a basic knowledge of cabinetry anatomy will come in handy. The following definitions and explanations will help you get to know typical cabinets inside and out.

Cabinet construction

The most traditional type of cabinetry is known as face-frame. The term refers to a solid-wood frame attached to the front edges of the cabinet box. Hinges that attach the doors to the frame may be either exposed or hidden. Because the frame overlaps the door and drawer openings, drawers and pullout inserts must be smaller than the actual width of the cabinet. This takes up some room inside the box. Frameless cabinetry, on the other hand, offers a more contemporary appearance and slightly more space inside. When you open the door of a frameless cabinet, you see the ends of each panel that make up the box. Door hinges attach to the inside of the cabinet sides and are not visible when the doors are closed. Though it's most typical to find frameless cabinets in laminate, some companies offer them in wood.

Door and drawer fronts

Three general categories offer three different looks. You'll find all of these in face-frame construction, but only full-overlay doors and drawers are used on frameless cabinets. **FULL-INSET CONSTRUCTION** means that doors and drawers fit flush with the face frame. Because this requires a precision fit, it's available only in custom cabinetry. **PARTIAL-OVERLAY DOORS AND DRAWERS** are large enough to cover the openings but small enough to reveal the frame around the edges. This is the easiest style to construct and the most affordable because it gives leeway in adjusting the position of doors and drawers. **FULL-OVERLAY DOORS AND DRAWERS** cover the face frame (or the entire box front on frameless cabinets), leaving only a sliver of space between doors and drawers for ease in opening.

Door styles

Three types of doors, *right*: solid-wood frame and panel; solid-wood slab; and solid-wood frame with veneer. The best joint for a cabinet box is a dado joint, *below*. The sides of the cabinet fit into grooves cut into the back and face frame. A corner gusset—a triangular brace—adds strength.

Doors

Despite the seemingly endless selection of door styles available, they all fall into one of two categories: frame-and-panel or slab.

The construction of a frame-and-panel door allows for the normal movement of solid wood because the panel "floats" within the frame. The panel within a solid-wood frame is either a flat veneer panel or a raised panel of veneer or solid wood. When glass, metal, or some other kind of insert is used instead of a wood panel, the frame construction generally features an open lip on the back. The insert is secured against the lip rather than within the frame.

Because of its clean lines and no-nonsense front, a solid-wood slab door offers a more contemporary look than a frame-and-panel door. Although a solid-wood slab door appears to be a single panel of wood, it's actually several pieces of wood glued together. Crosspieces screwed into the back add stability. Solid-wood slab doors are most often used in the full-overlay style, which leaves just a sliver of space between doors and drawers for ease in opening.

Cabinet boxes

A cabinet's side panels, back, and floorboard are made of plywood, particleboard, or medium-density fiberboard that's covered with veneer. The best joinery method for the cabinet box is a dado joint, in which the sides fit into grooves cut into the cabinet back and the face frame. This type of joint offers more strength and stability than a joint that simply has been butted and glued.

Corner gussets—triangular braces glued into the cabinet box's upper corners—add strength, as does the back panel, which also guards against insects and vermin. Plastic clips hold false drawer fronts in place.

Drawers

Durable joinery, materials, and glides keep drawers operating smoothly over time. The best drawer features dovetail or dowel joints, $1/2$- or $3/4$-inch solid wood sides, and a plywood bottom panel that has been glued into grooves.

High-quality glides account for most of the difference

CORNER GUSSET

DOVETAIL JOINT

Side-mount drawer glides are the most common, but drawers with a bottom-mount mechanism save space on both sides and offer a more upscale look. Similarly, full-extension drawers that offer you full access to the inside of the drawer without removing them from the cabinet are a step up from drawers with standard, three-quarter extension hardware.

Shelves

To avoid sagging under weight, the best shelves are made from $^3/_4$-inch high-grade particleboard. As in the interior of the cabinet box, shelves are covered with a durable material, such as laminate or melamine. Adjustable shelves are held in place with easily movable metal pins or plastic clips inserted into holes drilled along the inside of the cabinet box.

For added convenience, roll-out trays—a cross between a drawer and a shelf—are more commonly standard features. They make better use of space than a shallow shelf, and their low sides provide easy access to their contents. Often subjected to as much or more weight than drawers, roll-out trays require the same high-quality glides as drawers.

between satisfactory and superior drawers. Self-closing guides with a load rating of at least 75 pounds per pair are the most desirable. When a drawer is opened an inch, it should close on its own, and it should glide smoothly when opened all the way.

Drawers and shelves

Drawers constructed with dovetail joints, *top*, offer the most strength. Roll-out trays, *above left*, are a cross between a drawer and a shelf. They offer easy access to items stored in the back of the cabinet. Removable metal pins or plastic clips hold adjustable shelves in place, *above right*. Look for shelves made from at least $^3/_4$-inch high-grade particleboard.

Deciding which cabinets to buy may be the biggest (and most expensive) materials choice you have to make during your kitchen remodeling project, but choosing the hardware—the knobs and pulls for doors and drawers—might be the most fun. Although hardware won't set you back anywhere near what the actual cabinets do, it is not a minor purchase; the average kitchen requires between 30 and 60 pieces of hardware.

Even if you're reusing your existing cabinets, outfitting them with new hardware is a great and inexpensive way to add sparkle and new life to the old doors and drawers. See the sidebar on page 63 for more information.

Hardware is a bit like jewelry for your cabinets; it adds terrific and definable style to your kitchen. It obviously has an important function, too, and that should be your first consideration in choosing it. Whether you select glass, metal, rubber, wood, resin, ceramic, or stone, be sure the knob you attach to that roll-out pantry will be large, sturdy, and comfortable enough to pull when the pantry is stocked with heavy canned goods.

Some types of hardware are associated with particular architectural styles or historic periods—and there's no shortage of reproduction hardware on the market. Don't feel locked in by the era of your kitchen, however. You can personalize your kitchen with hardware or reflect a special interest you have, such as cooking, pets, or gardening.

Hardware styles

Form and function go hand in hand when it comes to cabinet hardware. Be sure the hardware you choose is comfortable to use and that it provides easy access to your cabinet doors and drawers, but don't forget the panache it can add to your kitchen, as these examples depict.

Geometric pulls made of wood, *left,* mimic the triangular inlay that helps create an exotic African style in this kitchen. Whether you're into bulldogs, music, cooking, or gardening (as these pea-pod pulls, *center,* suggest), there's a hardware design that expresses your interest.

These barely there wrought-iron door handles, *opposite,* enhance the rustic, organic look of distressed pine cabinets.

Hardware prices depend on the material the pieces are made of and how the hardware is made. A 1940s-style plastic reproduction knob may not cost much more than a burger and fries at your favorite fast food joint, but one custom-designed pewter knob may cost as much as dinner for two at a fancy restaurant.

Sometimes the best style is no hardware at all—sort of. If you like the clean, uncluttered and unfettered look, outfit your cabinets with invisible hardware. This hardware allows cabinet doors to open simply on the hinges, or they may be fitted with a spring-loaded hinge that pops the door open with a gentle push on the corner. Invisible hardware is generally associated with a more contemporary look.

New hardware, old cabinets

One common problem homeowners face when replacing pulls and knobs on their kitchen cabinets is that the existing holes in the cabinetry sometimes don't fit the new hardware. If that's the case in your kitchen, you can purchase backplates to cover the mismatch, then drill new holes. You also can buy a pull or knob that's large enough to conceal the variation in fit, or ask your designer about ordering custom hardware sized to fit, a more expensive option. If your cabinets are painted, fill the unused holes with filler compound, let it dry, sand it lightly, and touch up the spot with matching paint.

The look that cooks

Because it is situated in an island, this gas cooktop, *above,* with easy-to-clean sealed burners is surrounded by generous counter space and sits atop a unit that provides ample storage for pots and pans.

A period-style range, *below,* completes the look of this 1930s-era kitchen. If you can't locate an authentic antique range, don't despair; reproductions offer period style and modern convenience.

Buying a do-it-all range—a combination oven and cooktop—is one-stop shopping. The combination oven and cooktop is a practical and economical choice, as well as one that may be necessitated by limited space. In large kitchens, though, the all-in-one option often gives way to more specialized, strategically located cooking units. In addition to a conventional oven, new kitchens now boast one or two microwave ovens, island cooktops, convection ovens, and even warming drawers.

Ovens and ranges

Conventional ovens, with a baking and roasting element and a broiling element, are available as wall units or freestanding ranges with cooktops. Both gas and electric heat units are comparably priced. Uneven heating is a common complaint about conventional ovens, but new models do a better job of preventing that. If you do a lot of baking, consider a convection oven. Thermal, or radiant, ovens use heat elements to roast, bake, and broil; convection ovens use fans to circulate heated air for faster, more even cooking. Convection cooking produces crustier breads, juicier roasts, and three racks of cookies at one time. A popular choice is a combination conventional/convection wall unit.

The dimensions of your kitchen, the size of your family, and your cooking ambitions all help determine the size range you buy. Measure the space you have available before you go shopping. The standard freestanding range is 30 inches wide. Sleek, pricey restaurant-style models with features such as wider Btu ranges, built-in grills, and warming drawers are available in 36-, 48- and 60-inch widths. Remember to measure for cabinet depth: A range installed flush with the cabinets produces an attractive, built-in look.

Consider also what features are important to you in a range. Self-cleaning ovens use a high-temperature cycle to burn food stains into powder for easy wiping. Continuous-clean ovens have textured walls to absorb and burn spatters. Safety features include control locks to protect children and a hot-surface indicator, which is useful to everyone. Variable-temperature broiling lets you select the ideal temperature for anything from thick steaks to delicate fish.

User friendliness varies dramatically too. Some ovens and

ranges have electronic controls and easy-to-read graphics. Some offer one-touch controls preset to common cooking temperatures. Delay and time-bake cycles allow you to start and stop the cooking process even when you're not home.

Ranges endure a lot of wear and tear over their 10- to 15-year life spans, so look for heavy-duty oven racks able to support roasts and large casseroles; porcelain broiler pans; and durable, dishwasher-safe grids. Expect at least a one-year warranty—or five years on electronics and heating elements.

The kitchen is the heart of your home, so find a range that will fit your lifestyle now and in the future. Take into account both function and design. Some cooks love the decorative impact of a colorful period-style enamel range; others are enamored of commercial stainless steel. Still others prefer traditional, neutral styling that will match any kitchen decor.

Cooktops

Choosing a cooktop no longer is as easy as deciding between gas and electric, and your choice of heat source greatly affects the price at purchase and for utility bills. Electric-coil heat is the cheapest to purchase, followed by gas, solid element, sealed gas, halogen, and induction.

Many cooks prefer the control of gas cooktops to electric. Another plus is that traditional burner grates can be removed easily for cleaning. On electric ranges, coil elements accommodate almost any cookware; glass-ceramic cooktops have radiant elements sealed beneath the surface and are sleek looking and easy to clean. Some have flat-surface electronic control with no knobs around which to wipe. Or look for a dual-fuel model combining a gas cooktop with an electric oven. Also look for a mix of outputs—high Btus to sauté and a low setting to simmer sauces and melt chocolate.

Double or one?

As you select cooking equipment for your new kitchen, you may ask yourself, "Will I ever cook enough food at one time that I'll need two ovens?" Though you may never feed a small army, you still may appreciate the convenience of two ovens. Consider these instances when having two would be handy:

DIFFERENT COOKING REQUIREMENTS. Your menu may call for two dishes to be cooked at different temperatures or using different methods—baking or broiling, for instance. To get them to the table at the same time, two ovens are your best bet.

TWO COOKS. Each of you can be in charge of an oven. In this case, separate and strategically located ovens are better than stacked.

AN EAT-IN OR ENTERTAINING KITCHEN. If it's not uncommon to share your cooking space with family and guests, an auxiliary oven located outside the work core lets you avoid opening an oven door directly into traffic.

A PREFERENCE FOR DIFFERENT KINDS OF OVENS. If you want the option of both conventional and convection cooking, for example, you may consider a combination model. But purchasing these options in separate ovens offers the most flexibility and is often no more expensive. You're also in the market for two ovens if you'd like the option of a specialty oven, such as a steam oven or baker's proofing oven.

A DESIRE TO MAXIMIZE ENERGY. Buying two ovens of different sizes enables you to heat only as much space as necessary—the larger unit roasts a 20-pound turkey; the smaller oven bakes a single loaf of banana bread.

Microwaves

Microwave ovens have proven so handy and are now so inexpensive that you might consider two for your new kitchen: one in the work core to help with preparing meals and another near the refrigerator for heating beverages and snacks. Some of the "smarter" models cook by sensing doneness instead of only by time. Wall units put microwave power and convenience at an accessible height without gobbling up counter space. Some high-end microwave units are built to handle convection cooking too.

Ventilation

The ventilation system you choose for your kitchen is without a doubt a hardworking piece of machinery. It sucks out moisture, grease, and odors so the kitchen remains a cool, pleasant place to cook. But the right hood also enhances the decor of your kitchen. Ventilation products come as updraft or downdraft units. Their names indicate how they work.

Updraft vents come as over-the-cooktop fan hoods; they are more effective and more expensive than a downdraft device. Updrafts inhale steam and smoke as vapors rise, eliminating cooking odors.

An updraft hood can be ducted to the outside or it can be merely filtered. A ducted hood ventilates more thoroughly because it releases vapors and humidity to the outside in the same way a dryer duct does. A nonducted hood uses an internal filter to trap food and grease particles. It then recirculates the air back into the kitchen without cooling it. The filter must be replaced or cleaned often; some filters are dishwasher-safe.

The other option in ventilation is a downdraft vent. This device is great for an island or peninsula cooktop or any other place where a hood might be bulky or block views. Downdrafts are installed almost flush with the countertop; when not in use, they're practically out of sight. Pressing a button raises the device so it can draw moisture and odors from the cooktop and direct the vapors downward through a vent in the base cabinetry. Like an updraft system, downdrafts must also be vented to the outside of the house.

Ventilation products are rated according to how many cubic feet of air they vent per minute (CFM). How powerful a vent you'll need depends on the power of your appliances, as well as your cooking habits. An average cook with a residential-style range will find that a vent rated at 150 CFM is sufficient. If you own a commercial-style range or do a lot of frying, you'll need something with more power. Check with the maker of your range for recommendations.

The look of the hood

The size of the vent hood you buy depends on several factors. Choose one that complements the kitchen in size and finish. A large hood is best suited to a spacious custom kitchen, where a looming hood is in proportion to the rest of the room. Many are enameled to match the range; others are made of go-with-anything stainless steel. If you want something unique, a skilled carpenter can create just about any custom hood design for your kitchen by using molding, plaster, tile, cabinetry panels, or any of an almost countless selection of other materials.

Beauty or simplicity
Ventilation hoods can be purely functional, they can complement or blend in with the cabinetry, as this elegant curved hood does, or they can add artistic flair.

dishwashers

Without a doubt, the dishwasher is the most appreciated labor-saving device in the kitchen. Simply load and unload—most machines will do the rest, taking the drudgery out of cleanup.

The most basic, inexpensive models simply clean the dishes with the push of a button. Fancier models sense how dirty the dishes are and adjust the intensity of the wash cycle, which saves water and the energy needed to heat the water. Internal water heating saves energy, too, allowing you to keep your water heater set at a lower temperature while still thoroughly cleaning and sanitizing the dishes. A no-heat dry option features a fan that stirs room air through the dishwasher to dry the dishes. But even if this and other tempting features—including specialized cycles, built-in garbage disposals, and delayed starts—hold no appeal for you, consider the noise factor.

Though it may be the most-loved appliance in the kitchen, it is also, by far, the noisiest one. And as happy as you may be not to be doing dishes by hand, a roaring dishwasher can kill some of the happiness—not to mention interfere with your favorite TV program or your child's piano practice. With today's open floor plans, kitchen noise travels farther than ever. To minimize dishwasher din, choose a well-insulated model and expect to pay extra pennies for the quiet.

If possible, locate the dishwasher behind an island or in an alcove or some other place where there's a built-in noise buffer. It's also smart, energy-wise, to avoid installing the dishwasher next to the refrigerator. After all, a refrigerator is supposed to keep things cool, and a dishwasher creates heat. Having them side by side makes the refrigerator work much harder. The same principle applies to oven placement.

Other considerations include the interior of the washtub and how flexible the capacity is. Stainless-steel interiors are durable and easy to clean, and the finish resists nicks, chips, stains, and odor buildup, but they are more expensive than plastic or porcelain-enameled metal finishes.

Dish and glass racks are made of metal, coated with either nylon or vinyl. Be sure to check out the coverage on the tops of tines, which is where the coating usually wears off first. Adjustable-height racks allow you to move things around when you need to load large items. Most dishwashers hold 10 place settings; some hold 12.

The other important consideration concerns performance. Determine each model's number and type of wash cycles, as well as the sprayer mechanism's design. High-performance dishwashers usually have two or three spray arms that hit dishes with water from several levels and angles. Smaller holes in the arms mean the spray is more forceful.

When it comes to the exterior of your dishwasher, there is a wealth of options. You can get the stainless-steel restaurant look and make your dishwasher a focal point; or you can make it disappear with the option of adding trim panels to match the cabinets. Some manufacturers have even moved the electronic controls from the front of the machine to the top of the door to further disguise the appliance.

refrigerators and freezers

With all the money you're spending on your new kitchen, there is at least some good news on the financial front: Replacing a 15-year-old refrigerator with a new one will save you about $10 a month. Although refrigerators are still big energy consumers, today's versions are much more efficient than older models, using about one-third less electricity per year. They're more environmentally friendly, too, with most ozone-depleting refrigerants now eliminated from the insulation and compressors.

If you haven't bought a refrigerator lately (most consumers replace theirs every 15 years or so), you may be asking, "Which refrigerator is for me?" The answer to that question depends on many variables, including the size of your family, how often you shop for groceries, how often you entertain, and whether you own a separate freezer.

Size is just one consideration. As a rule, buy 12 cubic feet of storage space (between the refrigerator and the freezer) for two people; add 2 more cubic feet for each extra person. Ultrathin insulation now allows for maximum interior dimensions and energy efficiency. After you've determined the size, the next step is to consider the storage space configuration and what options you require.

Conventional models, with the freezer on top, are the most efficient, but you have to bend to get at some items in the refrigerator. Bottom-freezer models put the frequently used refrigerator space at a more comfortable height. Both are comparably priced. Side-by-side units with double doors require less space for opening the doors and generally offer more cubic feet of storage. Their shelves can make storing and arranging large or odd-shaped items somewhat difficult. They're also more expensive than conventional models.

What separates basic models from top-of-the-line units are the options. Some features, such as automatic defrost, are no-brainers, but the value of others depends on your needs. Pay a little more and you'll get adjustable door bins for large beverage containers, adjustable tempered-glass shelves, sliding shelves that allow easy access to items stored at the back, spillproof glass shelves that are easier to keep clean than wire shelves, window bins and see-through crisper drawers, front-door ice and water dispensers, additional insulation for noise control, and separate temperature and moisture-level controls for meat and produce bins.

Built-in refrigerators house the compressor on top rather than at the back, so they fit almost flush with 24-inch-deep cabinets. Some freestanding models are also designed to look built-in; many project 6 inches beyond the cabinet front. Before you go shopping for appliances, measure the area where the refrigerator will go.

If your needs are simple, you might decide that a basic, quiet, dependable unit is more important than all the extras; this choice lets you put your money elsewhere in your kitchen. If you do serious cooking or entertaining, though, you might want to splurge for a professional-style refrigerator, which generally holds twice as much as a standard unit. Or you might want to investigate specialty units, such as wine coolers or refrigerator drawers.

Cool choices

Built-in refrigerators fit almost flush with 24-inch-deep cabinets, *opposite*, keeping the traffic aisle clear. Side-by-side units, such as this stainless-steel model, *below*, offer the most cubic feet of storage for the space they take up.

Think of countertops as the canvas for your kitchen artistry—and the backsplash as its backdrop. There's no rule that you have to use the same material for all your creations. Mixing and matching materials not only gives your kitchen a distinctive look but also lets you use the surface that is best suited to a particular task.

As you shop for countertop and backsplash materials, remember that these are the surfaces you will come in contact with the most as you work in your kitchen. When working out your budget, consider the cost of installing and repairing specific surfaces as well as the look, durability, and ease of maintenance of particular materials. The up-front price doesn't always reflect a surface's value to you.

LAMINATE. Low-cost, low-maintenance laminates continue to be the most popular countertop choices. These thin layers of plastic bonded to plywood or particleboard offer durability and stain resistance in a wide variety of colors and finishes—at a reasonable price. Laminate is by far the least-expensive countertop option. Preformed laminate countertops are widely available at home centers, and installation is well within the capability of the do-it-yourselfer. However, some lower-end laminates contain patterns that don't penetrate below the surface. That means a stray knife blade or hot pan could ruin the surface. Solid-color laminates are less vulnerable to these scratches and chips. When possible, save laminates for less-used areas of the kitchen.

CERAMIC TILE. For more durability and even greater color choice, consider ceramic tile. Comparable in price to laminate, tile comes in myriad shapes and sizes, which allows for great design flexibility. Ceramic tile makes a terrific surface on which to set hot pans and dishes, although some cooks don't like the uneven surface created by the grout lines. Although keeping glazed tiles clean is easy, the grout lines can be a nuisance, as they tend to collect dirt and food particles and are easily stained. Patterned and hand-painted tiles add flair to your countertop and backsplash, but they are more expensive than stock tiles. Installing a sprinkling of custom tiles among a field of stock tiles is a popular, budget-smart strategy.

SOLID-SURFACING. This manufactured material comes in a vast range of colors and patterns that mimic granite and other stones. Part of its appeal is that it is less expensive and easier to shape and install than the natural material it mimics. At ½–1½ inches thick, solid-surfacing is nonporous and extremely durable, though not indestructible. Knives and hot pots can scratch or burn the surface, but

Mix it up or keep it seamless?

Your countertop and backsplash can be an eclectic mélange of materials such as this one, *below left*, or a seamless construction of one material, such as the ceramic tile countertop and backsplash, *below right*.

because the color runs all the way through, most minor damage can be repaired with sandpaper. Solid-surfacing is more malleable than stone and can be molded into practically any shape. A one-piece integrated sink and countertop is a popular option. Because there's no lip on this type of sink, there's nothing that collects food particles, making cleaning the sink and countertop much easier.

SOLID-SURFACING VENEER. Similar in structure to laminate, solid-surfacing veneer is made of a thin layer of solid-surfacing material bonded to a wood base. The veneer is durable, stain-resistant, and 20 to 30 percent less expensive than conventional solid-surfacing.

STONE. Nothing compares with the beauty and durability of granite or marble; but then, nothing compares with their price tags either. Even if you find salvaged pieces at a lower price, installation of the heavy, hard-to-cut slabs remains costly. A good alternative is granite or marble tiles, and even a tight budget should allow for this luxury. Marble is the ideal work surface for rolling out dough. If you're an ardent baker, consider installing a piece in your baking area.

Granite, less porous than marble, is the most popular stone for countertops. It holds up to almost anything: heat, water, knives, and most stains (sealing it will protect it from

Beautiful backsplashes

A backsplash can be beautiful, but it also serves an important function: It keeps splashes and spills from staining and spoiling your walls and from running down the back of your cabinets.

Backsplashes can be made from a material that matches your countertops or, for contrast, from an entirely different one. Good backsplash materials include ceramic tile, glass, stone, metal, wood, mirrors, laminate, stainless steel, copper, and solid-surfacing. Generally a backsplash doesn't get the same hard use as the countertop but should be maintained at the same time to keep it in good shape.

Whether you want your backsplash to stand out as a design statement or just stand up to stains, the right materials will help you do it with style.

all stains). Marble requires frequent resealing to resist staining. You'll need to wax both materials and polish their surfaces regularly to maintain a sparkling sheen.

BUTCHER BLOCK. A staple of the 1970s, butcher block is still the ideal surface for those who like the warmth of wood and want a great cutting surface. Butcher block is affordable but requires more care than most surfaces. Wood requires thorough disinfecting after food prep, as well as periodic mineral oil baths. Consider installing one section of butcher block in the kitchen's work area for chopping vegetables and slicing bread, in lieu of a cutting board.

STAINLESS STEEL. Serious cooks are drawn to stainless steel for its durability, immunity to heat, ease of upkeep—and the way it matches their professional-style appliances. Stainless steel is extremely easy to keep clean, but it can be scratched. Its main drawback: Some find the clank of utensils on the surface annoying.

CONCRETE. It's not just for driveways anymore. Tough, reliable concrete is growing in favor as a kitchen counter surface. It is as durable as natural stone and can be stamped with designs and colored any desired shade. A sealer protects the color and makes the surface easy to clean. Although concrete countertops are expensive because they are handcrafted, their popularity is beginning to drive the costs down.

A concrete option
Concrete may be textured and rustic, such as this countertop, *below,* or smooth and sleek.

Style and substance
This soapstone farmhouse sink and counter give a rustic look to this country kitchen—and provide room for potting plants.

More than mere plumbing, sinks and faucets are the lifelines of a kitchen, providing hot and cold water on demand. Although these fixtures should be dependable and easy to use, function doesn't have to preclude style.

Basin basics

So much is demanded from the kitchen sink these days that many homeowners are making room for a larger sink or even adding a second one. If you think all sinks are alike, you'll be surprised by the options available.

MATERIALS. Although more alternatives have become available in recent years—such as integrated granite or soapstone sinks, quartz or solid-surfacing sinks—the most popular types of kitchen sinks are still stainless steel or cast iron.

Stainless steel is lightweight, durable, easy to clean, and the least expensive of all sink options. It's popular for contemporary and professional-style kitchens. Though stainless, the shiny surface shows fingerprints, water spots, and scratches.

Cast iron provides a warmer, more traditional look. A little pricier than stainless or enameled steel, it's also more substantial. The weighty units can be a bear to install, but enameled cast iron resists chipping and stays shiny for years. White cast iron, its most popular shade, is a natural for all-white kitchens, though you can buy it in nearly any color to coordinate with your kitchen's decor.

Quartz composite, a material made from crushed or ground quartz, and solid-surfacing, made from acrylic- or polyester-base materials, are prized for their nonporous and stain-resistant surfaces that feature color throughout. These materials offer a distinctive look and incredible durability, allowing you to have the sink and countertop built as one easy-to-clean piece. Other than an integrated countertop/sink made of natural stone such as marble or quartz, however, quartz composite and solid-surfacing are also the most expensive options.

BOWLS. Double-bowl sinks have long been standard kitchen fare, but you can choose the number and size of bowls to fit your needs. A standard double-bowl sink is 33 inches wide and 8 inches deep. You might prefer a different configuration—for instance, one extra-deep (10-inch) basin for pots and pans and one shallow (6- to 7-inch) bowl for food prep. A three-bowl sink usually has two large bowls on the outside and a smaller prep sink in the center. The farm sink—one huge rectangular and very deep bowl with an exposed apron front—has become popular in recent years.

MOUNTING. The two ways of mounting a sink are by drop-in or undermount. Although most sinks are mounted from above with a ridge, or lip, that fits over the countertop, there are basins of all types that are recessed below the work surface. Undermount sinks pair well with solid-surfacing. There's no rim to collect food or dirt, and you can easily sweep water and crumbs from the counter into the bowls.

Faucet flair

Below the sink, most kitchen faucets are pretty much the same. Aboveboard, however, the variations in finish, height and shape of the spout, number and type of handles, and features such as sprayers and filters continue to increase.

The most basic option to consider is probably one handle or two. A single-handle faucet lets you mix water temperature with one hand, but the look of separate hot and cold controls, especially controls that feature cross-shape or large wing-shape handles for a period look, appeals to many people. Choose faucets made with replaceable cartridges or ceramic-disk valves instead of old-fashioned rubber washers.

Chrome and brass are the most common materials used for faucets, although pewter, nickel, and copper are available. Faucets with crystal or porcelain detailing mimic antiques.

Perhaps the biggest change in the modern faucet is the look of its spouts. Taller, longer spouts with high gooseneck arcs give you more clearance for filling or scrubbing large pots and pans. Spouts with pullout sprayers aid cleaning and let you fill large pans without putting them in the sink.

Concerns about water quality might lead you to consider a water filtration or purification system; you can incorporate it right into your sink and faucet setup. Faucets with built-in filters let you choose between filtered water for drinking and cooking, and unfiltered water for cleaning.

One bowl or two (or more)

The bowl configuration you choose depends on how you use your sink. The double sink, *below left*, has a large bowl for food prep and a small bowl for cleanup. The stainless-steel single-bowl undermount sink, *below right*, has a contemporary look.

Colorful, stylish flooring can make a strong design statement in this high-visibility room, but the material you choose must also be able to take a beating and handle heavy traffic, falling objects, and spills of all sorts.

So which materials will become the focal point of your new kitchen? Although you should put practical considerations first, color and pattern will no doubt be on your mind as you shop. If you haven't bought flooring in a while, you'll be pleasantly surprised by today's range of flooring choices. Manufacturers offer many different materials, in prices that range from low-budget to blow-the-budget. They look great, perform well, and require little care. Here's the lowdown on the many choices in the flooring market.

VINYL. Affordable vinyl has come a long way. While it has always been used to mimic other materials, such as stone or ceramic tile, new technology makes it more difficult to distinguish between the copycat and the real thing. Vinyl is also a good choice for families with young children. The softness of the floor cuts down on noise, increases the chances that a dropped glass will survive, and is easy on the cook's legs and feet. It also cleans up easily. Of all the available flooring options, vinyl is also the least expensive.

Vinyl comes in two forms—sheet or tile—and is available in hundreds of colors and patterns. Sheet vinyl is slightly more expensive than vinyl tiles, but it is also seamless. Vinyl tiles, usually 12×12-inch squares, are a good starting point for almost any geometric design. You can arrange two colors to form a classic checkerboard; buy several shades for a mosaic effect; or select tiles with diagonal corners and companion filler squares to mimic a ceramic tile floor.

LAMINATE. Popular for several decades in Europe, laminate has taken hold on this side of the ocean too. Laminate is the chameleon of the flooring world. It can mimic almost any other material—from stone to ceramic tile to (most commonly) wood—with lower cost and maintenance.

Spills just mop up—a saving grace in the kitchen. Laminate is made of medium- or high-density fiberboard and layers of paper and resin. It's available in planks, strips, and squares, which piece together easily.

Laminate is slightly higher in price than vinyl, and you will need underlayment and glue for some types. Installation is most often an easy do-it-yourself project.

CERAMIC TILE. A classic in the kitchen, ceramic tile is cool and smooth underfoot and has many fans because of its timelessness, durability, and design versatility. When you add grout in a complementary or contrasting color, the squares either fade into the background or pop onto center stage. Set on a diagonal, a ceramic tile pattern creates the visual effect of expanding a room.

Ceramic tile comes in sizes ranging from 1×1- to 12×12-inch squares, as well as geometric shapes in all sizes and unlimited colors. The tile itself is relatively inexpensive, but the cost of installing it depends on the pattern you choose and your subfloor and underlayment needs.

A couple of ceramic-tile caveats: Unless you use area rugs to trap dust and grit, tile requires regular sweeping. Ceramic tile is durable, but its hardness also means there's little "give." If you spend hours standing and cooking in the kitchen, your feet may begin to feel it—and a dropped glass or plate will shatter. One plus: Stains clean up easily.

WOOD. Wood flooring complements all styles and blends nicely with most color schemes and other wood elements, such as cabinets.

If you're concerned about the effect inevitable moisture will have on the wood, be assured that new moisture-resistant finishes make wood a practical choice for kitchens. Its forgiving surface is much loved by cooks who spend a lot of time on their feet.

Wood is a middle- to high-priced material for kitchen flooring, but it is also highly durable. Oak is the most popular wood for flooring. Pine is a favorite in country-style kitchens because dents and nicks give it an authentic old-time look. Walnut, cherry, ash, and maple are among the other varieties you'll often find.

Wood flooring comes in planks, strips, and parquet squares, either unfinished, stained, or painted any way you want. Simply seal your design with polyurethane to protect it against scratches, spills, wear, and household chemicals.

Solid wood should be cleaned and recoated—or refinished—every few years, depending on how much wear and tear it endures.

LINOLEUM. Although the popularity of linoleum has

What for the floor?
This rustic terra-cotta tile floor, *above left*, makes a perfect, patinaed transition from the kitchen to the garden.
Wood, *above*, is much loved for the warmth it imparts to a room and for its versatility; it goes with just about any kind of color or decor. Modern moisture-resistant finishes are making wood a popular choice for kitchen flooring.
Laminate flooring gives this kitchen, *left*, the look of wood without the price tag. Laminate's easy care and durability makes it great for kids and pets.

never waned in Europe, sales in this country suffered after vinyl flooring came out in the 1970s. Due to its design flexibility, low cost, environmentally friendly ingredients, and durability, linoleum has become chic again, moving from commercial applications back into residences.

The recipe for linoleum includes linseed oil, crushed limestone, wood shavings, and pine resin tapped from living trees. Linoleum floors give off no harmful gases, or VOCs (volative organic compounds), and because the linseed oil in

linoleum is constantly oxidizing, it retards the growth of bacteria. Another plus: Linoleum actually becomes harder the longer it is down—and it's durable.

Linoleum comes in a dazzling array of colors, and it is flexible enough to be cut into all kinds of original designs—as well as laid in the classic checkerboard. It costs about double the price of high-end vinyl sheet flooring but several dollars less than hardwood flooring.

STONE. Marble and granite have graced elegant homes

Go natural underfoot

Linoleum, *right,* which has experienced a renaissance of late, is a natural product. Made of linseed oil, crushed limestone, wood shavings, and pine resin, it gives off no harmful gases. It is relatively inexpensive and comes in a vast array of colors. One other boon: The longer it's down, the harder it gets—making it very durable.

Limestone tiles are set in a semi-random pattern in this kitchen, *opposite,* to emphasize each tile's one-of-a-kind beauty. Limestone most often comes in soft shades of gray or yellow; its neutrality makes it a good choice for nearly any type of decor. It is, however, one of the most expensive flooring options.

since the glory days of ancient Greece and Rome. Certainly there is nothing more durable than a real stone floor. But like any other material, natural stone has its good and less desirable points when it comes to kitchen flooring material. It has no "give" and is the most expensive option on the market. Its most positive point is its natural, one-of-a-kind beauty, borne out in soft, neutral colors and interesting striations. Real stone's look changes greatly depending on its finish. Marble and granite can be polished to a glossy sheen or "flamed"—a process much like sandblasting that exposes the stone's pores and gives it a rustic appearance. If you are going to use any type of stone, you will likely have to reinforce your subfloor to support the weight.

There are four basic types of stone that are quarried, polished, and cut into tiles for flooring:

■ Marble comes in a variety of colors, including green (the strongest and most popular type), black, white, blue, and yellow. Its smooth surface doesn't harbor dust or dirt, but it is porous, which means it can be stained or gouged fairly easily. It should be sealed or waxed periodically to protect it from staining.

■ Granite comes in speckled hues of gray, green, burgundy, black, and brown. Its timeless quality goes well with both contemporary and traditional styles. It is less porous and therefore more stain-resistant than marble and is durable and easy to care for. Like marble, granite must be sealed periodically to maintain the beauty of the natural stone surface.

■ Slate creates a rugged, outdoorsy look when used on the floor. You can choose from a natural irregular finish, or order it polished to look like marble. Colors vary from black and gray to purple, red, and green. Slate is fine-grained, durable and fights off stains well. It can be cold underfoot, but it

collects warmth in sunny locations. Slate has a naturally rustic matte finish. You can apply a low-sheen wax or acrylic sealer if you prefer a lustrous surface.

■ Limestone, usually found in shades of pale gray or yellow, boasts a soft texture that gets velvety with use. This sedimentary, calcified stone was once sea bottom, so it can contain visible fossils. Travertine, which is related, also contains mineral calcite but comes from precipitated deposits such as cave stalactites. The neutral color of limestone looks good with all kitchen styles and furnishings. Its hardness and porosity vary, depending on the conditions in which it was formed. In some cases, its pores can trap food particles, and it can be cold to walk on and slippery when wet. Like all natural stone, limestone is absorbent, so it should be sealed to protect the surface from stains. Some imported limestone is treated by the supplier for durability and stain-resistance.

CORK. Used frequently in the 1930s, cork tiles—made from the renewable bark of cork trees that grow along the coast of the Mediterranean Sea—are back in style. The kitchen is one of the most common rooms for a cork floor installation. Cork is similar to hardwood in that it can be sanded and refinished; and if a piece is damaged it can easily be popped out and replaced. Different shades of cork are created by baking each piece in a large commercial roaster; the longer a piece is heated, the darker it becomes. Cork can also be stained. The cork is then cut into tiles and covered with polyurethane. Cork is known for being durable but resilient and soft to walk on, resistant to water, quiet, and warm and insulating.

Light up your kitchen

Undercabinet lights provide task lighting for food prep and cleanup and lend a sparkle to granite counters, *above*. This kitchen, *below*, has a well-planned lighting scheme: Recessed cans in the ceiling for general lighting, pendants over the peninsula work area, and romantic ambient lighting in the form of a chandelier over the dining area.

A thoughtful lighting plan contributes many things to your kitchen—efficiency, beauty, and safety, to name just a few.

The ideal kitchen lighting scheme provides adequate general lighting as well as spot illumination for specific tasks. Even a simple touch—such as a row of undercabinet strip lights to illuminate a section of countertop—brightens the prospect of working in your kitchen. Here's a look at the two types of room lighting:

AMBIENT LIGHTING. This is soft, general light that spans an entire room. Ambient lighting can be natural, provided by windows or skylights, or artificial, from central ceiling fixtures, recessed fixtures, or cove fixtures that direct light upward to reflect off the ceiling.

The amount of ambient lighting you need depends on several factors, including the height of the ceiling and the color on your walls. Bright tones reflect light and require less illumination; dark tones absorb light and require more.

In the daytime, windows are the primary source of ambient light. Big windows help make a kitchen feel airy, cheerful, and spacious, but you must strike a balance between your need for windows and your need for cabinet space.

Indirect lighting can supplement the ambient light from your central ceiling fixtures, which, if used alone, create harsh shadows. Bulbs located on cabinet tops and aimed upward to reflect off the ceiling provide soft, sculpted light and expand the room's visual volume.

As a guideline, provide at least 100 watts of incandescent light or 75 watts of fluorescent light of ambient or general lighting for each 50 square feet of floor space.

TASK LIGHTING. Often placed directly above sinks, food preparation areas, or cleanup centers, task lighting usually takes the form of a strong beam focused on a specific location. Specialty areas such as baking centers or desks call for task lighting that is bright but not harsh. Lighting in a dining area should be soft and flattering. Install task fixtures in locations that are in front of you when you're working so your body doesn't create a shadow.

Task lights create concentrated, high-intensity beams that can be directed at specific work centers. Examples of fixtures that work well for task lighting include recessed down lights, track lights, hanging pendant lights, and undercabinet strip lights. Each work center should be lighted with a minimum of 100 to 150 watts of incandescent light or 40 to 50 watts of fluorescent light. For efficiency, lighting for each work center should be controlled by its own wall switch.

Ceiling-mounted task lighting cannot effectively illuminate the area between your upper cabinets and countertops. The solution is to install strip lighting, which is made specifically for underneath upper cabinets; it has a thin profile that allows the fixture to remain virtually hidden.

Undercabinet lighting consists of either fluorescent tube lighting or halogen bulbs. A fluorescent tube should extend along two-thirds the length of the counter it lights and provide about 8 watts of power per lineal foot of counter. For example, a 6-foot run of counter calls for a 4-foot fluorescent tube rated at 48 watts.

There are three types of bulbs. Each has its advantages:
■ Incandescent lights have a warm glow that enhances red and yellow colors and flatters skin tones. Incandescent fixtures come in a variety of styles, and the bulbs are inexpensive and easy to change. One advantage of incandescent lighting is that it can be placed on a dimmer switch, which allows you to vary the amount of light. An incandescent bulb in a pendant fixture over a dining area can be turned all the way up for homework or dimmed for a romantic dinner.
■ Fluorescent lights last up to 20 times longer than incandescent bulbs and produce up to four times more light as incandescent bulbs of the same wattage. Advancements have shortened the "hesitation period"—the pause between flipping the switch and getting full illumination, and there are now "warm white" bulbs available that more closely resemble incandescent tones than the old-style blue-green bulbs.
■ Halogen lights provide clean-looking, powerful illumination in a small size. They're up to three times brighter than comparable incandescents and last twice as long. Their compact design allows them to be installed in tiny, unobtrusive fixtures—one reason they're a popular choice for undercabinet lighting. Halogen bulbs burn at high temperatures, however, and become damaged by contact with oily substances. These bulbs are more expensive than either incandescent or fluorescent bulbs.

Illuminating ideas

In-cabinet lighting turns storage for a collection of glassware, *above*, into an artful display while imparting a warm glow to the whole kitchen.

Stylish pendant lights, such as this metal and glass lantern, *below*, hang from the ceiling and provide direct lighting for work areas such as islands and peninsulas.

Rooms with a view

Double-hung windows glide up and down and capture breezes with ease, *top left*.

A wall of windows in this airy white kitchen, *above*, makes alfresco cooking and dining an everyday experience. Consider this option if you have a garden or other lovely view you'd like to enjoy from your kitchen.

A three-paned picture window above the sink, *left*, is large enough to make standing at the island cooktop an eye-pleasing experience but small enough to allow for storage space above.

In the kitchen, light and aeration are more than aesthetic matters; they're necessities. Having enough windows provides ample sunshine and fresh air, which helps eliminate kitchen odors and heat.

If kitchen space is limited, you can boost illumination by replacing existing units with taller windows or by adding a fixed, arch-top window over an existing window. Either strategy adds a significant amount of daylight but doesn't require additional wall space. You also can add interesting architectural detail, though you'll have to be careful. Installing windows of different dimensions and shapes requires that you change the wall frame by moving the horizontal support, known as the header, over the window. If your walls are short, you may not have room to raise the header enough.

Another way to let light in is to install skylights, which also don't interfere with cabinet configurations. One thing to keep in mind: If you increase the amount of daylight your kitchen receives, also provide a way to shade windows and skylights to prevent overheating the space.

The following are the basic types of windows you'll find when you go window shopping:

DOUBLE-HUNG: The classic double-hung—named for counterweights on both sides of the housing—is perhaps the most common and popular window type. New versions combine traditional looks with the convenience of sashes that tip out for easy cleaning. Double-hungs are usually rectangular, which makes them adaptable to nearly any kind of architecture. They're basic and durable.

CASEMENT: This type of window opens on a hinge rather than sliding in a groove. It's a great choice above kitchen sinks because it's easier to open than other types of windows. A standard crank casement window is hinged on one side and opens from the opposite side.

TRANSOM: This type of window sits above a door or another window to provide extra light and, if operable, to allow air to circulate freely. It often opens and closes with a specially designed pole that hooks onto the crank. Transoms can be rectangles, half-circles, or even triangles.

BOW AND BAY: A bow uses several windows arranged in a radial or bow formation. A bay is a composite of several windows joined at an angle. Bay configurations work well over window seats or banquettes.

SKYLIGHT: Skylights installed in the ceiling are a great way to add sunlight and connect rooms to the outdoors while maintaining privacy. There's nothing like morning sunlight streaming into the kitchen to get your day off to a good start. Smaller tube-style skylights fit in places where traditional units would be too large.

GARDEN: Add a permanent touch of springtime to your kitchen with a garden window over the sink. Constructed much like a box, these windows are miniature greenhouses. Most have adjustable shelves that make room for small containers of flowers or herbs. Front-mount awning vents or side-mount casements let air circulate.

Let the sunshine in

Casement windows that crank out on a hinge work well above a sink because they're easier to open than standard double-hungs.

Tech talk

There's more to choosing a window than liking its shape or how it opens. Here's a quick overview of the features.

ARGON: An odorless, colorless gas inserted between panes of glass to boost energy efficiency by reducing heat transfer.

CLADDING: The material surrounding the window itself. It may be wood, vinyl, fiberglass, or a combination of two or more materials. Wood looks rich and traditional; vinyl is maintenance free, affordable, and available in many colors.

LOW-E (LOW EMISSIVITY) GLASS: Glass coated on one side with a transparent, metallic layer that helps reduce heat transference. It aids in insulating the window, thereby reducing utility costs.

MULLION: The vertical or horizontal divisions of joints between single windows in a multiple-window unit.

MUNTIN: A bar used to divide panes of glass in the same sash. Grilles or windowpane dividers simulate the look of true muntins.

NAILING FIN: A flange that runs around the edges of a window's exterior side. It simplifies attaching the window to a house during the remodeling process.

R-VALUE: The measurement of a window's ability to insulate. The higher the number, the more energy-efficient the window.

SASH: The part of the window that moves up and down, in and out, or to the left or right. In some cases, one sash may be fixed and the other may be operable.

VISIBLE LIGHT TRANSMITTANCE (VLT): An optical property expressed as a number between 0 and 1. The higher the VLT, more daylight is transmitted.

5

drawing your kitchen

ALL GOOD KITCHENS START WITH A PLAN. Whether you've painstakingly

redrawn your dream kitchen one hundred times, sketched it on a paper towel, or hired

a kitchen designer, remember one thing: This is *your* kitchen. Design it the way you

want it to function, the way you will use it, and as an expression of your lifestyle.

That doesn't mean you shouldn't seek the input of others. Friends can help you

visualize the different ways your kitchen could go together. Get professional advice,

too. You'd be surprised by what a certified kitchen designer, architect, or designer can

point out. The price of an hour's consultation may save the expense of a serious

mistake down the road. If you're buying new cabinets, see if the manufacturer or

home center has a designer on staff; he or she might review your plan for free.

You want your design to flow, look great, and function without flaw. It can, if you

follow these first concrete steps to outlining your new kitchen.

Whether your space is diminutive, like this apartment kitchen, *opposite*, or large, taking accurate measurements and putting a specific plan on paper is the first step toward seeing your vision come to life. This kitchen maximizes wall space to accommodate a surprisingly generous amount of storage without appearing overcrowded or feeling crammed.

step-by-step
measuring

Measuring seems like an easy enough task, but it's important to get precise and proper measurements before you buy expensive cabinetry and appliances. This measuring method will give you just that.

1. Draw a rough outline of your kitchen floor plan. Show all windows, doors, and jogs in the walls; do not include cabinetry and fixtures. This is a sketch on which you will write only exact measurements. Note all measurements in inches.

2. Designate the northwest corner of the kitchen with a star or some other symbol. Start here.

3. Measure from the star to the first opening, window, or door on the first (north) wall.

4. Measure the opening's width from outside trim edge to outside trim edge (i.e., include the woodwork around a window rather than the dimensions of the window itself). Measure the trim if it's wider than the standard 2 inches.

5. Measure from the trim edge to the next opening or to the far wall. Repeat Step 4 if necessary.

6. Measure the entire length of the first (north) wall and note the number of inches in the sketch. The measurements made in Steps 3–5 should equal the measurement made in Step 6.

7. Proceed to the northeast corner and repeat Steps 3–6 for the second (east) wall. Make the same measurements for the remaining two walls, starting from the appropriate corners.

8. Measure from the floor to the ceiling. If you have a cove or vaulted ceiling, note the variance in height.

Start your tape measures

Taking accurate measurements of a flat wall is enough of a challenge; measuring a wall of windows such as the one found in this kitchen, *right*, takes extra-special care. To get the most accurate measurements of an opening such as a window or door, measure its width from outside trim edge to outside trim edge. If you have doors in your kitchen that lead to the outdoors, as in the kitchen, *opposite*, or to another room of the house, note the direction of the swing, as well as the dimensions of the arc it makes.

9. Starting with the first (north) wall, measure from the floor to the bottom of any windowsill. Measure from that point to the top of the window (including trim). Measure from that point to the ceiling. This total should be equal to that of Step 8. Repeat for remaining windows or pass-throughs.

10. Make a notation for any existing mechanicals on the first (north) wall: hot and cold water lines and drainage line in the sink; gas line to the stove (if present); electrical outlet and switches; vent ducts. Make the same notations for the remaining walls.

11. Mark the location of overhead lights.

12. Note the swing of doors or casement windows.

13. Measure the depth, width, and height of any appliances you will be reusing.

Now go back and remeasure your kitchen—yes, repeat all 13 steps. (Better yet, have someone else measure the area.) Double-check any discrepancies. If the lengths of your north and south walls (and east and west walls) don't tally despite your best efforts, don't despair. Few rooms are perfectly square. If you're off by more than 1 inch, though, you may have to do some creative carpentry.

When you're satisfied that you have accurate measurements, use the figures to make an accurate layout of the room on a clean piece of ¼-inch graph paper. You will use this base floor plan as the foundation of all the kitchen designs you try, so either make photocopies of the finished layout or use sheets of tracing paper over the layout to create your designs.

drawing floor plans

Once you have made an accurate layout of your kitchen on a piece of graph paper, it's time to draw a final floor plan that includes the positioning of cabinets, appliances, special features, and utility connections.

A floor plan gives you an overhead, or bird's-eye, view of all the major elements in the kitchen: walls; windows; major appliances such as the cooktop, sink, and refrigerator; closets; dining areas; and wall and base cabinets. It gives you a good idea of how a certain layout occupies space. Before you draw the "after" design, it's helpful to draw a "before" picture so that you can clearly see what you'd most like to change.

Begin with the "before"

Using either a photocopy of your base floor plan or a piece of tracing paper positioned over your original ¼-inch graph paper plan, draw in your existing kitchen components. You don't need to be overly neat about this drawing; it's only for reference. Next to this plan, write down all the things you don't like about your current kitchen.

Draw the "after"

If you made photocopies of your base floor plan, sketch in as many potential designs as you can think of. Or if you're using tracing paper, remove your "before" plan and position a new sheet of tracing paper over the outline of your kitchen. There's one advantage to using tracing paper: You can overlap several designs at once, seeing at a glance whether a new configuration will work.

Consider the merits of each design. Sometimes the most surprising ideas come out of the worst concepts. Don't be afraid to throw all your preconceived kitchen plans out the window and start over.

When you've come up with the best design—the one that seems to address all your needs and wants—draw a final, accurate rendering of your dream kitchen. Write down all the things you like about the new kitchen.

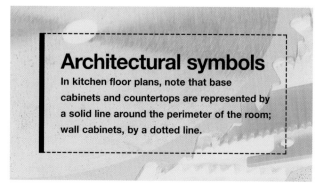

Architectural symbols

In kitchen floor plans, note that base cabinets and countertops are represented by a solid line around the perimeter of the room; wall cabinets, by a dotted line.

A bird's-eye view

One of the most helpful aspects of having a floor plan for the kitchen you intend to build is that you can easily see traffic flow from this vantage point. You can also make sure that space around an island is plentiful, that the work triangle is the recommended size, and that opening doors don't interfere with traffic patterns.

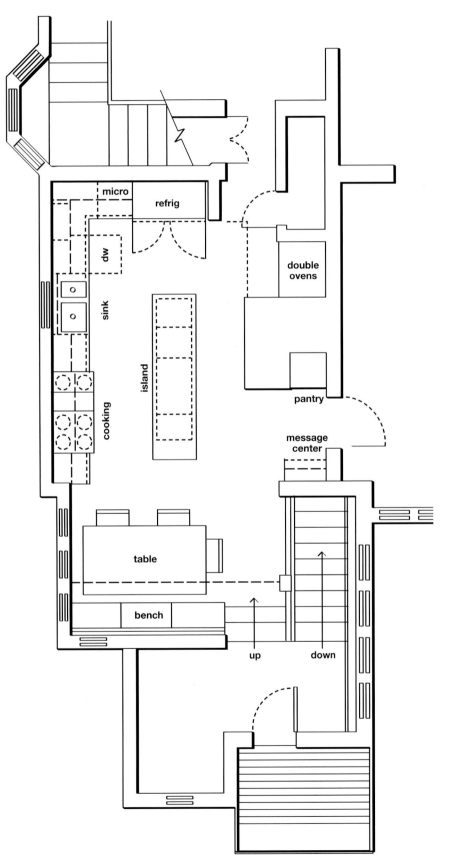

micro

refrig

double ovens

dw

sink

pantry

island

cooking

message center

table

bench

up

down

An elevation, which takes in one wall at a time, is a bit more tedious to draw than a floor plan, which shows a whole room at once. An elevation view shows what you'd see from floor to ceiling if you stood across from that wall. It represents what your kitchen will look like as you stand in it when it's completed.

Using your floor plan as a guide, take four pieces of ¼-inch graph paper and label each one as representing the north, south, east, or west wall. Draw in to scale all the elements of your new plan, including cabinets, appliances, fixtures, and outlets.

Study your elevation for problem spots, such as areas where a drawer may collide with another drawer, cabinet door, or appliance when it is opened, and make corrective adjustments as necessary.

Seek a second opinion

If possible, take your best design—both the floor plan and the elevation drawings—to an architect, certified kitchen designer, or other kitchen professional for an evaluation. Be sure to bring all your discarded plans with you too; they may have some good elements. A pro can help you fine-tune your layout to give you maximum efficiency and style.

An elevated view

Although the elevation, *below,* and the photograph, *right,* are not of the same kitchen, both images give the viewer a good idea of what it would feel like to stand in that space.

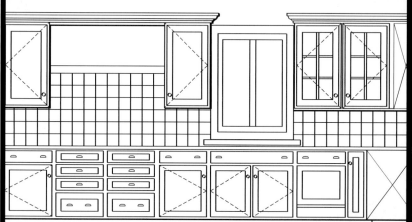

6

ready, set, remodel

HERE YOU ARE, WITH YOUR KITCHEN DESIGN IN HAND and cabinets and appliances selected. So what's next? A tip to help you cope with what's to come: Nowhere is Murphy's Law more in force than when you actually begin your kitchen remodeling project. The key to surviving is preparation—forewarned is forearmed.

Naturally each kitchen's rejuvenation varies with the extent of the project, the age and condition of the house, the layout, and so on. To give you a general idea of what to expect, we've divided the project into four phases and accompanied each with a prep and pep talk to get you ready for your house being (let's face it) in shambles. This information will help you make this difficult time as easy as possible. Prepare yourself: Everything that can go wrong probably will go wrong, but once you're standing in your new dream kitchen, everything it took to get there will prove well worth the effort.

Finishing touches, such as a decorative range hood or ceramic tile backsplash, *opposite*, don't have to be complete for you to begin using your new kitchen. See Step 3 on page 96, "A Kitchen Remodeling Chronology Checklist," for tips on setting up a practical temporary kitchen while you remodel.

Dream of days to come

When drywall dust covers everything and you think you can't stand another minute of the refrigerator being in the living room, take heart: Your family will soon bask in the sunshine of a brand-new kitchen, as these happy kids are doing, *above*.

Phase 1: Demolition

The ripping and tearing of the demolition phase can be loads of fun, particularly if you have laminate countertops and appliances in colors you've loathed for years, or vinyl flooring that has seen better days.

It can also be scary. That "little leak" under the sink may reveal rotten floorboards when the sink base comes out. Or worse, you could discover that some of the joists are beginning to give way; or perhaps the exterior wall of your kitchen is crumbling, thanks to the siding that trapped moisture inside. Or maybe you'll find the previous owners "rewired" by attaching new electrical outlets and thick nonmetallic-

sheathed cable to the original cloth-wrapped wiring.

The bad news? Unexpected extra repairs such as these cost money and cause delays; contractors may need more time to complete work, and you may need to postpone delivery dates of cabinets, flooring, and appliances.

There is good news, though. Doing the necessary structural work now means you won't have to do it after your beautiful new kitchen is complete. And you're fixing something that needed to be fixed; at least that problem can't get any worse. Installing your new kitchen in a room that's structurally and mechanically up-to-date makes for a sound investment. If you're going to spend all that money on a brand-new kitchen, you might as well do it right. That rot you uncovered and repaired won't spread to your new cupboards, and the updated wiring won't zap your appliances.

Even if you're hiring a pro to do some portions of the project, you can probably handle the interior tear-out phase yourself—though it is a tough, dirty job—and save a fair amount of money in the process.

Phase 2: Preparation

This may not be the most glamorous part of the job, but it is the foundation of your kitchen dreams. New drywall and plywood underlayment mean the undulation in your walls and the sag in your floors (if there are any) will be a thing of the past. Updated electrical systems and plumbing lines ensure that your kitchen will function smoothly. Extra lighting makes for a brighter, friendlier kitchen.

The assumption of this book is that you can do the simple updating of mechanicals yourself (see Chapter 8, "Building Blocks"), but in some parts of the country only certified electricians or plumbers are permitted to upgrade or install mechanicals. Check your local code. Even if you can do these jobs yourself, don't forget to schedule a visit from the building inspector to make sure your work is up to code and to ensure the quality and safety of the finished project.

Catch dirt at the door

If your home has a room adjacent to the kitchen, such as this mudroom, *below,* a lot of the mess from the remodeling stays out of the rest of the house. Outfit the room—or even the garage—with hooks for dirty workclothes and rugs for wiping shoes.

Phase 3: Installation

During this phase your barren room begins to look like a kitchen again. Nothing quite matches the thrill of the day you install your cabinets and appliances. To safeguard your investment, be sure to use a padded dolly to move these expensive items around, and take special care not to scratch or ding them with your tools.

You may install your flooring now or at the next stage. Sheet vinyl goes in more easily before the cabinets arrive, but tile and wood floors are usually installed afterward to conserve costs (generally these types of flooring are not laid under base cabinets because of their expense).

Phase 4: Completion

The dream is nearly a reality. With the cabinets and appliances installed, the flooring and countertops remain your two biggest hurdles, followed by sinks, faucets, and lights. All decisions and choices have been made at this point, and the items have been ordered or purchased. You may even be using your kitchen now; you just need a little more patience for the last pieces to fall into place.

Finally all the little details that may not be a necessity for the functioning of your kitchen take precedence. Those items, such as light covers, decorative hardware, switchplates, and minor trim, finish it off and give it personality. It's easy to run out of energy at this point, or you may have become used to living without them; but stay focused on these final touches, and when they're in place, you'll be glad you did.

After the last screw is turned, it's time for the really fun part: stenciling or wallpapering, picking out curtains, and displaying your collectibles. Relax—the kitchen is finished and it's yours.

The end is near

The installation of flooring, such as the laminate floor, *above right,* and countertops such as the laminate countertop, *right,* are two of the last major jobs in the remodeling process. After that, you've only to install the sink, faucet, and lights before the basic design of your kitchen is complete. Everything, including the kitchen sink, can be found in this recently remodeled kitchen, *opposite.* Now all it needs is a personal touch.

It won't be an easy job to remodel your kitchen. Having the heart of your home thrown into chaos can be hard on you and your family, but the checklist on these two pages will help keep you organized and on schedule.

STEP	ACTION
1	**GET THE BUILDING PERMIT.** If you're doing the work yourself, go to city hall or the county courthouse to find out what paperwork is needed. Post the permit where inspectors can see it easily.
2	**RENT A TRASH BIN.** Do this about a week before demolition. Compact the trash, which is usually paid for in cubic yards of waste, not by weight.
3	**SET UP A WORKING KITCHEN.** Move your microwave oven, indoor electric grill or hot plate, and a small fridge (or your old one) to temporary quarters. If you have to resort to storing food in coolers, you'll have to make a daily run for ice. Keep out microwavable containers, one large pot and fry pan, one knife, one serving spoon, one spatula, the can opener, and one place setting per person. Don't buy food that requires baking. Buy fruit, bread, and anything that's easy to store and eat (such as canned food). Wash each dish the moment you're done with it. Keep a ready supply of paper towels, plastic wrap, aluminum foil, and dishwashing liquid.
4	**CLEAN OUT THE KITCHEN.** Box and store all kitchen products and dishes. Pack breakables. Rent a storage unit to house kitchen items if you're tight on space.
5	**CLEAN OUT THE GARAGE.** You'll need space to store new components until installation. On the garage floor, put down a layer of sawdust or absorbent product over oil spots, then a layer of cardboard to protect items.
6	**WAIT FOR NEW CABINETS AND APPLIANCES.** Don't proceed to Step 7 until these items have arrived. Inspect each item before letting the delivery person leave. Note any damaged items and make arrangements to have them taken away and replaced. Check just-delivered cabinets for aesthetics too. A knothole or dark vein of grain in light cabinetry may prove irritating later. Replace it now.
7	**GET RID OF OLD APPLIANCES.** Run an ad in the paper, hold a garage sale, or arrange for Goodwill or the Salvation Army to haul them away.
8	**GUT THE KITCHEN.** Follow these steps for safe do-it-yourself demolition: •First. Shut off electricity, then water. Use heavy clear plastic sheets to cordon off the kitchen and keep debris and dust from scattering. Remove items in this order: sink, remaining built-in appliances, countertop, base cabinets, upper cabinets. •Second. Clean the kitchen and trash area, then tackle any soffits, walls, windows, and flooring. •Third. Make follow-up calls. Check arrival dates of workers (if any) and materials. Have work done in this order: electrical, plumbing, drywall installation, painting, cabinet installation, appliance installation, countertop installation, floor installation.
9	**PREP THE KITCHEN.** The following are common to nearly all kitchen projects: ELECTRIC. Update electrical service, if needed; all outlets must be grounded and outlets within 6 feet of the sink must have ground fault circuit interrupters. Install wiring for new appliances, switches, and lighting. PLUMBING. Route water lines and drainage pipes as needed to reposition or add sinks and appliances. DUCTWORK. Route new ductwork for vents. DRYWALL. Install sheets with drywall screws. FLOOR. Install underlayment, if needed. If putting in sheet vinyl, install now; put down canvas drop cloths or cardboard to protect the floor. PAINT. Seal new drywall with primer; use the same primer over existing walls for a uniform finish; paint walls with two coats of quality paint. Paint the ceiling while the kitchen is empty. **SCHEDULE BUILDING INSPECTOR.**

10   **INSTALL CABINETS AND APPLIANCES. If your appliances are built-in, they'll need to be on hand when cabinets are installed. Double-check and triple-check your measurements for built-ins.**

11   **FINISH THE KITCHEN. The following are common to nearly all kitchen projects:**
     COUNTERTOPS. Most laminates and all solid-surfacing countertops are made to spec. Granite may be more of an installation challenge than other surfaces.
     SINK AND FAUCET. Install after countertop is in place.
     CABINETS. Install doors and hardware.
     LIGHTING. Install or attach fixtures.
     FLOORING. Vinyl squares or linoleum can be installed in a day; hardwood, stone, or tile may take longer.

12   **DECORATE AND CELEBRATE. Congratulations! You have a new kitchen.**

The maiden voyage

With its vibrant lime-green enameled metal cabinets and two-toned wall treatment, little additional decorating is needed in this kitchen, *above*. A clean style in which utensils add decorative interest also keeps them within easy reach.

tools

YOU CAN'T DO THE JOB RIGHT UNLESS you have the right tools. You've heard it said, or maybe you've said it yourself. It's a sentiment some may dismiss as justification for obsessively collecting all kinds of gadgets to play with, but there's no denying the truth in it. This chapter outlines which basic tools you'll need for each phase of remodeling and for particular tasks, including demolition; framing; plumbing; wiring; installing drywall; hanging cabinets; installing countertops, flooring, and molding; tiling; and painting. Variations on all tools abound; you may be faced with three or four choices at your local hardware store or home center. The tools shown here are representative of tools recommended for use by the do-it-yourselfer, not the professional. Every tool you might need to complete the step-by-step projects in Chapters 8 and 9 isn't necessarily listed, and don't feel as if you have to go out and buy every tool shown. There are often two or more different tools you can use for the same task, or one tool you can use for multiple tasks. You may already own a tool other than what is suggested that will do a particular job just fine, and some of the larger power tools can be rented.

A good hammer, *opposite*, is perhaps one of the most indispensable tools to have in your toolbox. You're going to pound and pull a lot of nails during your kitchen remodeling project. A collection of hammers of different weights and sizes provides many options, but generally, a quality 16-ounce hammer that feels comfortable in your hand is a good place to start.

safety & demolition

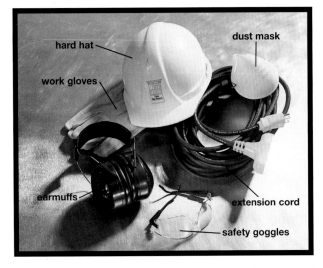

hard hat
dust mask
work gloves
earmuffs
extension cord
safety goggles

The tools you need for demolition depend on the degree of demolition to be done. If you're keeping your old cabinets and giving them a facelift with a fresh coat of paint, the tools you'll require are entirely different than if you're tearing out all of the walls and building a breakfast room. Check the list below to see which ones apply to your situation.

BALL PEEN HAMMER AND COLD CHISEL. For chipping away ceramic tiles and masonry.

CAT'S PAW NAIL REMOVER. Also called a nail puller, this is another indispensible demolition tool that makes it easy to pull nails—though it will damage wood.

CIRCULAR SAW. For general cutting.

DRILL BITS, ELECTRIC DRILL. For quickly removing screws that hold up the old cabinetry.

DROP CLOTH. For protecting surfaces you plan to save.

DUST MASK. To protect your lungs from dust.

EARMUFFS. To protect your ears from damaging levels of noise from power tools.

EXTENSION CORD. To prevent dragging a taut cord across the room, where it can be tripped over, or where it can knock over power tools, ladders, sawhorses, and so on.

FLOOR SCRAPER. For peeling up vinyl flooring.

HACKSAW OR MINI-HACKSAW. For cutting metal.

HAMMER. For removing nails and tearing down walls.

HANDSAW. For cutting door thresholds.

HARD HAT. To protect your head from falling debris.

METAL OR PLASTIC PUTTY KNIVES. For scraping up old glue, adhesive, and caulk.

PRY BAR, CROWBAR, OR SLEDGEHAMMER. For removing walls and flooring.

RATCHET WRENCH AND SOCKETS. For quickly removing nuts and bolts.

RECIPROCATING SAW. An indispensible demolition tool, this saw can cut studs and galvanized pipe in places no other saw can reach.

SAFETY GOGGLES. To protect your eyes from dust.

UTILITY KNIFE. For making razor-sharp cuts.

WORK GLOVES. To protect your hands from splinters, rusty nails, and general wear and tear.

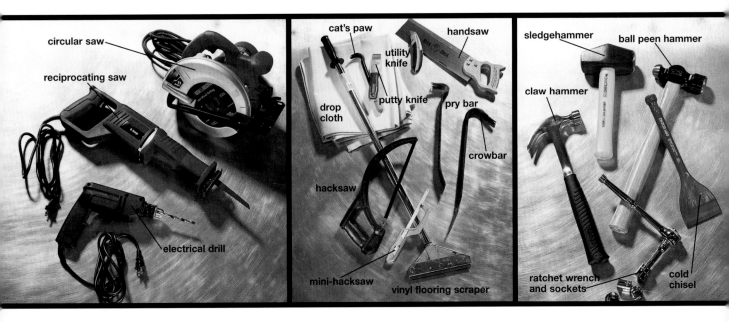

circular saw
reciprocating saw
electrical drill

cat's paw
handsaw
utility knife
drop cloth
putty knife
pry bar
crowbar
hacksaw
mini-hacksaw
vinyl flooring scraper

sledgehammer
ball peen hammer
claw hammer
ratchet wrench and sockets
cold chisel

tools for framing

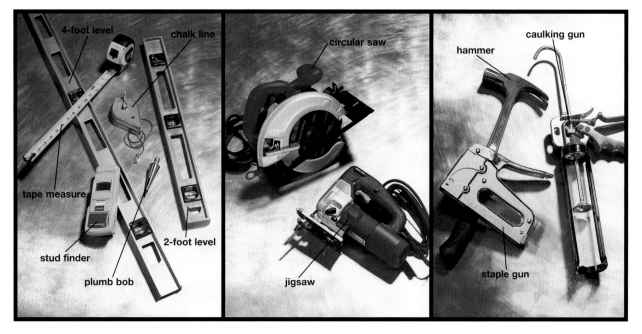

Nearly every tool you'll need for framing your new kitchen walls is a basic tool you may already own. Some of the power versions of manual tools, such as a power nailer, simply make the job go faster.

CARPENTER'S LEVEL. For checking that the floor is level and the corners of the room are square. It's a good idea to have a couple of different sizes on hand.

CAULKING GUN. For applying panel adhesives when attaching drywall to the framing.

CHALK LINE. For snapping a long, straight line that marks the intended location of the wall on the floor.

CIRCULAR SAW. Perhaps the most basic power tool of all, the circular saw crosscuts, angle-cuts, rips (cuts lengthwise), and bevels lumber easily and cleanly. Purchase a circular saw that takes a 7¼-inch blade. It will let you cut to a depth of 2½ inches at 90 degrees to cut through a piece of 2× lumber even when the blade is set at 45 degrees.

FRAMING SQUARE. Also called a carpenter's square, this tool is used to check corners for square and to establish a perpendicular line when framing up walls.

HAMMER. For nailing 2×4s together to make a stud wall.

JIGSAW. Nimbler than a circular saw, the jigsaw (also called a saber saw) allows you to make curved cuts and cuts in areas where space is tight.

PLUMB BOB. Basically a weight on the end of a string,

this simple tool establishes true vertical lines for plumbing walls. Dangle the weight from the string just above the floor. When the weight stops moving, the line is plumb.

POWER DRILL OR CORDLESS DRILL. Be sure to get a variable-speed, reversible power drill with a standard ⅜-inch key chuck. Buy one that pulls at least 3.5 amps. A cordless drill frees you to work without tripping over an electrical cord. Buy one that uses at least 9.6 volts.

SAWHORSES. For holding lengths of lumber elevated and steady as you cut them to size. Have at least two sawhorses on hand that are strong and don't wobble.

STAPLE GUN. For attaching sheets of plastic vapor barrier or for installing fiberglass insulation batts.

STUD FINDER. For locating joists if ceiling is finished.

TAPE MEASURE. For all measuring tasks, including making sure studs are 16 inches on center.

Plumbing doesn't require a lot of expensive or complicated tools, and even those you may use only once are well worth the cost. The money you save by doing your own work pays for them many times over. With the tools shown on this page, you can tackle basic kitchen plumbing.

ADJUSTABLE-END WRENCH, PLIERS. For fitting and removing nuts on faucets and other fixtures.

ADJUSTABLE PIPE WRENCH. Essential for working with threaded iron pipe.

BASIN WRENCH. For getting at faucet and sink nuts that you can't reach with pliers.

CAULKING GUN. For applying caulk and sealant around plumbing fixtures.

FLARING TOOL. For making flare joints in copper tubing. Flare joints are useful where it's difficult to solder.

HACKSAW. For cutting pipe; the blades dull quickly when used for this purpose, so have a supply on hand.

LEVEL. For setting the proper incline of drain pipes.

NEEDLENOSE PLIERS. For delicate jobs, such as working with O-rings and clips.

PLASTIC TUBING CUTTER, PLASTIC PIPE CUTTER. For cutting supply pipes.

PROPANE TORCH. For soldering copper pipe. If you have a lot to do, pay the extra money for a self-igniting model. Otherwise get an inexpensive spark lighter.

TAPE MEASURE. For measuring the dimension of pipe; measure the inside diameter of the pipe and round off to the nearest $\frac{1}{8}$ inch.

TONGUE-AND-GROOVE PLIERS. To disassemble and connect pipes; they adjust to grab almost any size pipe.

TUBING BENDER. For bending flexible copper tubing without kinking it.

TUBING CUTTER. For cutting copper pipe or tubing.

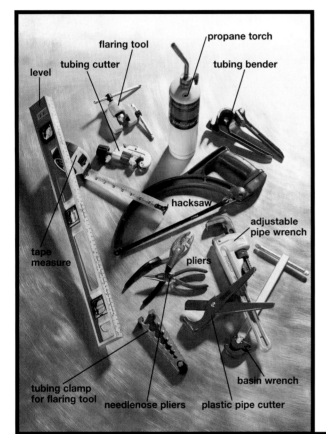

flaring tool
propane torch
level
tubing cutter
tubing bender
hacksaw
adjustable pipe wrench
tape measure
pliers
tubing clamp for flaring tool
needlenose pliers
plastic pipe cutter
basin wrench

tongue-and-groove pliers
adjustable-end wrench
standard pliers

tools for electrical

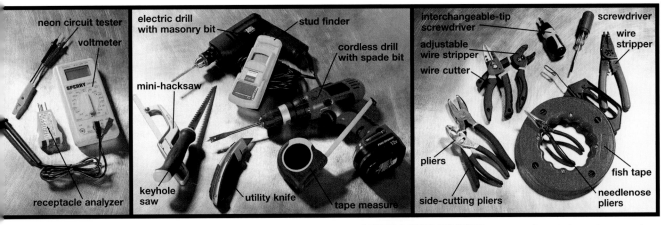

neon circuit tester • voltmeter • receptacle analyzer • electric drill with masonry bit • mini-hacksaw • keyhole saw • utility knife • stud finder • cordless drill with spade bit • tape measure • interchangeable-tip screwdriver • adjustable wire stripper • wire cutter • pliers • side-cutting pliers • screwdriver • wire stripper • fish tape • needlenose pliers

Many of the required tools for electrical work are toolbox standbys; others, you'll note, can be used for both plumbing and electrical jobs.

ADJUSTABLE WIRE STRIPPER. For stripping the sheathing off wires without nicking them.

BIT EXTENSION. For drilling holes deeper than the length of your spade bit.

BX CUTTER. For making easy and safe work of cutting through metal-sheathed cable. This tool can be rented.

CABLE RIPPER. For removing the sheathing from nonmetallic cable without nicking the wires.

COMBINATION TOOL. This tool will strip wire, as well as crimp and cut it.

CONTINUITY TESTER. For testing fuses, switches, and sockets with the power off.

ELECTRIC DRILL WITH SPADE BIT. For making holes in the walls for cable to pass through.

FISH TAPE. For running cable through finished walls and ceilings or running wire through conduit.

FUSE PULLER. If you have cartridge-type fuses in your fuse box, use this tool to pull them out of the box. Never pull fuses by hand.

HACKSAW OR MINI-HACKSAW. For cutting conduit and metal-sheathed cable.

INTERCHANGEABLE-TIP SCREWDRIVER, SCREWDRIVER WITH INSULATED HANDLE. For connecting cable to electrical boxes.

KEYHOLE SAW. For cutting drywall when running cable in finished spaces.

LINEMAN'S PLIERS. For neatly twisting wires together, and for cutting wire.

MASONRY BIT. For drilling holes through masonry for cable to pass through.

NEEDLENOSE PLIERS. For bending wires into the loops required for many electrical connections, and for cutting wire.

NEON CIRCUIT TESTER. An absolute safety essential, to make sure electricity is shut off before you start working on your home's electrical system.

RECEPTACLE ANALYZER. This small but handy device tells you if your receptacle has a faulty connection and if it is properly grounded and polarized.

SIDE-CUTTING PLIERS. These make it easy to snip wires in tight places and are the perfect tool for cutting the sheathing off cable.

SOLDERING GUN AND LEAD-FREE, ROSIN-CORE SOLDER. If local codes permit you to—or require you to—solder, you'll need these tools to make a soldered splice of two or more wires.

STANDARD PLIERS. For pulling and twisting wires.

STUD FINDER. For locating studs when running cable in finished space. Studs need to be located, then notched to accommodate the run of cable.

TONGUE-AND-GROOVE PLIERS. For tightening connectors when working with electrical conduit.

TUBING CUTTER. For making clean cuts in conduit.

VOLTMETER. This device works with the power on or off; indicates the amount of voltage at a particular outlet.

tools for
drywalling

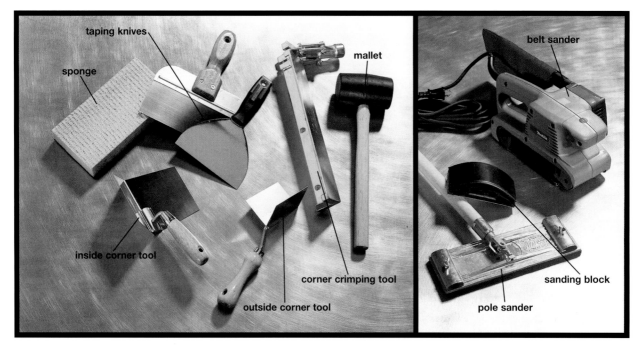

sponge · taping knives · mallet · belt sander · inside corner tool · corner crimping tool · outside corner tool · sanding block · pole sander

Hanging drywall is a difficult job because drywall is so heavy and cumbersome. In addition to the tools listed below, one of the most helpful tools may be a human who assists you in lifting and placing the drywall. Finishing drywall is a one-person job. Though it's tricky to get a perfectly smooth finish, having the right tools helps immeasurably.

BELT SANDER. For quick initial sanding of large areas.

CORNER CRIMPING TOOL AND MALLET. For attaching corner bead to outside corners of new walls.

CORNER TAPING TOOL. For applying and smoothing drywall tape and making sure it fits snugly inside, or around outside, corners.

DRYWALL LIFTER OR HOIST. This tool isn't a necessity, but it makes moving drywall sheets easy. Rolled across the floor on wheels, it lifts and carries heavy drywall sheets into place.

DRYWALL SAW. For cutting curves in drywall, and for cutting holes in the drywall to acommodate pipes.

DRYWALL T SQUARE. For making straight cuts in drywall panels. This tool quickly pays for itself in time and labor savings. For crosscuts, simply make one measurement, set the square in place, and run the knife along the square's blade for a square cut. It also simplifies parallel rip cuts (those that are the same width all along their length).

FRAMING SQUARE OR T SQUARE. For checking corners for square.

POLE SANDER. For sanding hard-to-reach heights on large walls and ceiling areas after drywall mud has dried.

SANDING BLOCK. For detail sanding in tight areas.

SCREW GUN. For screwing drywall to studs.

SPONGE. For smoothing on tape and mud to finish joints between panels of drywall.

TAPING KNIVES: 6-, 8-, AND 12-INCH. A variety of taping knives allow you to smoothly apply wallboard compound to any surface.

TIN SNIPS. For cutting and trimming metal corner bead.

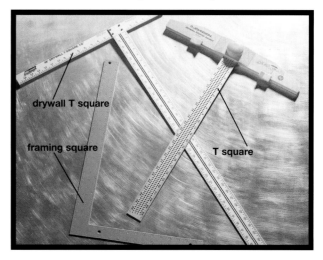

drywall T square · framing square · T square

tools for
cabinet installation

Many of the tools listed here for cabinet installation you'll also need for installing a laminate countertop (see page 106).

ADJUSTABLE-END WRENCH. To tighten and loosen nuts and bolts, usually found only on the sink and faucet.

CLAMPS. Hold adjoining cabinets together for installation.

CORDLESS OR ELECTRIC DRILL. For drilling pilot holes and driving screws.

FRAMING SQUARE, PLUMB BOB, CHALK LINE. For squaring up corners, checking walls for plumb, and chalking a level line on which to begin installation.

HAMMER. For driving shims behind wall cabinets or under base cabinets to ensure they're plumb in all directions.

LEVEL. For making sure wall cabinets are plumb in all directions and base cabinets are level and plumb in all directions before you drive the first screw.

RUBBER MALLET. For gently tapping adjacent cabinets together as tightly as possible before fastening them to each other or to the wall.

SCREWDRIVERS. For attaching hardware to cabinets. For this task, it's best to use manual drivers; because of the high speed, bits attached to electric drills can slip and damage hardware or cabinets.

STUD FINDER. For locating studs on which to hang the cabinets. Cabinets must be hung on studs.

TAPE MEASURE. For all measuring tasks, including measuring the distance from the bottom of the wall cabinets to the floor—usually 54 inches.

UTILITY KNIFE. For cutting shims, thin strips or wedges of wood used to fill a gap between two adjoining components, to help establish level or plumb.

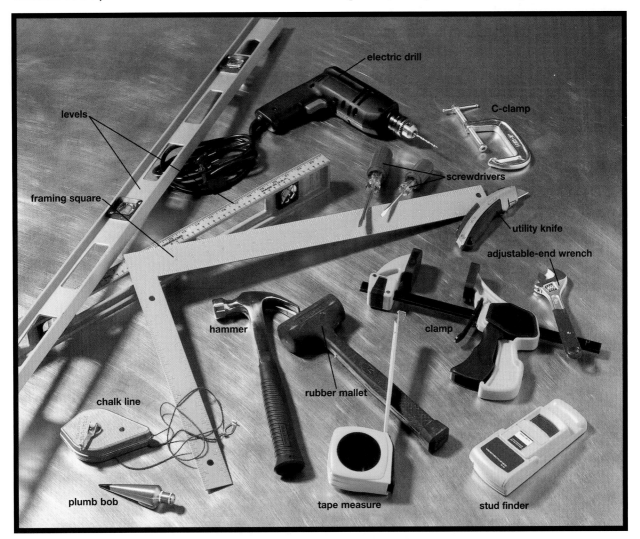

tools for
countertops

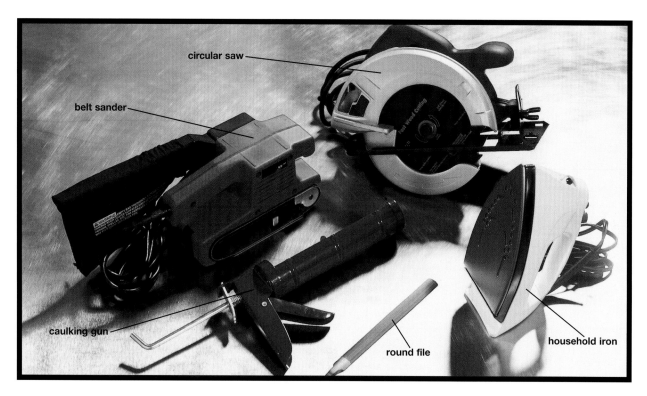

circular saw

belt sander

caulking gun

round file

household iron

Most of the tools needed to install a laminate countertop are used to install cabinets (see page 105), but the job also requires these additional tools.

BELT SANDER. For shaving the counter backsplash so it's flush against the wall.

CAULKING GUN. For applying caulk where the top of the backsplash meets the wall.

CIRCULAR SAW AND/OR JIGSAW. For cutting a sink hole in the countertop. You can use either one, but if you have both, you'll probably use both.

HALF-ROUND FILE. For filing the end-splash laminate flush with the countertop.

HOUSEHOLD IRON. For heating the laminate end-splash to apply it to the ends of the countertop.

Working safely with tools

A degree of danger comes with every remodeling project. In order to work safely, exercise common sense and follow safety guidelines for working with tools.

When you're working with a powerful electric tool, such as a drill or saw, even one moment's lapse of concentration can lead to disaster. To minimize the risks of getting injured, heed these safety tips:

USE TOOLS only for the jobs they were made to do. If your power tool came with an instruction manual, read it. Understand what the tool will do and what it will not do.

MAKE SURE THE TOOL is in good condition before using it. A dull cutting edge or a loose-fitting hammer head spells trouble. Inspect the cord of a power tool to make sure it's not damaged.

DON'T WORK WITH TOOLS if you're tired or in a hurry.

DON'T WORK WITH TOOLS after you've consumed alcoholic beverages.

ALWAYS WEAR GOGGLES when the task you are performing could result in an eye injury from dust or debris.

DON'T TAMPER WITH the safety mechanisms on power tools; they're there for your protection.

DON'T WEAR LOOSE-FITTING CLOTHING or dangling jewelry when using tools.

KEEP OTHER PEOPLE—especially children—at a safe distance while you're using tools. Before you let children use a tool, instruct them on how to use it and don't ever let them use it without supervision.

BEFORE SERVICING OR ADJUSTING a power tool, unplug it and let the moving parts come to a complete standstill.

You'll need most of the following tools for laying out and installing your new floor, no matter what the material. Most of these tools are used to prepare the subfloor. Ask a salesperson at your hardware store about the specific tools you'll need for the flooring material you've chosen.

BELT SANDER. For sanding rough patches on a plywood subfloor to get it as smooth and level as possible.

CHALK LINE. For establishing perpendicular lines at the center of the room as a starting point for laying flooring.

CIRCULAR SAW AND JIGSAW. For cutting plywood panels and cement backerboard underlayment panels to size.

COMBINATION SQUARE OR FRAMING SQUARE. For measuring short distances and marking square corners; you can get by with one or the other.

ELECTRIC DRILL. For installing underlayment.

HALF-ROUND FILE. For gently filing any rough edges on molding or trim after flooring is installed.

NOTCHED TROWEL, SQUARE TROWEL. For patching old underlayment and applying adhesive when laying cement backerboard.

PLUMB BOB. For establishing whether where the walls meet the floor creates a true vertical line.

PRY BAR. For removing old underlayment.

PUTTY KNIFE. For pushing vinyl flooring into tight corners and under cabinets.

TAPE MEASURE. For measuring new underlayment.

VINYL FLOORING KNIFE. For cutting sheet vinyl or vinyl tiles to size.

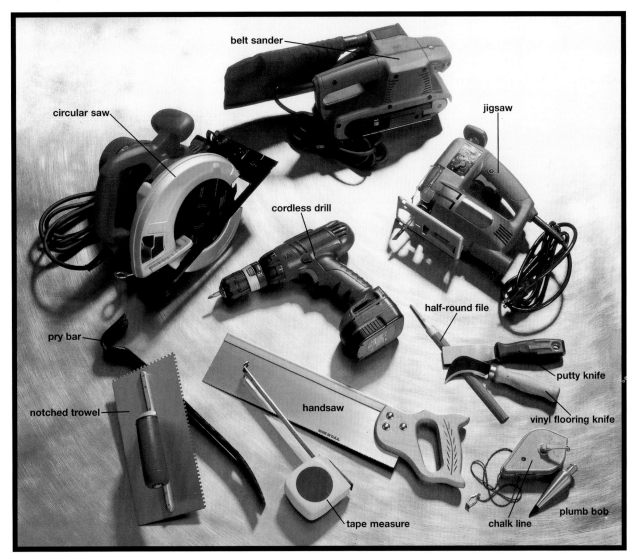

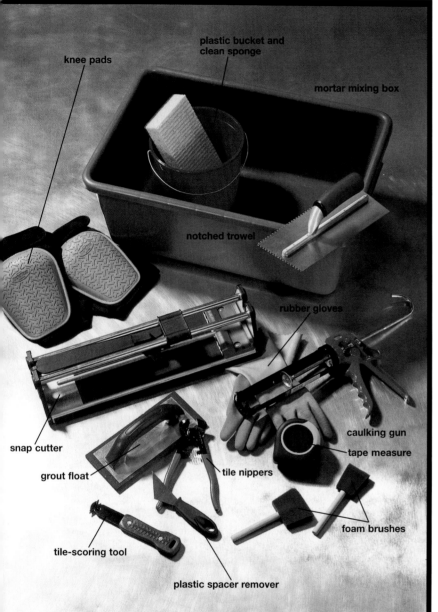

knee pads

plastic bucket and clean sponge

mortar mixing box

notched trowel

rubber gloves

snap cutter

grout float

caulking gun

tape measure

tile nippers

foam brushes

tile-scoring tool

plastic spacer remover

gently pressing tiles evenly and firmly into the adhesive.

CAULKING GUN. For applying caulk and sealant around edges.

FOAM BRUSH. For applying grout sealer.

GROUT FLOAT. A rubber-backed trowel used for spreading grout into the joints.

MASON'S TROWEL OR PUTTY KNIFE. For finishing grout joints to give them a neat appearance.

MORTAR MIXER. If you have two or more gallons of thin-set mortar or grout to mix, this tool is a great time-saver. It's mounted like a drill bit on an electric drill.

MORTAR MIXING BOX. For small jobs, an empty, clean drywall compound bucket will suffice, but if your job is larger (such as a floor) a mortar mixing box is the best choice.

NOTCHED TROWEL. This tool has two smooth sides for spreading adhesive and two notched sides for combing it to the right depth. Check the tile and adhesive manufacturer's recommendations for the proper notch size.

PLASTIC BUCKET, CLEAN SPONGE. For washing residual grout off tiles.

PLASTIC SPACER REMOVER. For neatly and cleanly removing plastic tile spacers.

RUBBER GLOVES. To protect hands when working with mortar and adhesive.

RUBBING STONE. For smoothing rough edges on cut tiles.

Most of the tiling tools you see here are for cutting, installing, and grouting tile. The tools needed to lay out the job include many items you've already used many times before: pencil, eraser, graph paper, ruler, framing square, level; plumb bob, chalk line, tape measure, and combination square. One goal in setting tile is to lay out the job in a way that minimizes the need for cutting, though it's inevitable that you'll need to cut tiles for corners and around fixtures.

BEATING BLOCK AND RUBBER MALLET. For

SNAP CUTTER. For cutting tiles. Set the the tile in the cutter and score it along the snap line. Press down the handle to snap tile along the score line.

TAPE MEASURE. For laying out and marking individual tiles for cutting.

TILE NIPPERS. For cutting tiles. They resemble pliers but have carbide-tipped edges that are ideal for making small notches and curves in tile.

TILE-SCORING TOOL. For marking cut lines on tiles.

Painting tools are perhaps the least complicated and most familiar tools of all. Quality is a concern for paintbrushes. Don't skimp or you'll be disappointed in the results. Cutting molding doesn't really require more than a simple miter box, although if you've got a lot to do—or if you want more precision than you can get with a miter box—you might consider renting a power miter saw.

ANGLED SASH BRUSH. For precise trim painting; minimizes the amount of paint that gets on window glass.

BUCKET. For holding clean water to rinse paintbrushes when using acrylic paint.

DROP CLOTH. To protect finished surfaces from paint drops and spills.

LOW-TACKING MASKING TAPE. For protecting any surface you don't want painted. Especially helpful around trim and on cabinetry.

MITER BOX OR POWER MITER SAW. For cutting trim pieces at perfect 45 degree angles; your trim will look sloppy if it's off by even a degree.

PAINTBRUSH COMB. For thoroughly cleaning brushes and maintaining the separation of the bristles.

PAINTBRUSHES: 2-INCH AND 3-INCH. Use narrower brushes for painting trim and wider brushes for painting in tight spaces where a roller won't reach.

PAINTER'S HAT. To protect hair from inevitable splatters

ROLLER HANDLE EXTENSION POLE. Attaches to a roller handle to reach the top of the walls and the ceiling.

ROLLERS AND HANDLES. For applying paint to wide swaths of surface area. Rollers cater to a variety of surface materials. Use thicker, woolier rollers for rough textures such as brick or stucco; use thinner, smoother rollers for smoother textures, such as finished drywall, plaster or wood.

ROLLER TRAY AND LINER. For applying paint to a roller. Disposable liners make clean up a snap.

WINDOW SCRAPER. For scraping paint off glass.

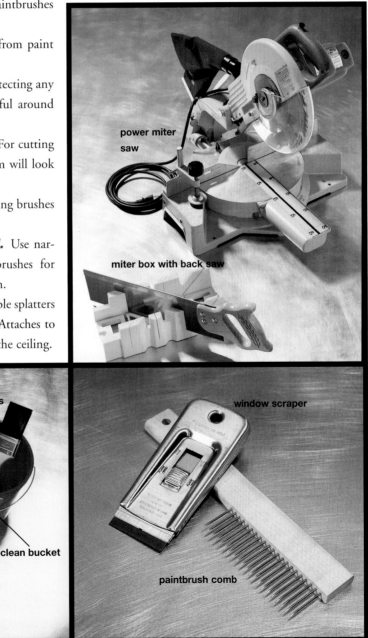

power miter saw

miter box with back saw

drop cloth

rollers

brushes

angled sash brush

roller tray liner

masking tape

clean bucket

roller tray

window scraper

paintbrush comb

8

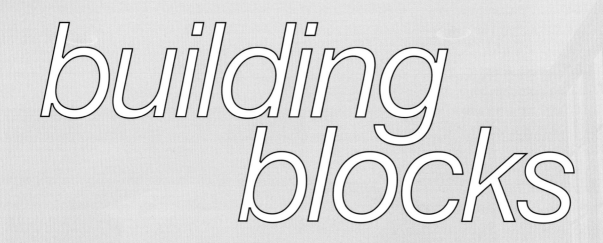

building blocks

THE MONTHS (OR YEARS) OF DREAMING, PLANNING, ASSEMBLING TOOLS

and materials, paint and tile samples are over. It's time to take hammer in hand and

make your dream kitchen a reality. Part of that reality is understanding that the kitchen

is perhaps the most complex room in the house. It must be wired specifically for

various appliances and plumbed adequately to handle cooking and cleanup every day.

To accommodate its many uses, it must be constructed with more materials than any

other room: wood for cabinets; ceramic, linoleum, or vinyl for flooring; laminate,

granite, or solid-surfacing for countertops; chrome or brass for faucets; and stainless

steel or cast iron for sinks. Step-by-step, this chapter shows you how to tear out the

old and build the new, starting from the ground up. That means how to build walls,

how to wire and plumb them, and how to install windows, hang cabinets, and build an

island. If you've never done any of this, fear not: Here's everything you need to know.

It won't be long before the only work you do in your kitchen will be washing garden tomatoes or arranging a vase of flowers. A stellar example of good design, this breezy white kitchen, *opposite*, boasts an efficient work triangle; an island for casual dining; a transom window above the door that, when open, allows for good air flow through the house; and decorative molding on the island and above the window.

Before you begin building your new kitchen, you have to take out the old one. But before you can remove the ugly old range or tear into the dented and peeling vinyl, first things first: Turn off the water, electricity, and gas. Following are step-by-step instructions.

Turning off the power

1 A BREAKER PANEL has a set of switches that shut down if the electrical circuits are overburdened. To figure out which circuit you're working on, turn on the electrical fixtures and appliances in the area where you're working. Switch breakers off until you find the ones that control power to the area; you'll know you have the right ones when everything you turned on goes off. Leave those breakers off while you work.

2 IF YOU HAVE AN OLDER HOME, you might have a fuse panel. It usually has a main fuse block, a series of fuses that protect the individual 120-volt circuits, and two fuse blocks for 240-volt circuits. Turn on the electrical fixtures and appliances. Remove fuses or blocks until you locate those that control fixtures and appliances in your work area; you'll know you have the right ones when everything you turned on goes off. Leave those fuses out while you work.

3 DON'T LEAVE ANYTHING to chance. To be absolutely sure the power is off, test the circuit with a neon circuit tester. Plug the prongs into the outlet. Hold the tester with one hand, so if there is live current, the power won't travel through your body. If the light comes on, the circuit is still live. To find the correct breaker or fuse, plug a lamp into the outlet and turn it on. Pull fuses or switch breakers until the circuit is off.

Turning off the water

1 MOST SINKS have water shutoff valves on the supply pipes leading to the fixture. Generally they are under the basin on the hot- and cold-water supply pipes. Turn the valves clockwise as far as they will go to close the shutoff valves

2 IF YOU NEED TO DRAIN the whole water system, or if your fixtures don't have individual shutoff valves, you'll have to shut off the

water meter

water supply to the whole house. The main water valve is located next to the water meter. Turn the valve clockwise as far as it will go. Use a pair of pliers if you have to. Once the valve is shut—but before you begin working— turn on all of the faucets in the house to drain the plumbing system.

Turning off the gas

The gas valve for most gas stoves is on the supply line behind the appliance. To shut off the gas, turn the handle of the valve so it's perpendicular to the pipe. Open the windows and doors, then turn on the burners to free any gas still left in the stove. When you turn the gas back on, you'll need to relight the pilot lights. Local codes usually require that a plumber reconnect the old stove or connect a new one.

Removing cabinets

If you're starting from scratch, you'll need to remove the cabinets and counters. Take out anything that isn't permanently attached to the cabinets.

That includes drawers, doors, and shelving. You'll need the space when you reach inside to remove the screws that hold the cabinets to the wall.

If you plan to reconfigure and reuse your cabinets, be sure to put any hardware, fasteners, and corner blocks in a safe place. Tape the end of your pry bar and cover the counter surface to avoid scratching it while it's in storage.

1 **COUNTERTOPS ARE USUALLY screwed to corner blocks. Remove the screws that run through the blocks and any other fasteners you see. If you have older cabinets, the counter may be nailed to the cabinet from above. In that case, you'll need to pry the counter loose (see Step 2).**

2 **USING A UTILITY KNIFE, slice through any caulk that seals the backsplash and wall. With a pry bar, leverage the countertop off the cabinets. If the countertop has been glued down, you'll need to pry it in several spots along the edge to completely break it loose.**

3 **TO TEAR OUT BASE CABINETS, remove screws that hold adjacent cabinets together, then remove screws that hold the cabinets to the wall. You'll need a helper to pull the cabinets apart from each other and away from the wall.**

4 **TO REMOVE WALL CABINETS, take out the screws that connect the wall cabinets to each other. With a helper holding the cabinets from underneath, remove the screws that hold the cabinets to the wall. If the screws are difficult to remove, drill around them with a hole saw. Place the center bit just to the side of the screw, drill to the wall, then lift the cabinet off the wall.**

Removing the faucet and sink

Before you remove the old faucet and sink, gather the tools you'll need and some penetrating oil in case the faucet's mounting nuts are stuck. Turn off the water-supply stops or turn off the water to the whole house and drain the lines.

If your faucet has a sprayer, remove the nuts that secure the hose to the faucet body and the spray head to the sink. Unhook the supply lines and move them out of the way. Use a basin wrench to loosen and remove the mounting nuts that hold the faucet body to the sink. Lift out the faucet.

To remove the old sink, disconnect the supply lines and the trap that joins the sink to the drainpipe. Remove the mounting clips from underneath the sink by unscrewing them and pushing them to the side, then pry up the sink.

Removing walls

If you are expanding your kitchen, or if the existing drywall or plaster is damaged beyond repair, you'll be stripping walls down to the studs. Tearing down walls isn't complicated work—just very dusty and loud—but it does require that you know whether the wall you've marked for demolition is a structural, or load-bearing, wall.

To figure out if a wall is structural, knock a little plaster away at the top of the wall. If there are studs running into two 2×4s and a floor joist, the wall is load-bearing. It cannot be removed without bolstering the existing framing, a job for a pro.

If the wall is not load-bearing, you can tear it down yourself. The only tools needed are a pry bar and hammer. As always, first shut off the power and turn off the water and gas. Begin by removing cover plates from switches and outlets, and from heat registers. If you have baseboard heaters or an old-fashioned radiator, call a plumber to remove them. Take mirrors and pictures off nearby walls; pounding may knock them loose. Tape plastic sheeting over doors and heating vents to keep dust from circulating throughout the house. Wear goggles and a dust mask.

If your house was built prior to 1978, the paint might contain lead. If your house was built prior to 1979, the plaster and flooring might contain asbestos. For information on lessening health risks during renovation, call the Enviornmental Protection Agency: 1/800-424-LEAD for lead and 1/800-368-5888 for asbestos.

basic framing

Walls are pretty simple constructions. Behind the drywall, plaster, or paneling, they consist of vertical members, called studs, that butt at the top and bottom against horizontal members, called plates. Building a wall, however, takes thoughtful planning. When you cover the framing with drywall, for instance, the seams between sheets must fall in the center of studs. There must be a nailing surface for the sheets at the corners, and all framing members must be aligned along a flat plane.

If your kitchen floor and ceiling are nearly level, it's easy to assemble a stud wall on the floor and raise it into position, as shown here. If your floor and ceiling are uneven, or if you're working in tight quarters, build the wall in place, custom-fitting each stud and toe-nailing it to the top and bottom plates (see page 117).

Either way, attaching your wall to the ceiling is a must. If the wall runs perpendicular to the ceiling joists, fasten the wall's top plate with two 16-penny (16d) nails at every joist. If it's parallel, install crossbraces so you can nail the top plate into solid material.

Building a wall

1 USE A FRAMING SQUARE and a chalk line to mark the exact location of the new wall on the floor. For long walls, check for square using the 3-4-5 method, which is based on the Pythagorean theorem. Here's how: On one side of the floor, mark a point 3 feet from the corner. On the other side, mark a point 4 feet from the corner. If the distance between the two marks is exactly 5 feet, it is square. Using a level and a straight 2x4 that is as high as your ceiling, mark the wall location on the ceiling, joists, or crossbracing. These marks will help you position the wall before you plumb it. Be sure the ceiling has adequate framing to which you can nail the top plate.

2 USING THE FLOOR LAYOUT as your guide, mark and cut 2×4s for the top and bottom plates. Place them on edge next to each other and mark for the studs. The first stud will be at the end of the wall. The rest of the studs will be either 16 or 24 inches on center, which means that the measurement from the edge of the wall to the center of each stud will be a multiple of 16 or 24. Make a mark every 16 inches; then, with a combination or speed square, draw lines ¾ inch on each side of your first marks. Draw an X in the middle of each mark to indicate where to nail the studs.

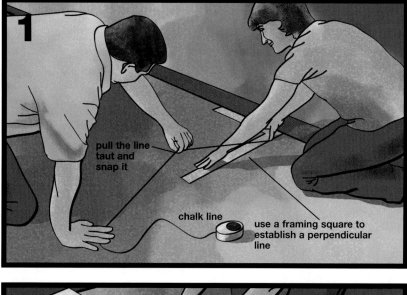

pull the line taut and snap it

chalk line

use a framing square to establish a perpendicular line

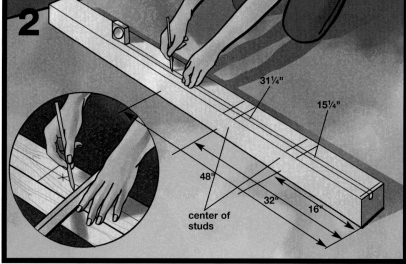

31¼"

15¼"

48"

32"

16"

center of studs

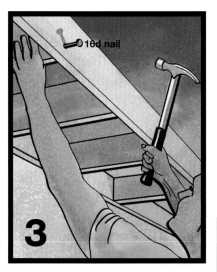

16d nail

3 **IF THE NEW WALL RUNS** parallel to the ceiling joists, cut pieces of 2×4 wood to fit tightly between the ceiling joists and attach them with a 16d nail every 2 feet or so. Measure for your studs and cut them to length.

4 **WORKING ON A FLAT SURFACE,** lay the studs on edge between the top and bottom plates. If possible, while you hammer butt the bottom edge of the new wall against something solid, such as a wall, to keep the wall from sliding. For speed,

nail one plate at time to the studs. Drive two 16d nails through the plate and into the ends of each stud. Because hammer blows tend to knock studs out of alignment, double-check your work as you nail. Keep the edges of the studs flush with plate edges. If any of the studs are twisted or bowed, replace them.

5 **RAISING THE FRAME** can be cumbersome, so have a helper on hand. Position the bottom plate about in its final resting place and tip the wall into position. If the wall fits so tightly against the ceiling that you have to hammer it in place, protect the framing with a scrap of 2x4 as you pound. Tap both ends of the frame until it is roughly plumb in both directions.

6 **IF THE WALL IS SHORT** in places, drive shims between the bottom plate and the floor or between the top plates and the ceiling joists. Have your helper steady the framework while you drive the pieces into place. Drive shims from both sides,

drive shims from both sides

thin edges facing each other, to keep the plate from tilting.

7 **ONCE THE FRAME IS SNUG,** use the level to make sure the wall is plumb in both directions. Check both ends of the wall and every other stud. Fasten the top plate to the ceiling by driving a 16d nail through the plate and into each joist. Fasten the bottom plate to the floor with the right kind of nail for your situation. Use 16d nails if your floor is wood; use masonry nails or a power hammer if your floor is concrete.

Building a wall in place

1 **IF IT'S NOT POSSIBLE TO BUILD a** wall on the floor and raise it into position, begin by cutting the top and bottom plates and mark them for studs (see page 114). Transfer the marks to the faces of the plates, making sure the marks are clear so you can easily see them to align the studs while toenailing.

Nail the top plate to the joists with 16d nails. Use a level and a straight board to mark the location of the bottom plate, or use a chalk line if you're using a plumb bob. Mark the floor in two places and make an X to indicate on which side of the mark the plate should be positioned. Use masonry nails or a power hammer to fasten the bottom plate to the floor.

2 **WITH THE TOP** and bottom plates installed, measure each stud individually. Add $\frac{1}{16}$ inch for a snug fit and cut. Tap each stud into place. If you have to whack it very hard to get it into place, it's too long.

Don't risk splitting the stud; take it down and trim it a hair.

3 **TO SECURE THE STUDS**, drive 8-penny nails at an angle through the side of the studs and into the plate; this is called toenailing. Tap the nail once or twice while holding it parallel to the floor or ceiling. When the nail tip bites into the wood, change the angle of the nail to 45 degrees. Drive four to six nails into each joint: two on each side, with an optional one at the front and back. The first nail may move the stud, but the second nail, driven from the other side, moves it back.

If you have a difficult time toenailing, you can drill pilot holes for the nails, using a $\frac{3}{32}$-inch bit. Or place a $14\frac{1}{2}$-inch board between the studs to serve as a temporary nailing brace.

4 **WHEN FRAMING CORNERS**, be sure a nailing surface exists for

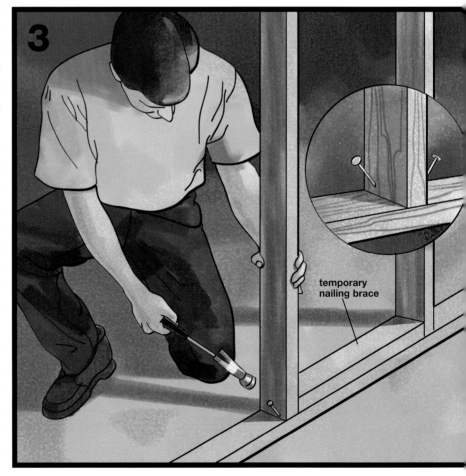

temporary nailing brace

every piece of drywall to be installed. This means you have to add nonstructural nailers. How you do this will depend on your particular situation. Look at the examples below to find one similar to what you have in your own kitchen.

In Situation 1, the extra stud is turned sideways to offer a nailing surface and to strengthen the corner. Drive 16d nails through end stud #1 and into the extra stud, then through end stud #2 and into the extra stud and end stud #1.

In Situation 2, several foot-long 2×4 scraps (usually three in a stan- dard 8-foot wall) serve as spacers between two full-length studs placed at the end of one wall. Tie wall sec- tions together with 16d nails.

Situation 3 shows two intersecting walls. Nail three studs together and nail to the plates, then attach to the adjoining wall.

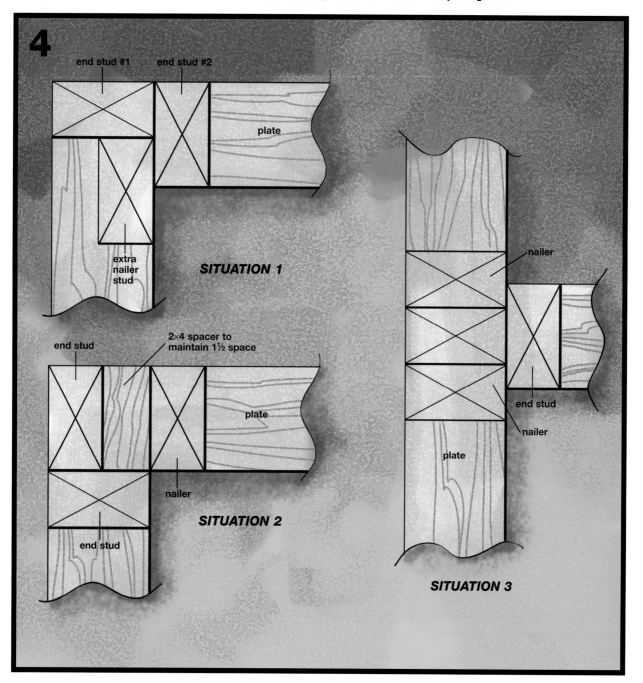

4

end stud #1   end stud #2

plate

extra nailer stud

SITUATION 1

2×4 spacer to maintain 1½ space

end stud

plate

nailer

end stud

SITUATION 2

nailer

end stud

nailer

plate

SITUATION 3

installing windows

A kitchen awash in sunlight is a wonderful place to be. As important as windows are in the rest of the house, they are especially important in the kitchen, both for light and ventilation. If your kitchen remodeling involves adding or replacing windows, you'll be pleasantly surprised at the benefit-to-hassle ratio of installing them. They're not terribly difficult to put in—and having big, bright windows in good working order in the kitchen is a big plus.

1 TAKE OUT THE INTERIOR WALL surface (usually drywall or plaster) around the window opening, then test-fit the new window. Be sure to center it in the rough opening.

Support the weight of the window with blocks and shims placed under the bottom jamb. Make sure the window is plumb and level, adjusting the shims as necessary.

2 TRACE THE OUTLINE of the window molding on the exterior of the house. If you have vinyl or metal siding, you'll need to enlarge the outline to accommodate the required extra J-channel moldings. Remove the window after you've finished the outline.

3 WITH A RECIPROCATING SAW held at a shallow angle, or with

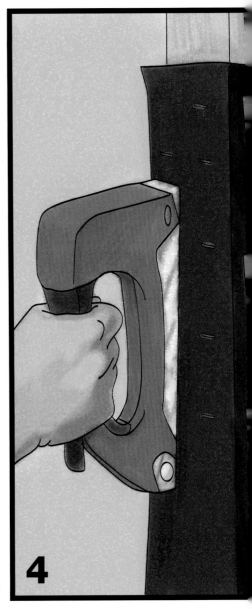

a circular saw adjusted so the blade depth equals the thickness of the veneer or siding, cut along the outline from Step 2. Use a sharp chisel to complete the cuts at the corners.

4 CUT 8-INCH-WIDE STRIPS OF building paper and slip them between the siding and sheathing around the entire window opening. Wrap the paper around the framing members and staple it in place.

drip edge

5 **CUT A LENGTH OF DRIP EDGE** to fit over the top of the window, then slip it between the veneer or siding and building paper.

6 **PLACE THE WINDOW** into the opening, then push the molding firmly against the sheathing.

7 **CHECK FOR LEVEL AND PLUMB** and follow these next steps to adjust as needed.

8 **IF THE WINDOW IS LEVEL,** predrill and nail both of the bottom corners of molding with 16d casing nails. If the window is not perfectly level, nail just the higher of the two bottom corners.

9 **IF NECESSARY,** have a helper adjust the shim under the lower corner of the window from inside the house until the window is level.

Drywall installation is not technically complex, but it helps to learn some basic techniques. The most difficult thing about working with drywall is that it is heavy and unwieldy. Many older rooms are out of square, so cutting and fitting drywall can be a challenge. Achieving a smooth surface takes professionals three compound applications and sandings, so you might want to count on four or five.

Before you begin, study the framing to be sure you can attach the drywall at all points. If you're covering an existing wall, locate all the studs and clearly mark their locations.

Local building codes specify how many nails or screws to use to hang drywall and in what pattern. Codes even vary from room to room.

If you don't use adhesive, the general practice is to install two nails into the wall studs at 16-inch intervals and a single nail every 7 inches along edges. When using adhesive, install two nails at 24-inch intervals and one nail at 7 inches along the edge. Keep adhesive 6 inches away from the top and bottom of the drywall sheet. Check with your local building department for code specific to your area.

1 **LAY THE DRYWALL SHEETS on** top of scrap lumber to keep them off the floor. Before you cut, you may have to turn some pieces over so the finished side faces you. Mark the sheet ¼ inch shorter than the measured length. Stand the drywall on edge and set your drywall square in place. Clasp the square firmly on top and press your foot against the

trap square with foot

cut backing after breaking

bottom of the square's blade to be sure it doesn't move. With the blade against the square, cut downward most of the way, then finish by cutting up from the bottom. Snap back the cut segment, away from the cut, then slice through the backing paper.

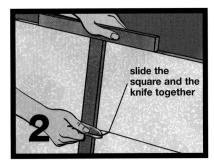

slide the square and the knife together

2 **TO CUT ALONG THE LENGTH of** a sheet of drywall, set the drywall square on the edge of a sheet and hold the knife against it at the correct spot. Slide the square along as you keep the knife in position. If the rip cut must be wider at one end, chalk a line and cut it freehand.

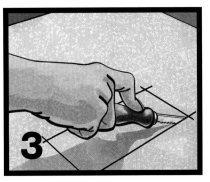

3 **TO MAKE A HOLE for an electri-** cal receptacle box, measure from the box's edges, top, and bottom to the edges of the adjacent sheets of existing drywall. Transfer measurements to the new sheet and draw a rectangle. Score outline with a utility knife; cut the hole with a drywall saw.

4 **TO CUT A HOLE FOR A PIPE,** measure and mark the sheet for the center of the pipe. Draw a circle and cut it out with a drywall saw or knife. Or drill a hole using a hole saw that's slightly larger than the diameter of the pipe. Bore small holes with a power drill.

5 **TO INSTALL SHEETS** horizontally, butt the upper sheets firmly against the ceiling. Cut sheets so they fall midway across a stud. Butt the lower panels firmly against the upper panels, tapered edge to tapered edge. When covering existing plaster, apply drywall adhesive and drive screws into the lath only at the edges of the drywall.

lever panel with wood scraps

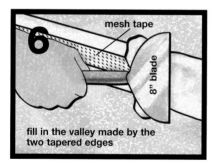

mesh tape

8" blade

fill in the valley made by the two tapered edges

6 **WHEN ALL OF THE SHEETS** are hung, finish the drywall by taping and mudding the joints. Press the mesh tape in place. Load an 8- or 10-inch taping knife with joint compound. Make sure the knife blade more than spans the valley created by the tapers. Fill in the taper only, to create a flat wall surface. For butt joints, feather out the compound 8 to 10 inches on each side. If you end up with a small ridge in the middle of the joint, you can sand it off after the compound dries.

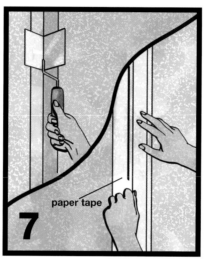

paper tape

7 **TO FINISH INSIDE CORNERS,** apply compound to both sides with a 6-inch blade. Cut a piece of paper tape, fold along its crease, and pat into the corner. Run a corner blade down its length to embed tape. In spots where it doesn't adhere, lift the tape, add compound, and embed. Feather later coats with a 10-inch taping knife.

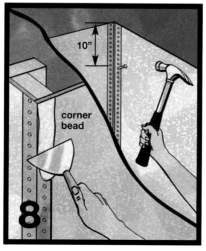

10"

corner bead

8 **TO FINISH OUTSIDE CORNERS,** cut metal corner bead to fit, using tin snips. Fasten it to the walls with nails or screws at 10-inch intervals. Be sure the flange does not stick out at any point; test by running a taping knife along the length of the bead. When applying compound, let the knife blade ride on the bead. Use a 6-inch blade for the first coat, then 10- and 12-inch blades.

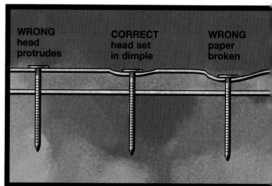

| WRONG head protrudes | CORRECT head set in dimple | WRONG paper broken |

Drywall nailing 101

When attaching drywall to the studs, driving the nails properly is harder than you might think. If you simply drive a nail in flush, you won't be able to cover it with joint compound. If you drive it too deeply, you'll break the drywall paper. If the paper is broken, the nail won't hold; it tears right through the inner core of gypsum.

The correct way lies somewhere in the middle. Try to drive the nail so the nailhead is set into a slightly dimpled surface. No portion of the nailhead should protrude above the surface of the drywall.

To make sure your nails are deep enough, run a taping blade along the surface of the wall. Nailheads should not click against the blade as you pull it across. Also, pull any nails that miss a stud, then swat the hole with your hammer to dimple it, and fill with joint compound for a smooth wall surface.

The instructions from here through page 131 describe how to run a new electrical circuit in a finished space. If you've taken your kitchen walls down to the studs, any electrical work will be much easier. The method for installing electrical circuits in unfinished space is similar to the method shown here but is admittedly far less difficult. Most of the materials for both situations are the same, although there are receptacle boxes and fixture or junction boxes specifically designed to minimize damage caused by installation.

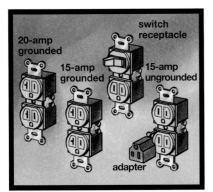

Standard receptacles

Standard duplex receptacles have two outlets for receiving plugs. Each outlet has a long (neutral) slot, a shorter (hot) slot, and a half-round grounding hole. This ensures the plug is polarized and grounded. Receptacles are rated for maximum amps. A 20-amp grounded receptacle has a T-shape neutral slot; use it only on 20-amp circuits. For most purposes, a 15-amp grounded receptacle suffices.

When replacing a receptacle in an ungrounded outlet box, use a 15-amp ungrounded receptacle, intended only for use in older homes where circuits lack ground wires.

The switch in a combination switch/receptacle can be hooked up to control the receptacle it's paired with.

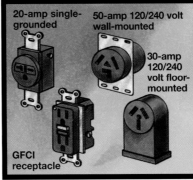

Specialized receptacles

The kitchen requires installation of specialized receptacles. Any receptacle located within 6 feet of a water fixture must be a ground-fault circuit interrupter (GFCI), a safety device that senses any shock hazard and shuts down a circuit or receptacle. Electric ranges require a 240-volt receptacle. Plugs required for appliances of 15, 20, 30, and 50 amps will have different prong configurations. Although it's not a necessity, a 20-amp single-grounded receptacle makes it nearly impossible to overload a critical circuit.

Choosing wire

Wire, cord, and cable—the conductors—provide the routes along which electricity travels. Wire is a solid strand of metal wrapped in insulation; cord is a group of small metal strands wrapped in insulation; and cable is made of two or more wires encased in protective

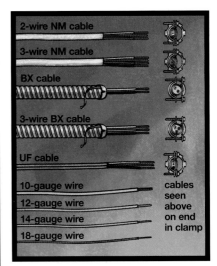

sheathing of metal or plastic, while flexible armored cable (BX) contains wires wrapped in a flexible metal sheathing; underground feed (UF) cable is watertight.

Different sizes, or gauges, of wires carry different amounts of electricity. For instance, 14-gauge wire carries a maximum of 15 amps, 12-gauge wire carries up to 20 amps, and 10-gauge wire carries up to 30 amps.

Coding printed on the sheathing tells you what's inside. For example, "14-2 G" cable has two 14-gauge wires inside plus a bare ground wire (the "G" stands for ground).

Color=function

COLOR	FUNCTION
white	neutral, carries power back to service panel
black	hot, carries power from service panel
red, other colors	also hot, color-coded to help identify which circuit it's on
white with black tape	a white wire being used as a hot wire
bare or green	a ground wire

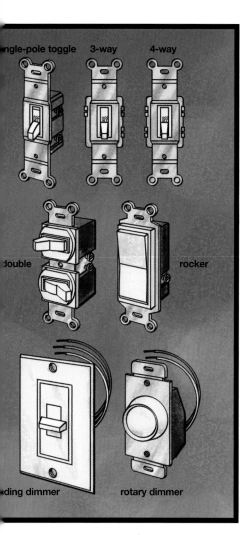

single-pole toggle   3-way   4-way

double   rocker

ding dimmer   rotary dimmer

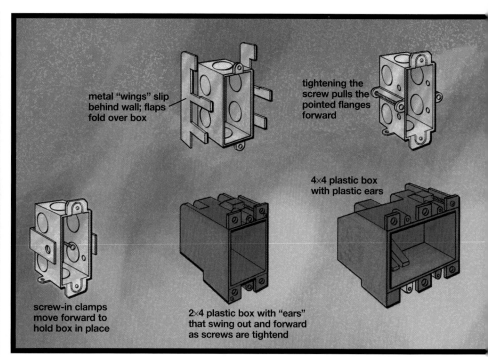

metal "wings" slip
behind wall; flaps
fold over box

tightening the
screw pulls the
pointed flanges
forward

4×4 plastic box
with plastic ears

screw-in clamps
move forward to
hold box in place

2×4 plastic box with "ears"
that swing out and forward
as screws are tightend

Which switch?

For most needs, a single-pole toggle switch works fine. You'll need a three-way or four-way switch if you want to control a light from two or three separate switches. If you want to add a switch without putting in a larger box, a space-saving double switch may be the solution. A rocker switch functions the same way a standard toggle does but is slightly easier to use. A dimmer switch allows you to adjust light levels to suit your needs. It's a nice option to have on pendant lighting over a dining area or on in-cabinet fixtures.

Retrofit switch, receptacle boxes

When installing new electrical service in finished walls, use boxes designed to minimize damage to the wall. If the clips don't work, try attaching the boxes to framing pieces with screws driven through holes inside the box.

Retrofit fixture, junction boxes

Adding new wiring to old walls is a challenge. It's not easy to secure a fixture box when there's drywall or plaster in the way. For heavy ceiling fixtures, use a brace bar that can be slipped into the hole and expanded from joist to joist.

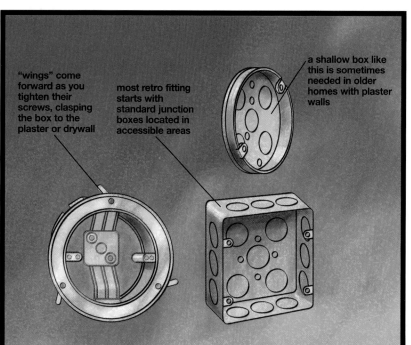

"wings" come
forward as you
tighten their
screws, clasping
the box to the
plaster or drywall

most retro fitting
starts with
standard junction
boxes located in
accessible areas

a shallow box like
this is sometimes
needed in older
homes with plaster
walls

The patching and painting that accompanies electrical work in a place where the walls and ceilings are finished can take more time than the electrical work itself. A few tips to make it go as smoothly as possible:

■ Plan the placement of the boxes carefully so you can avoid making unnecessary holes.

■ Use special boxes designed for installation in a finished wall or ceiling.

■ Before you begin, plan how you're going to get cable to the new location.

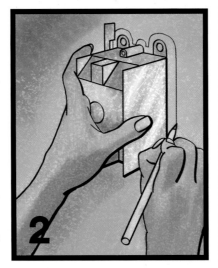

4 SIDE-CLAMP BOXES grip the wall from behind as you tighten the screws. Pull 8 inches of cable through the box and insert the box into the hole. Hold the box plumb as you tighten the clamps. Alternate from side to side as you work so the box seats evenly. Don't overtighten the clamps.

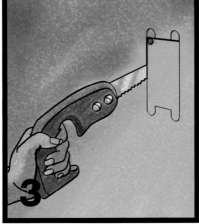

Center the box on the hole you successfuly rotated the wire through. Be sure the template or box is plumb before you mark the outline. If it's not, make a new outline.

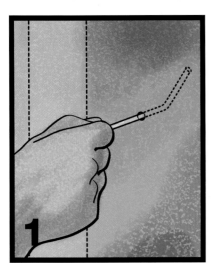

3 CUT AROUND the traced outline. If the surface is drywall, use a utility knife. If you have to cut into plaster walls, use a keyhole saw. If the plaster is crumbly, mask the outline with tape to support it and keep it intact as you saw. If the wall is wood, drill a ¼-inch access hole in each corner and use a saber saw. Run the cable (see pages 129–130).

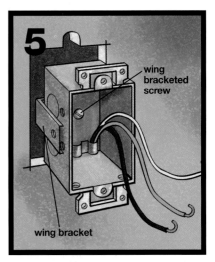

1 TO DETERMINE the box location, drill a small hole in the wall. Insert a bent wire and rotate it. If you hit something solid, you've probably found a stud. Go 6 inches to one side and try again. If you hit wood again, you might have hit a fire block. Drill another hole 3 inches higher or lower. Keep trying until you can rotate the bent wire freely.

2 SOME BOXES COME WITH a template that can be held against the wall and traced around. If yours doesn't, use the box itself.

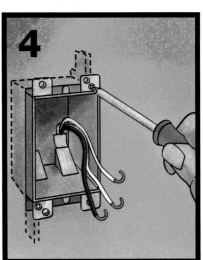

wing bracketed screw

wing bracket

5 ALTERNATELY, YOU'LL NEED TO tighten the wing clips on the box. Loosen the screw that's centered in the receptacle box until the wing bracket fully extends from the

back. Hold the wings against the body of the box and push it into the hole. Tighten the screw until the box is held firmly in place.

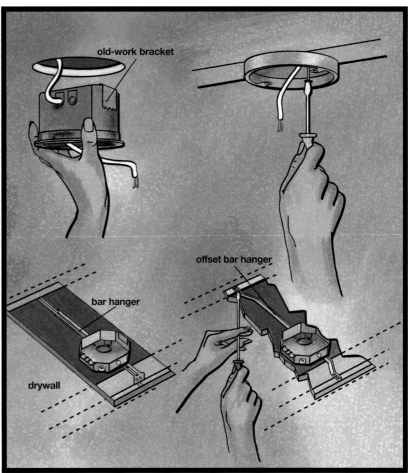

old-work bracket

offset bar hanger

bar hanger

drywall

For access from the attic

A ceiling box must support a light fixture or fan, so it must attach very securely to the framing. If you are fortunate enough to have attic space above your kitchen, the job can be done without damaging your ceiling. Mark the location of each box on the ceiling and drive nails as reference points. Cut the hole for the box. If there is a joist nearby, attach an L-bracket box directly to it. If not, use a bar hanger or frame in a 2×4 support.

No access from above

If you don't have access to the ceiling above your kitchen, you have other options. If your light fixture weighs 5 pounds or less, use an old-work bracket. Cut a hole the size of the box, slip in the bracket, telescope it to fit

between two joists, and attach the box. If your fixture weighs more than 5 pounds, make an opening in the ceiling and install hanging hardware. With a drywall ceiling, cut a large rectangle and install a bar hanger. For plaster, chip a path and use an offset bar hanger.

Test first, then patch

After testing the electrical installation, patch the ceiling. With drywall, you may be able to use the piece you cut out. Nail the panel to the joists and tape seams with joint compound (see pages 120–121). For a plaster ceiling, fill the hole with patching compound.

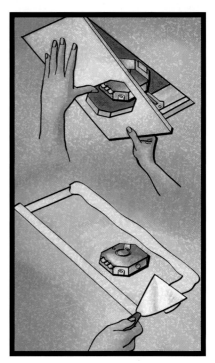

stripping wire

Before you make electrical connections, you'll need to remove some of the sheathing that encases the three or four wires of the cable and strip some of the insulation that covers the individual wires. Stripping wire is a simple job, but it must be done with great care or you could end up with dangerous electrical shorts.

If you think you have damaged the insulation, cut the cable back to a place behind the potentially dangerous spot and start again. Strip wires before, rather than after, the cable is pulled into the box, so if you do make a mistake you can cut off the damaged portion and try again.

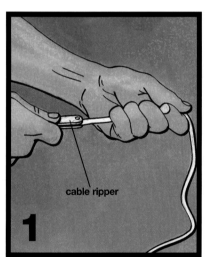

1 TO REMOVE PLASTIC SHEATHING from nonmetallic sheathed cable, use a cable ripper. Slip 6 to 8 inches of cable into the ripper's jaws, squeeze, and pull. This slits the sheathing without damaging the insulation of internal wires.

2 PEEL BACK THE SHEATHING you have slit, as well as the paper wrapping or strips of thin plastic,

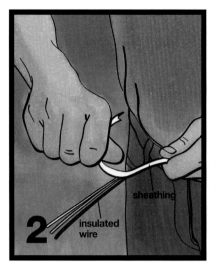

if any. You'll find two or three separately insulated wires, as well as a bare ground wire.

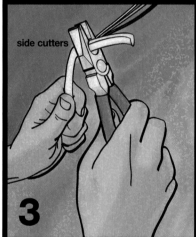

3 CUT OFF THE SHEATHING and paper. Remove the slit sheathing with a pair of side cutters.

4 TO STRIP INSULATION from the wires, use a combination tool, which has separate holes for different wire sizes. Place the wire in the correct holes, clamp down, give it a twist, and pull the tool away from you. You can use the same technique with an adjustable stripper; once it's set

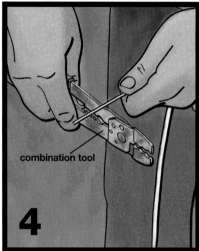

for the correct wire size, you don't have to look for the right hole every time. You can also strip wire with a utility knife, but be very careful not to dig into and weaken the copper wire. Place the wire on a scrap piece of wood, hold the blade at a slight angle, and make several light slices.

Working with wire

The most satisfying phase of an electrical installation comes when you get to tie wires together and attach them to the switches, light fixtures, and receptacles. As with any other facet of an electrical job, don't take shortcuts with wire connections and splices. Cap splices with both wire connectors and tape—not just one or the other. Make pigtails (see page 128) wherever they're needed instead of trying to connect two or more wires to a terminal. Finally, don't overcrowd a box with too many wires. Check your local electrical code to see how many wires you can install in a box.

To make a splice of two or more

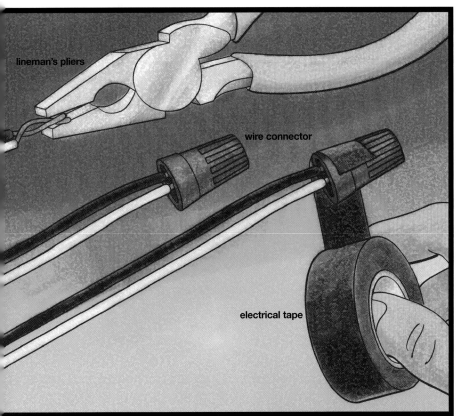

lineman's pliers

wire connector

electrical tape

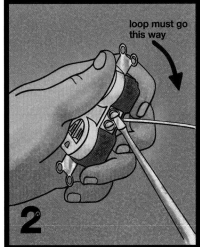

loop must go this way

2 Hook the wire clockwise around the terminal so that the loop closes when the screws are tightened. With receptacles, the black wires go to the brass side, the white wires go to silver. Tighten firmly but don't overtighten, which can crack the device. If the device suffers damage, throw it out.

wires, use wire connectors. They come in a variety of sizes and are color-coded to help decipher how many wires of what thickness can be used with them (see chart below). Wire connectors firm up the splice and protect bare wires better than tape. Twist the wires firmly together. Don't depend on the connector to do the joining. Twist on the wire connector, turning it by hand until it tightens firmly. As a final precaution, wrap the connector clockwise with electrical tape, over-lapping the wire.

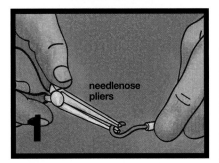

needlenose pliers

1 TO CONNECT A WIRE to a terminal, strip just enough wire to wrap around the terminal, about ¾ inch. Then form it into a loop using needle-nose or lineman's pliers. It takes a little practice to make loops that lie flat and that are the right size.

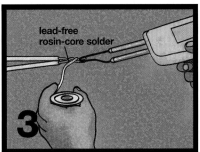

lead-free rosin-core solder

3 SOME CODES REQUIRE splices to be soldered. More often, however, the soldering of house wiring is prohibited. If you need to solder a splice, start by twisting the wires together. Heat the wires with a soldering iron, then touch lead-free, rosin-core solder to the splice. The solder melts into the splice.

How many wires can a connector hold?

Connector color	12-gauge wire	14-gauge wire
red	2–4	2–5
yellow	2–3	2–4
orange	2	2–4

connecting wires

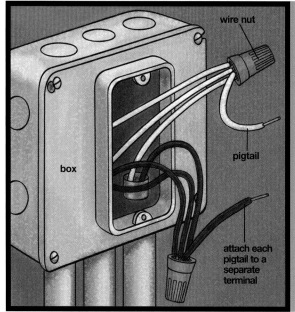

wire nut

box

pigtail

attach each pigtail to a separate terminal

Most receptacles and switches have connection holes in the back. To make a connection this way, strip the wire (a stripping gauge is often provided, showing how much insulation to remove) and thread it into the correct hole. Receptacle holes are marked for white and black wires, but most professional electricians don't use these holes. Wires inserted this way are not as secure as those screwed to a terminal, the method is shown below.

Never attach more than one wire to a terminal. Codes prohibit it. It's unsafe—terminal screws are made to hold only one wire. If you have to join multiple wires to a terminal, make a pigtail. Cut a short piece of wire (about 4 inches), strip both ends, and splice it to the other wires with a wire nut. Then attach the free end of the pigtail to the appropriate terminal.

Alternately, make a soldered splice, but only if your local code permits soldering. Twist wires together so one extends 1 inch beyond the splice. Solder the twist and loop the extended wire. Tape the soldered splice before screwing the wire to the terminal.

Ground receptacles and switches in one of several ways, depending on the type of wiring you're using and the type of box. With flexible armored cable (BX), Greenfield, or rigid conduit, the metal of the wiring casing and the metal of the box substitutes for the grounding wire. Simply by attaching the device firmly to the box, you have grounded it. Some local codes require that you also attach a short grounding

Do as the professionals do

Although the holes on a receptacle are marked for white and black wires, most professional electricians don't use them. Instead they screw the wires to the terminal as shown below, a method that is much more secure.

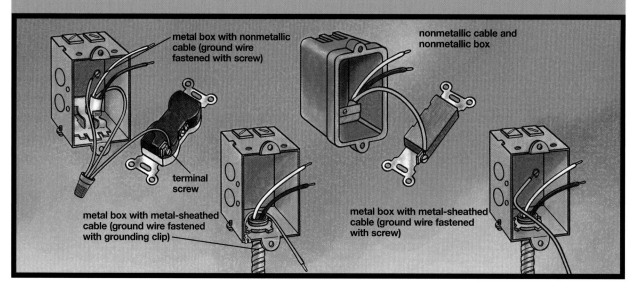

metal box with nonmetallic cable (ground wire fastened with screw)

nonmetallic cable and nonmetallic box

terminal screw

metal box with metal-sheathed cable (ground wire fastened with grounding clip)

metal box with metal-sheathed cable (ground wire fastened with screw)

wire. If you're working with nonmetallic sheathed cable (Romex) and metal boxes, connect short ground wires to the box and device. With nonmetallic boxes, the cable's ground wire connects directly to the device.

Running cable

Do some investigative work before running cable through finished walls or ceilings. As best as you can, figure out what's in the wall or ceiling cavity.

Try to find access from an unfinished attic floor or basement ceiling above or below your kitchen. Check for insulation that might be blocking the way. Determine if it's possible to run the cable parallel to the joists and studs. Finally try to make as few holes in the drywall or plaster as possible.

The most time-consuming part of running cable often is patching holes in the walls and ceilings. Use patching plaster, drywall tape, and compound to patch holes you do have to make.

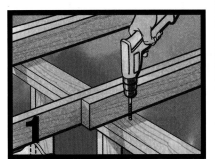

1 IF YOU FIND ACCESS from above or below your kitchen, drill into the top or bottom plates of the wall frame. For a double plate or awkward angle, use a bit extension. After you drill the hole, feed the cable through the hole to the box opening. If you hit

blocking (horizontal pieces between studs), you'll need to notch the blocking (see Step 5).

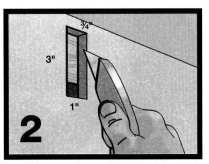

2 IF YOU DON'T FIND ROOM to drill through the plates from above or below, you'll need to enter from the side instead. At the top of the wall, cut an opening to expose the single or double plate. At the bottom, you'll find only a single plate; remove the baseboard and cut the opening ¾ inch above the floor.

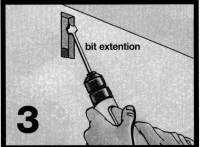

3 USING A BIT EXTENTION, drill a hole into the bottom of the plate, angling toward the center. Bore slowly to avoid burning out the drill. Watch for nails and always wear goggles to protect your eyes.

4 PUSH THE CABLE UP or down to the box opening, then loop it through the plate. Pulling cable through walls is a two-person job. One person tugs gently—not too hard

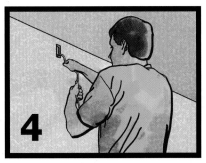

or the sheathing might tear—from the attic or basement. The other person uncoils the cable and feeds it through the opening, taking care to prevent kinks and knots.

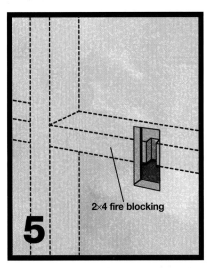

2×4 fire blocking

5 TO LOCATE FIRE BLOCKING, slip a tape measure through the hole and push it until it strikes the blocking. Measure to that point and make an opening that straddles the blocking. Chisel a notch that's large enough to accommodate the cable easily. After you've run the cable and before you patch the hole, install a nail plate. A nail plate prevents live wires from being pierced by nails or screws. Simply tap the nail plate into place with a hammer.

For short runs of cable

If you need to run only a short line of cable, it's often easiest to "fish" cable from a nearby outlet rather than to run a whole new circuit. Before you tap into an outlet, however, be sure that doing so won't overload the circuit (see "How much wattage?" on page 50). Turn off the power, remove the cover plate, and see if the receptacle has an unused set of terminals. If it doesn't, add pigtails (see page 128) before reconnecting.

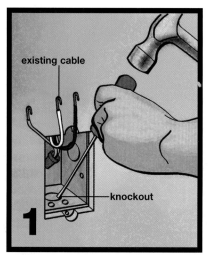

1 DISCONNECT THE RECEPTACLE. See if it has a cable clamp or other device that will attach the new cable to the box. If necessary, remove a knockout with a hammer and

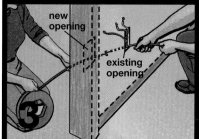

screwdriver and install a clamp.

2 USE AN ELECTRICAL BOX as a template to mark the new outlet opening and cut it open with a utility knife (for drywall) or keyhole saw (for plaster walls). If possible, place the new box in the same wall cavity as the source box.

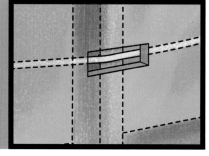

3 THREAD ONE FISH TAPE through the knockout hole and another fish tape through the new

opening in the wall. Wiggle one or both until they hook.

4 PULL THE TAPE FROM the existing box through the new opening. Strip some sheathing from the cable (see page 126), hook the wires on the fish tape end, and wrap with electrical tape to secure them.

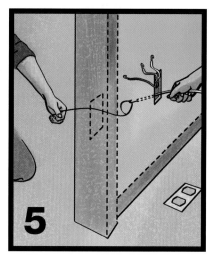

5 FINALLY, PULL THE CABLE through the new opening and into the old box. Connect the cable to the old box (see page 131) and install the new box (see pages 124–125).

Cutting notches

To run cable past studs, cut openings that span each of the studs. Save the cutouts for patching later. Chisel a shallow notch in the stud. Install a nail plate (see Step 5 on page 129) to protect the cable. Patch the wall.

connecting cable to boxes

The most common ways to connect nonmetallic cable to boxes follow. (This is the most common kind of cable used inside walls, ceilings, and floors.) Other connectors are needed for metallic sheathed cable, Greenfield, and conduit. Leave at least ½ inch of sheathing inside the outlet box.

1 **NONMETALLIC BOX with clamp:** Some have internal clamps. Clamping isn't always necessary, however. Some local codes require only that the cable be secured within 8 inches of the box.

2 **METAL BOX with saddle clamp:** Some have internal saddle clamps. Simply tighten the saddle-clamp screw, and one or two cables are quickly secured.

3 **PLASTIC CONNECTOR:** A plastic connector works like a clamp connector, but it's quicker and easier to use. Just snap it into the knockout hole, insert 6 to 8 inches of cable, and tighten the capture screw. Other connectors grab the cable when you pry up a wedge or squeeze the unit with pliers.

4 **METAL BOX with clamp connectors:** Remove a knockout hole in the box, insert a clamp connector in the hole, and secure it with a locknut. Slide cable through the clamp connector and into box. Tighten the saddle onto the cable.

5 **QUICK CLAMPS:** Some boxes have internal quick clamps. Pry up a spring-metal tab and slip the cable through. The clamp springs back to hold the cable securely.

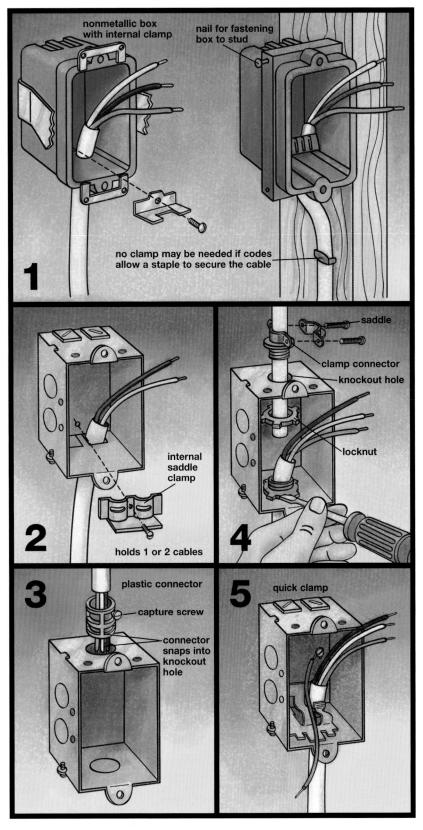

1 nonmetallic box with internal clamp — nail for fastening box to stud — no clamp may be needed if codes allow a staple to secure the cable

2 internal saddle clamp — holds 1 or 2 cables

4 saddle — clamp connector — knockout hole — locknut

3 plastic connector — capture screw — connector snaps into knockout hole

5 quick clamp

tapping into plumbing

Tapping into existing lines

Before you start any plumbing improvement in your kitchen, read about plumbing requirements on page 50 to see just what you're getting into. Then consider whether you might want to hire a professional.

If your home is older and has cast-iron pipe, for instance, you may well want to call in a professional. Cast iron is heavy, can shatter, and has sharp edges. Some plumbers may be willing to make the cast-iron connections only, allowing you to save some money by making the plastic connections yourself. Similarly, you might want a pro to tap into the main stack for a new vent, leaving only the new drain and supply projects for you.

If you're adding a sink close to or on the opposite side of a wet wall (the wall that contains the working plumbing lines), you can tie into copper supply lines and plastic drain lines. To locate your home's drainpipes, start in your basement or crawl space. Look for a 3- to 4-inch round stack. It most likely runs straight up through the roof to release sewer gases into the air. Or you can look for a plumbing-access panel. You may find one on the other side of the wall behind your bathroom fixtures. Take off the access panel and peer inside with a flashlight.

Another way to locate drainpipes is to assess the thickness of your walls. If a wall is thicker than the standard $4\frac{1}{2}$ inches, chances are good that it contains drainpipes.

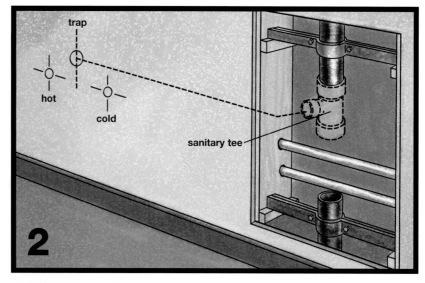

2

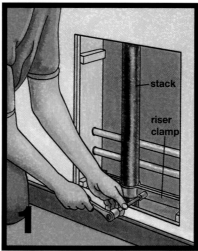

1 **SHUT OFF THE WATER and drain** the lines (see page 112). Open the wet wall to the center of a stud on either side to have a nailing surface for patching later. You may have to make a separate hole to access the supply pipes. Anchor the stack by attaching riser clamps above and below the section you will be cutting.

2 **LAY OUT THE FIXTURE'S rough-** in dimensions and mark them on the wall. Be sure the location doesn't exceed the maximum distance from the stack allowed by local codes. To determine at which point the fixture ties into the stack, draw a line that slopes from the center of the drain trap at $\frac{1}{4}$ inch per foot. Cutting squarely, use a hacksaw or reciprocating saw to remove a section of stack that's 8 inches longer than the sanitary tee you'll be installing.

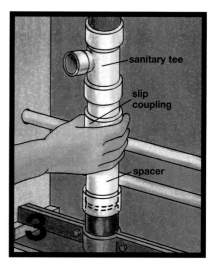

3

3 **IN MOST KITCHEN SITUATIONS,** the sanitary tee must be sized to accept $1\frac{1}{2}$-inch pipe. Fit the tee, two spacers, and two slip couplings into place, as shown. Slide the couplings up and down to secure the spacers. Only dry-fit the pieces at this point. Don't cement them until the rest of the run is complete.

4 CUT OUT A STRIP OF DRYWALL and notch the studs just deep enough to support the pipes. It's important not to weaken wall studs by cutting deep notches in them. In most cases, a 45-degree elbow and a short spacer at the stack, and a 90-degree elbow and a trap adapter at the trap, work best. Once you're sure the pipe slopes at ¼-inch per foot, scribe all the pieces with alignment marks, disassemble, prime, and cement the drainpipe pieces together (see pages 136–137).

5 TAP INTO COPPER OR PLASTIC supply lines using spacers, slip

couplings, and tees similar to those on the drainpipe. (For soldering in copper joints, see pages 138–139.) If you tap into galvanized steel supply lines, you may have to remove sections of pipe and install unions. Be sure to use transition fittings when connecting different pipe materials.

When making a transition from steel to copper, use a special dielectric fitting or the joint will corrode.

6 RUN PIPES to the fixture location using 90-degree elbows and pipe, as needed. Use 90-degree elbows and short pieces to bring lines beyond the wall surface. Stuff a rag in the drain to seal off sewer gas. Solder caps on the ends of supply lines (see pages 138–139), turn on the water, and test for leaks. To eliminate the possibility of poking a hole in a pipe when nailing the drywall back on, protect drainpipes by installing a metal nail plate over notches in the studs. Then close up the wall, turn off the water again, add stop valves (see page 135), and install the fixture.

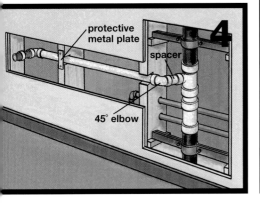

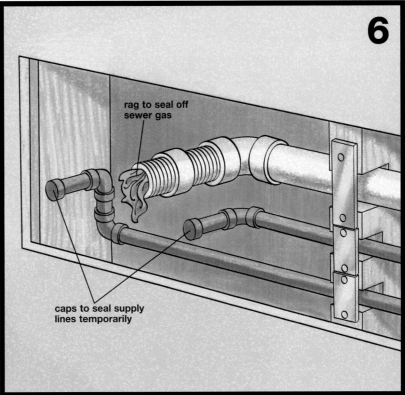

Running the drain lines

Cutting, moving, and refitting plastic pipe are all simple jobs, as long as you have a plastic waste stack and easy access to the drainpipe. Every drain line must be properly vented. Be sure you have this planned before you start cutting drainpipe. You may need to tap in at a second, higher point for the vent.

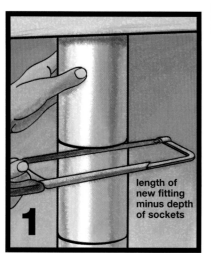

length of new fitting minus depth of sockets

1 MEASURE THE NEW SANITARY tee to see how much of the old pipe you need to remove, and subtract the depth of its sockets so that the pipe will have adequate length to fit solidly inside the tee. Be sure both sides of the existing pipe are supported so they'll stay in position after the cut is made. Cut with a hacksaw or fine-toothed saw and remove any burrs with a utility knife.

2 INSTALL THE TOP END of the sanitary tee, then the bottom. You may have to loosen some of the support straps to provide enough play in the pipes to do this. Once the sanitary tee is dry-fit in the desired

position, make an alignment mark with a marker.

3 RUN PIPES TO THE LOCATION of the new fixture. If you need to run the drainpipe through wall plates or framing, cut holes to accommodate the pipe. Leave at least $5/8$ inch of wood on any side that will receive drywall. This way, nails or screws driven through drywall and into the plate won't pierce the pipe.

4 CONNECT THE DRAINPIPE to the sanitary tee with elbows and lengths of pipe. Dry-fit the pieces, draw alignment lines, disassemble, prime, and cement the pieces together (see pages 136–137). Support the

run of pipe with at least one strap for the horizontal run.

Running the supply lines

Extending the supply lines to meet the new location of a sink is one of the easier plumbing jobs for the do-it-yourselfer. Turn off the water and drain the lines (see page 112). If you are tapping into old galvanized pipe, open it up at a convenient union and dismantle it back to the nearest fitting. Or tee-in the supply by cutting a supply pipe and removing both ends (see pages 132–133).

1 IF YOU ARE GOING from galvanized to copper or plastic pipe (check your local code to be sure it

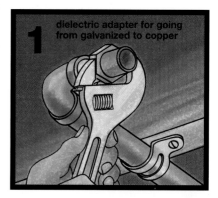

dielectric adapter for going from galvanized to copper

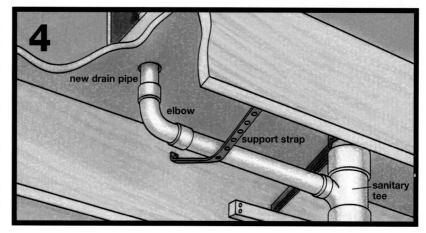

new drain pipe

elbow

support strap

sanitary tee

permits the use of plastic), use a dielectric adapter such as the one shown here. Never hook copper pipe directly to galvanized pipe. A reactive process called electrolytic action will corrode the connection.

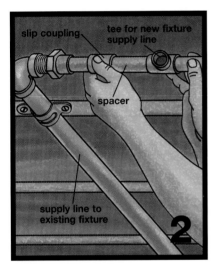

slip coupling

tee for new fixture supply line

spacer

supply line to existing fixture

2

2 REPLACE THE RUN OF PIPE you removed with copper or plastic pipe and a tee fitting. Splice with a slip coupling and spacer. Solder (pages 138–139) or cement (pages 136–137) the pipes and fittings. As you install the pipes that lead to the new service, slope the lines slightly so the system easily drains.

3 AT THE NEW FIXTURE, use drop ells instead of regular elbows. Attach them with screws to wood that is firmly anchored to the framing. Position them between 6 and 8 inches apart. See directions on pages 138-139 for soldering copper pipes, or see pages 136-137 for cementing plastic pipe. Cap the lines, turn on the water, and check for leaks. Don't refinish the wall; the building inspector will want to look at the pipes.

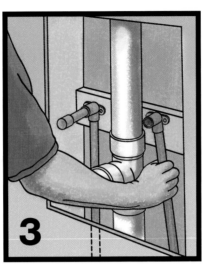

3

Installing stop valves

Any time a water line bursts or a faucet needs repair, you'll be grateful to have a stop valve on each individual fixture so you can shut off the water supply to just that fixture and not to the whole house.

If you have an older home that lacks stop valves, plan to add them to all of your home's plumbing fixtures at the same time you're installing one on your kitchen sink and dishwasher.

Whatever the material or size of your pipes, there's a stop valve made to order. For copper lines, use brass valves; galvanized and plastic pipes take steel and plastic stop valves respectively. If the valve will be in view, use the kind with an attractive chrome finish.

To make a connection from a stop valve to a sink, use flexible copper or plastic line. Or throw away the nut and ferrule that come with the valve and use the handy plastic or braided-metal flexible supply lines that simply screw on.

1 SINKS REQUIRE A STOP VALVE on both the hot and cold lines.

2 DISHWASHERS REQUIRE a stop valve on the hot line only.

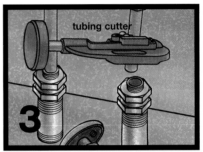

tubing cutter

3

3 IN THE EXAMPLE ABOVE, the existing plumbing consists of galvanized pipe and flexible copper tubing. To make room for the stop valve, cut the tubing. Leave enough tubing to fit the compression fitting and allow for tightening the stop valve on the steel pipe.

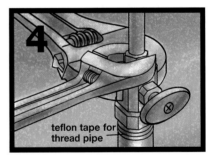

4

teflon tape for thread pipe

4 ONE END OF THE STOP VALVE is sized to fit regular pipe; the other receives compression-fitted flexible lines. Wrap the galvanized pipe clockwise with Teflon tape and install the stop valve. Slip the copper line into the other end and, holding the stop valve in place with a second wrench, tighten the compression fitting.

Working with rigid plastic pipe

Do-it-yourself plumbers like plastic pipe because it's inexpensive and fairly easy to work with. It goes together without any special tools or techniques and is cut with a hacksaw. Simply clean the burrs from the cut with a utility knife, prime the pipe, and glue all the parts together.

The most difficult thing about installing plastic pipe is the preplanning and attention to detail it requires, as well as a willingness on your part to adhere to a certain order of doing things. If you do make a mistake, the parts can't be taken apart; you simply have to cut out the faulty section, throw it away, and start over.

Several types of plastic pipe exist; check your local codes to be sure you're using the right type for your job. In most places, either ABS or PVC are accepted (and sometimes required) for drain lines. Many localities do not allow plastic pipe for supply lines; others specify CPVC. Do not mix ABS with PVC. They expand and contract at different rates, and each uses a specific type of cement. Plastic pipe is not as stiff as metal, so it requires additional support. Be sure to secure horizontal runs every 4 to 5 feet.

1 WHEN MEASURING PIPE for cutting, the socket depth of the fitting must be taken into account. Add the depth of the fitting's socket to the length of the pipe to ensure a solid fit. Cut the pipe in a miter box, using any fine-tooth saw. Use a straight cut; diagonal cuts reduce the

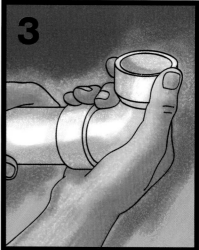

amount of bonding area at the deepest part of the fitting's socket—the most critical part of the joint.

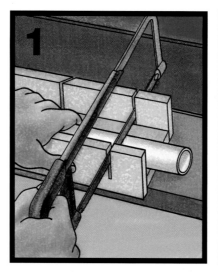

utility knife

2 AFTER THE PIPE HAS BEEN CUT, use a utility knife or file to remove burrs from the inside and the outside of the cut end. Burrs scrape away cement when the pipe is pushed into the fitting, seriously weakening the bond.

3 DRY-FIT THE CONNECTION. The pipe must enter at least one-third of the way into the fitting. If the pipe bottoms out and feels loose,

try another fitting. Unlike copper components, plastic pipes and fittings are designed with tapered walls on the inside of the socket so that the pipe makes contact well before the pipe reaches the socket shoulder.

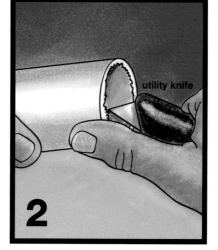

alignment mark

4 WHEN YOU CEMENT the pieces together, you'll have less than a minute to position the pipe and fitting before the cement sets. Draw an alignment mark across the pipe and fitting of each joint. When you fit the pieces together, you'll know exactly how to position them.

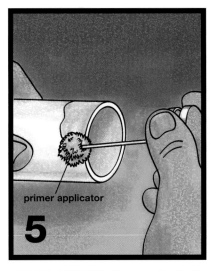

primer applicator

5

5 TO ENSURE the most sturdy bond, all components should be as clean as possible. Wipe the inside of the fitting and the outside of the pipe end with a clean cloth. If you are working with PVC or CPVC (but not ABS), coat the outside of the pipe end with a special primer. Many inspectors require purple-colored primer so they can tell the joints have been properly primed.

cement

6

6 USE THE CEMENT designed for the particular plastic you're using. Immediately after you've

primed, swab a smooth coating of the cement onto the pipe end.

7

7 REPEAT THE PROCESS on the inside of the fitting socket. Apply the cement generously, but don't let it puddle. Reapply a coating of cement to the pipe end.

quarter-turn twist

alignment marks

8

8 FORCEFULLY PUSH the two pieces together to ensure the pipe moves fully into the socket. Twist a quarter-turn as you push to help spread the cement evenly. Keep twisting until your alignment marks

come together. Hold the pipe and fitting together for about 20 seconds to allow them to fuse into a single piece. Wipe away any excess cement.

9 IF YOU MISALIGN a connection, saw it off; cut it squarely. Install a new fitting with a spacer and slip coupling, as shown. Cemented joints are strong enough to handle after 15 minutes, but don't run any water in the line for about 2 hours after you've assembled it.

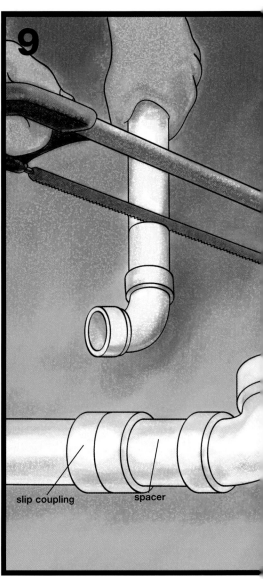

9

slip coupling   **spacer**

Working with rigid copper pipe

The job of soldering pipe may seem daunting but with practice it is faster than screwing together threaded pipe.

Soldering, sometimes called "sweating," relies on capillary action to flow molten solder into a fitting. Just as a blotter soaks up ink, a joint absorbs molten solder, making a watertight bond that's as strong as the pipe itself.

Important: Before soldering copper, open every faucet on the run so heat and steam from the torch can escape. Otherwise it may burn out washers and other parts, and built-up steam may rupture a fitting or pipe wall.

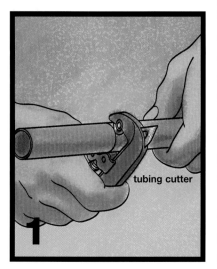

1 TO CUT COPPER PIPE, use a tubing cutter or hacksaw. A tubing cutter makes a cleaner cut. Clamp the cutter onto the tubing, rotate a few times, tighten, and rotate some more. Make hacksaw cuts in a miter box, taking care not to nick the metal, which may cause a future leak.

2 REMOVE ANY BURRS on the inside of the pipe by inserting

the reaming blade of the tubing cutter and twisting. If you don't have a tubing cutter, use a metal file.

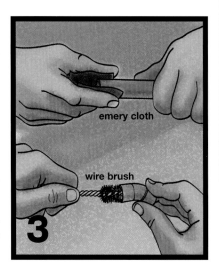

emery cloth

wire brush

3 USE EMERY CLOTH, steel wool, or a wire brush to remove anything—grease, dirt, or rust—that could impede the flow of solder from the outside of the pipe and the inside of the fitting. Stop polishing when the metal is shiny, then avoid touching the polished surfaces. The oil from your fingers could interfere with the solder and cause a leak.

4 DRY-FIT A NUMBER OF PIPE pieces and fittings to make sure they are the correct length. If you have trouble pushing pieces together, the pipe may have been squeezed out of shape when it was cut. Cut a new piece. Once you are satisfied with the way everything fits, take the pieces apart and set them on a clean, dry surface.

5 BRUSH ON A LIGHT, even coating of flux (also called soldering paste) to both surfaces you intend to join. Flux retards oxidation when the

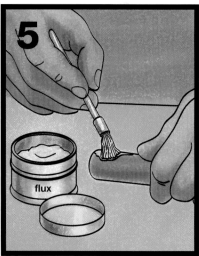

flux

copper is heated. As solder flows into the joint, the flux burns away. Be sure to use rosin-type flux, not the acid type, for plumbing work.

cookie sheet

6 PROTECT FLAMMABLE surfaces. Always remember, you're working with an open flame. If you're working near wood framing, paper-sheathed insulation, or other flammable materials, shield them from the propane torch flame with an old cookie sheet or piece of sheet metal.

7 UNWIND ABOUT 10 INCHES of solder, straighten it, and bend 2

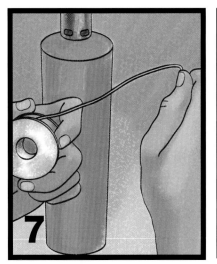

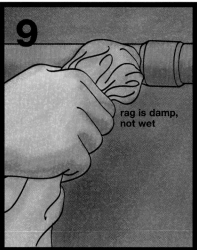

inches at a 60-degree angle—enough so that it's easy to work with but long enough to keep your fingers away from the flame. Light the torch. Adjust the flame until the inner (blue) cone is about 2 inches long.

heat the fitting, not the joint

8 ASSEMBLE THE CONNECTION and heat the middle of the fitting—not the joint—with the inner cone of the flame. Touch the solder to the joint. If it is hot enough, capillary action will pull solder into the joint. Remove the flame when solder drips from the pipe.

9 TO KEEP YOUR PIPES looking neat, lightly brush the joint with a damp rag. Be careful not to burn your fingers. It's a good idea to lay out an entire run of copper, first cut-

ting and dry-fitting all of its components. After dry-fitting, go back to clean, flux, and solder each joint.

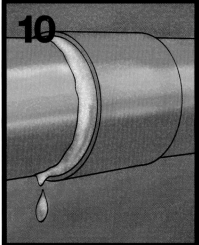

10 AFTER THE NEW RUN is installed, test the system by turning on the water. If you find a leak, there is no easy way around it. Shut off the water, drain the line, and disassemble the joint by heating both sides of the fitting (but not the soldered joint) with a 2-inch-long blue flame. When the pipe is hot, grasp the fitting and pipe with pliers and pull the joint apart. To remove the old sol-

der, heat the end of the pipe, and quickly (and very carefully) wipe it with a dry rag. Let the pipe cool, then polish the end with emery cloth. You can reuse the pipe but not the fittings; only a new fitting will provide a watertight seal.

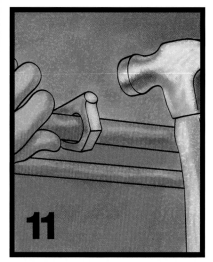

11 COPPER SUPPLY LINES must be supported at least every 6 feet. One way to support them is with the plastic type of hanger shown here. It's easy to install, helps quiet noisy pipes, and because it is slightly flexible, it doesn't damage the pipes.

Before you solder

When adding to existing plumbing, you'll have to dry the inside of the pipes to create a tight joint.
•Stuff piece of crustless white bread just upstream of the connection. It absorbs water and later dissolves when the water is turned back on.
•Insert a waxy capsule specially made to plug the line. When you're done soldering, apply heat where the capsule was lodged to melt it away.

Lay out the cabinets

Before you drive a single screw, carefully mark the location of each cabinet on the walls. Draw lines to show the location of each stud. Mapped out beforehand, the actual hanging of the cabinets becomes a smooth job with few mistakes.

Measure twice, cut once

As with many household tasks, preparation for hanging wall cabinets can be more involved than actually hanging them. It's easier to hang the wall cabinets before setting the base cabinets because you'll have more room to work and lift the cabinets into position.

Once you've removed the old cabinets and appliances, install and check the drain and supply plumbing lines. Run the gas line if needed for a gas cooktop, oven, or range. Rough in the electrical outlets, switches, and cables for dishwashers. If you will be installing undercabinet lights (see page 176), pull standard electrical cable out of the walls at points just below the bottom of the wall cabinets. You may need to drill holes in the back lower lip of the cabinets for the electrical cable to slip through. Cut out a vent hole for the range hood (see page 170).

Smooth and prime all wall and ceiling surfaces, especially those that will show after the cabinets are in place. In most cases, it's a good idea to install the flooring before installing the cabinets. Piecing around cabinets is difficult and time-consuming. You may waste some flooring material in places cabinets will cover, but having a smooth finished floor to work on makes installation easier. If using particularly expensive flooring, you may want to leave the area under the cabinets uncovered. In that case, be sure to overlap the footprint of your base cabinets with the flooring. Add pieces of flooring at all four corners to level each cabinet.

Carefully mark the location of each cabinet on the walls. Allow for small spacers at the corners so you will not have to cram things in too tightly. Mark the location of the wall studs.

If you purchased your cabinets ready-made, inspect them carefully. It's not unusual to find imperfections, and you won't be able to return them once you've driven screws into them.

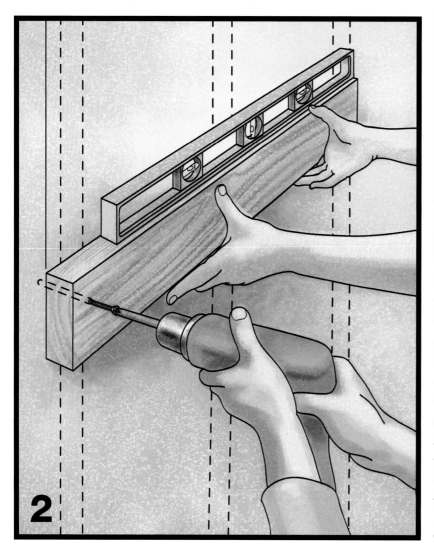

2

3

at the point where you want the bottom of your cabinets to be. The standard distance is usually 54 inches above the floor (18 inches above the countertop). Level the ledger and attach it with just a few screws or nails so you won't create a big wall-patching job when you remove it. Alternately, you can make a 2×4 frame of the appropriate height and rest the cabinets on top of it until they are all fastened to the wall.

3 BEGIN ATTACHING CABINETS in a corner. While a helper holds the cabinet, check for plumb in both directions. Use shims, as shown, as necessary. Once the cabinet is positioned, drive $2^1/2$- to 3-inch screws through the top and bottom framing pieces and into the wall studs. If your cabinet has a lip on top, drive the screws into it so the screws won't show. If you like, use trim or finish washers for a more finished look on the inside of the cabinet. Some manufacturers supply plastic screw-head covers.

4 TO ENSURE TIGHT, even joints between cabinets, make sure

You also need to take a good look at your walls and floor. If your walls are not plumb or square and your floor is not level, you may end up with cabinets that don't fit. Check in advance and reposition your layout carefully and accordingly.

When you actually start the installation, always work with a helper, and have a stable stepladder on hand. One person can hold a cabinet in perfect alignment and the other can drive the screws. If the cabinets are very heavy, remove the doors and shelves to lighten the weight and

reduce the chances of damaging the cabinets or injuring yourself.

1 YOU'LL HAVE FEWER MISHAPS and restarts if you mark the wall to show where each cabinet will go. Draw lines with a pencil to show the stud locations. (Draw lightly wherever your marks will not be covered by a cabinet.) Remove any moldings or other obstructions that might prevent the cabinets from fitting tightly against the wall.

2 TO BE SURE CABINETS ALIGN with each other, secure a straight piece of 2×4 lumber with its top edge

each cabinet you install is flush with the next one, not only along their faces but also at the top. Clamp them in place before fastening. Drill pilot holes and countersink them, then drive screws to hold the units together firmly (see "Drilling 101," opposite).

5 WHERE THE LAST CABINET meets up against a side wall, hold the cabinet in place and measure for a spacer. Spacers can easily be hidden in corners. Cut the spacer and attach it, using clamps to hold it firmly while you drill pilot holes and drive screws from the cabinet into the spacer. Then remove the clamps and attach the cabinet to the wall.

6 YOU'LL WANT TO USE A SPACER in an inside corner. If you simply attach two cabinets at an inside corner, it's very likely that at least one of the doors won't open fully. To provide space for each cabinet to fully function, attach a spacer to one of the cabinets (see Step 5), then attach the other cabinet to the spacer. Drill pilot holes and drive in screws through the spacer and into the frame of the adjacent cabinet.

Seek out the studs

If you've ever carried a stack of 10 or 12 dishes, you know how heavy they are. Cabinets that hold dishes or canned goods bear a surprisingly heavy load, and they do it with ease when safely and properly installed. Unlike base cabinets, which rest on the floor, wall cabinets don't rest on anything. The screws that hold them to the wall carry all the weight, which is why fasteners driven into drywall or plaster alone will not do the job. Only screws that are embedded at least 1 inch (2 inches is better) into wall studs will support fully loaded cabinets. Be sure to drive the screws into the wall studs. If you're attaching the cabinet to a masonry wall, use metal masonry shields.

Drilling 101

When you use wood screws to fasten two pieces of material together, take the time to drill a starter, or pilot, hole for the screw to ensure easy driving and to avoid splitting the wood. Using a bit that's slightly smaller than the screw, drill a pilot hole through both pieces. Then select a bit that's as thick as the screw shank and drill through the top board. The screw will slide easily through this top hole and grip tightly as it passes into the smaller hole. Use a countersink bit to bore a space for the screw head. When you drive the screw, it will fit without cracking the wood.

If you're driving a lot of screws—as is the case with cabinet installation—consider a combination countersink-counterbore bit, which drills three holes in one action. Be sure to get the correct bits for the screws you'll be driving. If you want the screw head to be flush with the surface, simply drill until the spot marked on the bit is even with the surface. To counterbore the screw head, drill deeper.

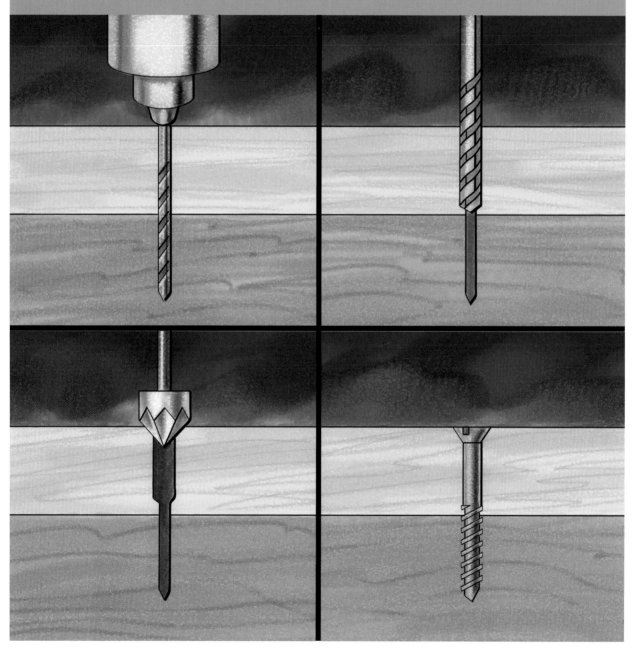

Despite how eager you might be to see your cabinets completely installed, take the time to ensure that all of the base cabinets are level from the beginning. If you cheat just a little, you'll run into frustrating problems later, both in installing the other cabinets and putting on the countertop.

Find the highest point of your floor by using a level and a long, straight board such as a 2×4. (Sight down its length to see that it's not bowed.) Set the board upright on the narrow side of its length. Place a carpenter's level in the center on top of the board. Raise one end or the other until the bubble is centered between the two lines.

Slide the board around the floor until you are sure you have found the high point. Level the board from this high point and measure the distance from the floor to the bottom of the raised end of the board to see how far out of level the floor is. Start installation at this point; you can shim the cabinets up but not down.

If a baseboard or molding is in the way, cut and remove it; don't cut the cabinet to fit the molding. If you installed the wall cabinet first, watch your head as you work.

1 FIND THE HIGHEST POINT on your floor (see method, above). Set the first cabinet in place and check it for level in both directions. Make sure the stiles, or door faces, are plumb. Use shims at the floor to level and solidly support the cabinets. If your wall is out of plumb or wavy, you may need to shim the back

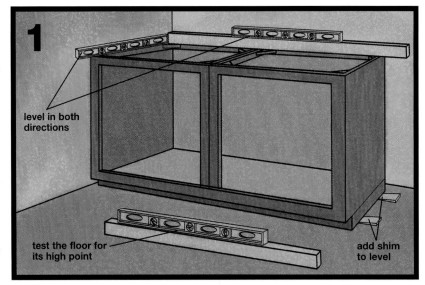

level in both directions

test the floor for its high point

add shim to level

of the cabinet as well. When you drive in the screws to attach the cabinet to the walls, be sure that you don't pull the cabinet out of level.

2 DRIVE IN SCREWS through the back of the cabinet frame and into the wall studs. When possible, screw through solid framing pieces. After driving the screws, check to see if the cabinet is still sitting flat on the floor. If not, back out the screws and adjust the shims before driving the screws back in. Check for level and plumb again.

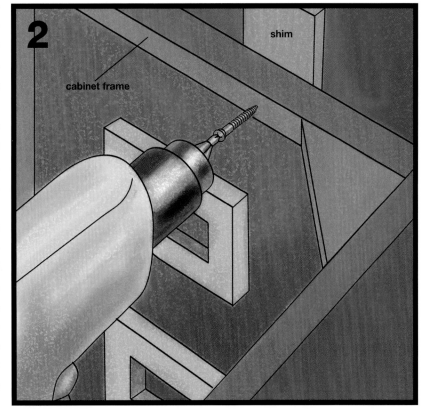

shim

cabinet frame

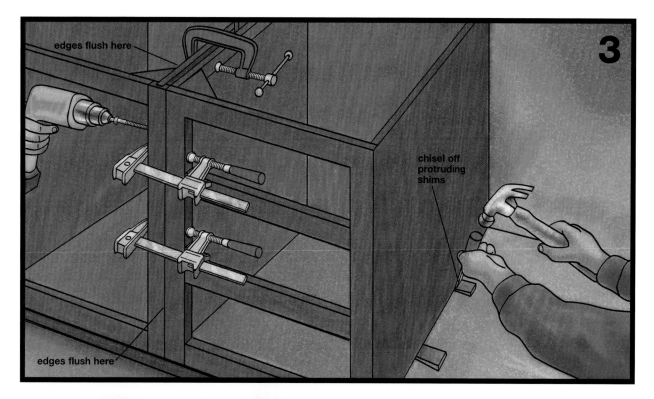

edges flush here

chisel off
protruding
shims

3

edges flush here

wall cleats

door frame

base

4

3 **AFTER THE FIRST CABINET is** installed, use clamps to hold the next one firmly in alignment while you join the cabinets together. Make sure their surfaces are flush with each other, not just the face frames but the top edges as well. Use screws of a length that will hold the cabinets firmly together but aren't so long they poke through the stiles. To keep the surface of the stiles smooth, drill pilot and countersink holes, then drive in the screws. Most of the time, you can use a hammer and chisel to nip off protruding shims. If you layer shims, cut them with a handsaw.

4 **YOUR CABINETS** may include a complete corner cabinet with sides or a less-expensive knockdown unit like the one shown at left. For this kind of corner cabinet, install the base first, then set the two adjoining

cabinets in place on either side. Insert the door frame and join it to the adjoining cabinets. Install 1×2 cleats on the walls to support the countertop.

5 YOU CAN ALSO JOIN two base cabinets. This approach provides less usable space, but it saves money. Install at least one spacer between the two base cabinets so both doors swing freely (see Step 6 of installing wall cabinets on page 142.) Clamp, drill pilot and countersink holes, and drive in screws.

6 IF YOU ARE INSTALLING an island or peninsula, you'll need to provide strong framing on the floor because there is no wall to attach it to. Lay the cabinet on its side and measure its inside dimensions. Then measure, cut, and nail 2×4 cleats to

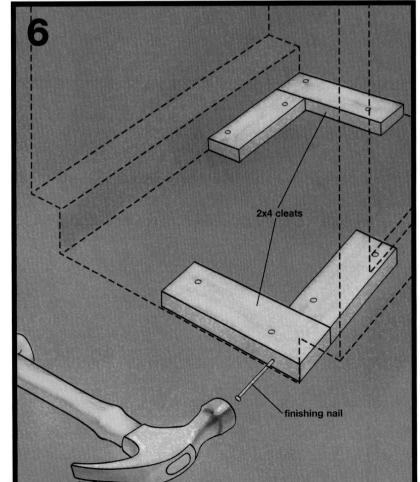

the floor for the cabinet to slip over tightly. Use finishing nails for exposed areas; otherwise, drill pilot holes and use screws.

7 WHEN YOU COME TO AN inside wall, measure the distance between the cabinet and the wall at both the top and the bottom. Rip a filler piece to fit snugly in that space and position it flush with the cabinet face. Drill pilot and countersink holes and drive in screws. If the filler piece is more than 4 inches wide, it must be attached to the wall.

8 IF YOUR KITCHEN DESIGN leaves an exposed edge other than the side of a cabinet—as is the case when a dishwasher ends a run— install an end panel. End panels are made for the purpose of creating a seamless run. Instead of nails, use clips at the floor, countertop, and wall so that the panel can be removed to service the dishwasher.

9 IF YOU HAD TO SHIM the cabinets or if your floor is out of level or wavy, an unsightly gap probably exists between the bottom of the base cabinet and the floor. If the toe-kick was preinstalled, remove it by gently prying it off, and reinstall it flush to the floor. Don't worry: Any gap created along the top of the toe-kick will be hidden by the overhang of the base cabinet. If the toe-kick was not preinstalled, simply nail it flush to the floor. You can also put a vinyl cove base over the toe-kick.

cleats

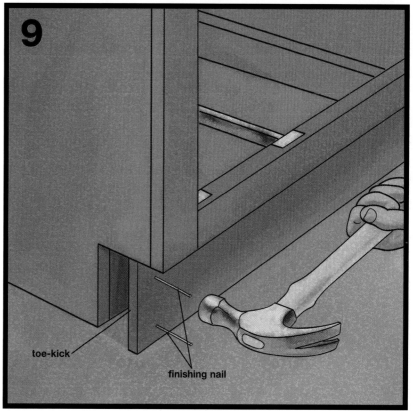

toe-kick

finishing nail

building an island

Where there is ample room, a center island or peninsula has become an option many homeowners choose for the food-preparation, dining, and socializing space it adds to the kitchen. If you plan to purchase custom cabinets, you can design an island to suit your needs exactly. If your budget doesn't support custom cabinets, you can still have a very functional island made from standard-size base cabinets. Either way, you'll need a countertop.

The simple island shown here is made of two base cabinets, side panels, and a veneered plywood back panel. The countertop is something most do-it-yourselfers can accomplish. The trickiest aspect of the project comes with outfitting it for a cooktop or sink, which requires the installation of electrical cables, gas pipe, plumbing supply and drains, and the vent duct.

1 IF YOU'RE USING stock base cabinets, you'll have access to the shelves from one side only. If you want the countertop to feel comfortable for people sitting on stools, lower the cabinets slightly by cutting off the toekick. To join the cabinets, clamp them together, drill pilot holes, and install bolts. You can also drive general-purpose screws through the frames, being careful not to pierce the exterior side. Install panels on the sides using construction adhesive. Cover the back with a single panel. Finish the corners with corner molding. If you're building a peninsula instead, you'll have to reconfigure the design so it butts against your wall-attached base cabinets.

2 IF YOUR ISLAND COUNTERTOP is to serve as an eating counter, make it wide enough to accommo-

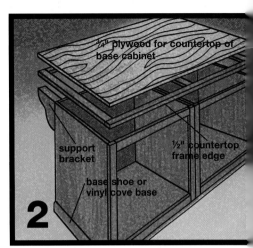

date comfortable seating but not so wide that it impinges traffic flow. (See pages 46–49 for specific guidelines from the National Kitchen & Bath Association.) To avoid painful encounters, be sure to round off exposed corners.

Countertops are usually made of chipboard, which means they can't handle much weight if they're not supported from underneath. To make a cantilevered countertop stronger, attach plywood to a 1×2 frame to thicken the edge. If you want to extend the top to make a stool-height informal eating area, add bracket supports. Install wood base shoe or vinyl cove base at the bottom. Attach the island to the floor, as shown on page 146.

3 A SECONDARY SINK in an island is a great place to redirect some of the traffic from the main kitchen sink. If your island design includes a sink, you'll need to figure out how to get the drain and water supply to the sink. If you have a basement with exposed joists below your kitchen, the job will be pretty easy. If not,

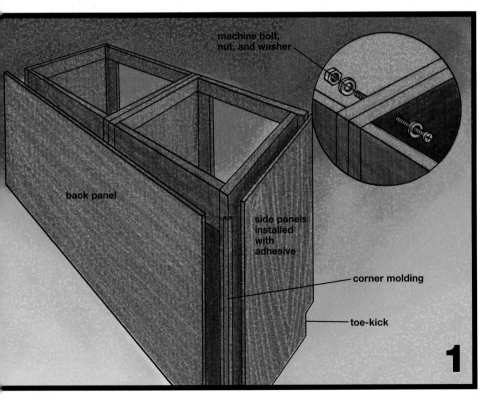

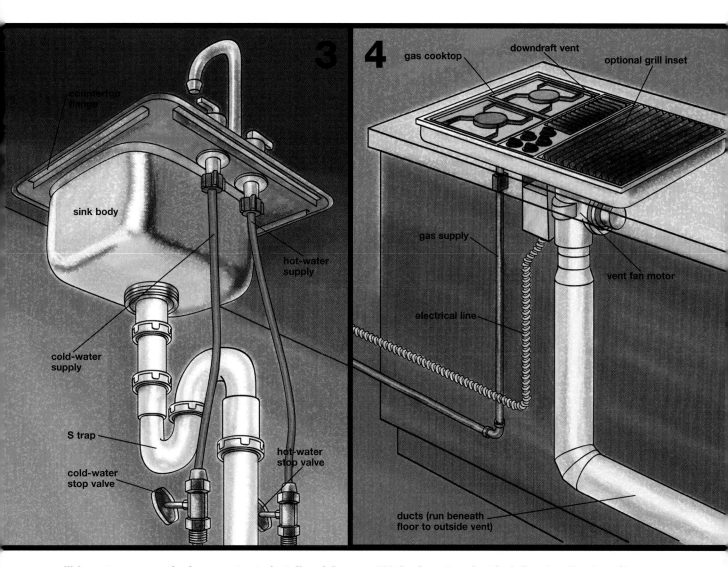

3

countertop flange

sink body

hot-water supply

cold-water supply

S trap

cold-water stop valve

hot-water stop valve

4

gas cooktop

downdraft vent

optional grill inset

gas supply

electrical line

vent fan motor

ducts (run beneath floor to outside vent)

you'll have to open up the basement ceiling or the kitchen floor. Drain pipes must run downhill.

Drains also must be properly vented (see page 51). If the drain is more than 5 feet away from a vented waste stack, you will most likely have to install a new vent (check your local codes), a job that probably requires the help of a professional plumber.

Water-supply lines are less problematic, especially if you have a basement or crawlspace under the kitchen. See pages 158–159 for how to install a sink, page 160 for faucet installation instructions, and page 135 for how to install stop valves.

4 WHETHER YOU HAVE A COOK-TOP in your island, or simply a built-in grill and griddle, all island cooktops must be vented. If your island or peninsula has overhead cabinets, you can install a vent hood. Usually, though, a downdraft range is the preferred choice. These ranges have a vent fan already installed. If you buy a gas cooktop, you will need to run not only a gas line but also an electrical line for the fan. (For an electric range, hire an electrician to run a 220-volt line to the unit.)

The ductwork is easy to understand but difficult to install. The most foolproof installation requires running it through the basement or crawlspace below the kitchen. If that is not a possibility, you may have to cut large holes in the floor joists—but only if the structural integrity can be maintained. The vent exits the house the same way a range hood vent does (see page 170).

9

form and function

AS EACH STEP OF YOUR REMODELING IS COMPLETED, the vision you had for your kitchen begins to take form. The walls are up, wired, and plumbed, and the cabinets have created the basic shape of the room. The "bones" of your new kitchen are in. The projects that come next, such as installing countertops and backsplashes, sinks, flooring, and trim, as well as beautiful lighting to illuminate it all, clarify and refine your vision. These aspects of your kitchen are functional but also begin to help personalize the space, to make it very much about you and your family's lifestyle, needs, and preferences. You may have chosen a laminate countertop for its economy and easy upkeep, ceramic tile for its timelessness, or granite tile for its beauty. Whatever materials you've chosen to make your kitchen hardworking and aesthetically pleasing, you'll find detailed instructions on these pages for installing them easily— and correctly—so they'll function beautifully in your kitchen for years to come.

A hammered copper backsplash, *opposite*, adds a warm glow to this kitchen while protecting the space between the cabinets and countertops from splashes and spills. After the walls are up and the mechanicals are in, many of the materials you choose for your kitchen have both aesthetic and functional aspects, giving you the opportunity to forge a space that's both beautiful and hardworking.

Install a laminate countertop

With the wide variety of colors available in post-form laminate countertops these days, it's probably not worth the time and effort to make your own laminate countertop. If your countertop configuration and sizing are fairly standard and your walls are not more than ³/₈ inch out of square, you can save money and frustration by buying a readymade countertop at your local home center. Made with precut corners, it can be trimmed to fit most base cabinets.

1 LEVEL YOUR BASE CABINETS all the way around so the countertop will sit flat on them. If necessary, install cleats on the walls, as shown, or end panels (see page 147) to support the countertop firmly. Also lay a straightedge down the full length of each wall to be sure walls are square with each other and free of major bulges. Most post-form countertops have a lip of laminate, called a scribe, that can be trimmed (see Steps 3 and 4) to compensate for variations of up to ³/₈ inch. A square-edged top will allow you to compensate for up to ³/₄ of an inch. If you have wavy walls or if they are more than ³/₈ inch out of square, a premade countertop may not fit flush against them. In such a situation, you may need to hire a professional countertop maker to take precise measurements, prepare, and install a custom-fitted countertop.

face-side down to avoid nicking the laminate. Be sure the blade on your circular saw is square to the base and use a clamp-on guide to ensure that your cut will be straight. Support the waste side so it doesn't fall off before the cut is complete—a sure way to damage the laminate.

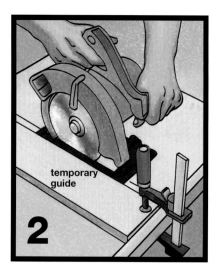

temporary guide

2 IF YOU MUST CUT your countertop to length, do so with great care. (It stands up to hard use but can be damaged during installation's cutting process.) Use a circular saw with a fine blade and cut the countertop

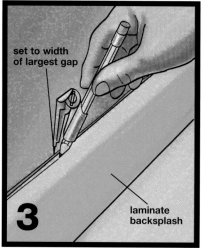

set to width of largest gap

laminate backsplash

3 IF THE COUNTERTOP doesn't fit snugly against the wall, because the walls are wavy or slightly out of square, push the countertop as firmly as you can against the wall, making sure it is aligned correctly with the base cabinets. Use a compass to scribe a line that's as wide as the largest gap between the countertop and wall on top of the laminate backsplash.

4 USE A BELT SANDER with a fairly coarse, 36-grit sanding belt and light pressure to slowly sand away material up to the scribed mark. Don't try to cut to the scribed mark with a circular saw or saber saw—you'll almost certainly chip the countertop.

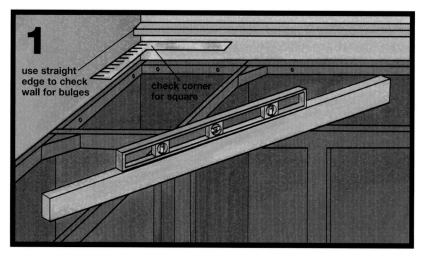

use straight edge to check wall for bulges

check corner for square

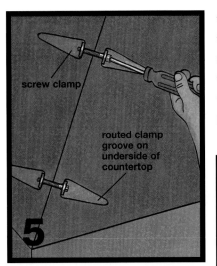

5 IF YOU MUST SPLICE PIECES at a corner or in the middle of a run, it's a good idea to have a professional make the cuts and rout the grooves for the clamps. Apply waterproof glue to the edges of the pieces, line them up, and begin tightening the clamps. Check the countertop as you work to be sure it doesn't slide out of alignment.

6 NOW YOU'RE READY to attach the countertop to the cabinets. Screws should extend as far as possible into the countertop without poking through. Drill pilot holes every 2

to 3 feet along the front and rear of the countertop and drive in the screws. Be sure to screw into structurally sound sections of the cabinet framing. Don't let the countertop move as you work.

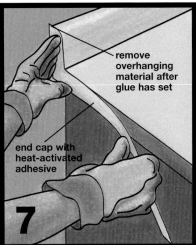

7 AT THE END OF A RUN, you'll attach a precut end cap. If it has heat-activated glue, hold the end cap in place so it overhangs the countertop edge (you will remove the excess later) and slowly run a hot laundry

iron over it, being careful not to burn the laminate, until the glue adheres. File, sand, or rout away the excess end cap material.

8 IF YOU'VE BOUGHT a square-edged countertop and your walls are not square, the square-edged countertop will cover the gap between countertop and the walls. (See side view of countertop in illustration 8.) Set the top so it overhangs the cabinets evenly. Cut the backsplash pieces to fit and set them in place. Carefully mark their positions on the countertop, then pull the top away from the wall. Run a bead of caulk along the bottom of the edging, set the edging in place, and fasten it with screws from underneath. Attach the top from below, as shown in Step 6. If your wall is bowed, fasten the countertop in place, then glue the edging pieces to the wall with construction adhesive. Brace the pieces with pieces of 1× or heavy objects so the edging conforms to the curve of the wall.

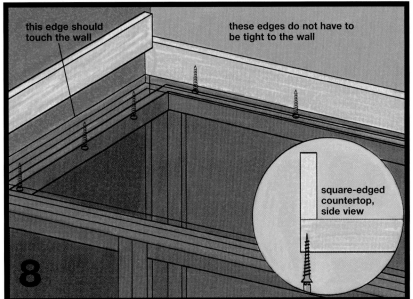

Installing a ceramic tile countertop

Manufacturers make a variety of ceramic tiles for nearly every surface in the house. Be sure you buy tiles specifically made for use on countertops. Ceramic countertop tiles generally are ½ inch thick and glazed to ward off stains. Unless you are supremely confident in your ability to set a countertop without the slightest imperfection, use a light-colored grout or one that approximates the color of the tile, rather than a dark or contrasting color.

To make sure the tile color and finish are consistent, work with a dealer who provides all the types of tile you'll need: field tiles (those that cover the bulk of the counter); decorative or bullnose tiles for the front edge; and bullnose pieces for the backsplash. Each tile that has an exposed edge must have a rounded edge, called a bullnose, or cap, on that edge.

Be sure to use the mastic recommended by the tile dealer, usually a thin-set mortar. All-purpose tile adhesive fails to hold up on countertops.

1 **TILES MUST BE SET on a firm, level, and perfectly flat surface.** Measure to make sure the total thickness of the underlayment, or substrate (including the mastic), will be covered by the edging you choose. Securely attach ⅝- or ¾-inch plywood to the cabinet tops. Check the substrate for level and square. To protect the plywood substrate from the inevitable moisture that seeps through grout joints, cover it with a

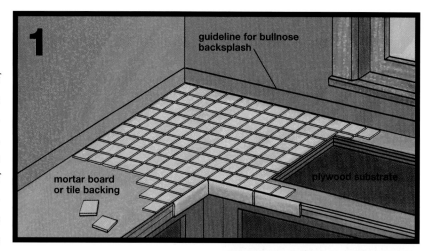

layer of mortar board or tile backing attached to the plywood with screws placed in a grid pattern no more than 4 inches apart.

If your backsplash or edging tile has a large radius, provide backing for it by fastening a strip of mortar board to the wall. Try to find a metal screed for the front edge; it offers both a straight line for setting tile and a surface to which the mastic can adhere.

2 **DO A DRY RUN. Establish your** starting point by using a chalk line to create two lines that are perpendicular to each other at the center point of the countertop. Set the tiles in place, positioning them exactly as you will when it's time to install them. Use plastic tile spacers, and check that all lines are straight. To determine which tiles to cut, set them in place and mark accordingly. Remember to allow for the thickness of the grout joint.

3 **TILES THAT RUN the perime-** ter of the wall or backsplash will invariably have to be cut. For straight cuts, use a tile cutter, which has a glass-cutting wheel that scores

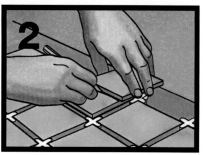

the tile and a level that breaks off a straight cut. Your tile supplier may provide a cutter free of charge. If not, rent or buy one. (If a project will take more than a weekend or two, buying a cutter might be less costly.)

To cut a tile, position it on the cutter and bear down firmly as you score a single line. Then snap the cut by pushing down on the handle. The best tile cutters have adjustable guides, which allow you to quickly cut a series of same-size tiles.

If you have a lot of straight cuts to do, rent a tile-cutting wet saw. For the occasional cutout or curve, you can use pliers or a nibbling tool to bite away the tile bit by bit.

4 **MIX THE THINSET MORTAR** according to package directions. If the powder does not contain latex additive, mix it with latex rather than water. Allow the mixture to "slake," or hydrate, for 10 minutes, then mix again. Working one small section at a time, pick up a set of the dry-laid tiles and apply the mortar to the surface with a comfortable-size notched trowel. Set each section before you move to the next one.

5 YOU CAN ADD COLOR and interest to your countertop by edging it with a combination of decorative border strips, called dadoes, overlapped by bullnose tiles.

A sink cap gives the countertop a slight lip that keeps water from running down the edge of the counter. It may have a bullnose edge of its own, or you may have to add a row of bullnose tiles under it.

Two bullnose edging pieces—one on the counter surface and one on the edging—can be used in place of a sink cap. Install the edge piece and surface tiles at the same time to keep them aligned.

Wood edging is different in that it goes on after the tiles are set. It looks great but has some maintenance issues, so protect it with a durable finish. Set the top edge of the wood slightly below the tile, so

the counter can be wiped easily. Join edging to plywood with trim screws, or use a biscuit joiner so no screw holes have to be puttied.

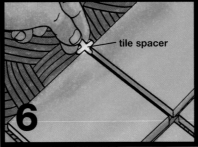

6 AS YOU SET the tiles in place, try to avoid sliding them around too much. Use plastic spacers to keep the joints even. As you work, make sure the tiles evenly overlap, or line up with, the edge pieces.

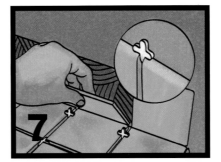

7 IF YOUR BACKSPLASH TILES are the same width as the surface tiles, line them up so the grout joints match. Backsplash tiles don't get the same wear and tear as the top tiles, so they can be glued directly to the wall without attaching a plywood substrate first.

8 AFTER YOU'VE FINISHED one section, bed the tiles to make sure they are set down into the mastic and that they form a smooth, even surface. Buy a bedding block or make

one from a scrap of wood wrapped with a piece of carpet. Place the block over the tile and tap gently with a hammer or rubber mallet.

9 ALLOW THE TILES TO SET at least 24 hours before grouting. Mix the grout according to package directions. Mix colored grout thoroughly to avoid streaking. Use latex grout additive instead of water to keep grout from cracking. Mix, let slake for 10 minutes, then mix again. Using a float, apply the grout in two steps. First push grout into the joints by holding the float fairly flat. Move float in at least two directions so all the cracks completely fill in. Second, tip the float up at a fairly steep angle and wipe away the excess grout.

Use a damp sponge to further wipe away excess grout, checking each grout line to ensure it's filled evenly. Rinse the sponge often; it will take two or three swipes with the sponge to remove most of the grout that remains on top of the tiles. When the grout is dry, remove the grout dust from the tile surface by rubbing it with a soft, dry cloth. The tiles will shine. (See pages 180–181 for information about sealing the countertop.)

Setting a granite tile countertop

A granite slab makes an elegant and highly durable countertop, but it also can be very expensive. You can get the same look for a fraction of the cost by using granite tiles. Standard granite tiles are 12 inches square and ⅜ inch thick, with one side polished smooth.

To minimize chipping, manufacturers bevel the exposed edges of granite tiles, making them so smooth and straight that the grout joint between the tiles can be very thin to create a nearly seamless look. If desired, you can eliminate the grout completely by butting the tiles tightly against one another. The silicone caulk used as an adhesive has the added benefit of protecting the plywood substrate (see page 154 for how to install) from moisture. Before you apply adhesive and lay the tiles, make sure your substrate is absolutely level, square, and smooth, and do a complete dry run.

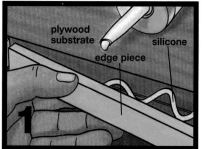

1 **CUT AND GLUE EDGING FIRST.** Cut narrow strips of granite of equal depth to give the countertop edge a uniform appearance. This requires careful cutting. Plan to discard several miscut pieces. The pieces should fit under the overhang-

ing surface pieces and hang about ¼ inch below the edge of the substrate.

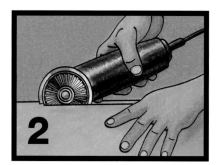

2 **THE BEST TOOL** for making neat rectangular cutouts such as edging pieces is a small stonecutter with a diamond blade. Rent or borrow one from the tile dealer or a rental store. After cutting in each direction, knock the cutout free; use tile nippers and a rubbing stone to clean up the corners of each piece.

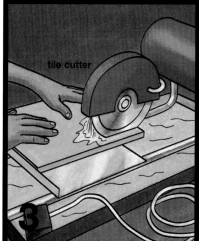

3 **GRANITE TILES** must be cut with a wet saw, which you can rent. Because silicone caulk sets quickly, do a complete dry run by cutting and placing every tile before you start gluing. Natural stone sometimes breaks along existing fissure lines

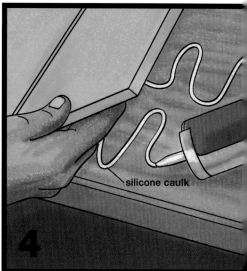

when it's cut. If this happens, cut the tile through only two-thirds of its thickness, then turn it over and finish the cut from the other side. As with any tiling project, establish your starting point by using a chalk line to create two lines that are perfectly perpendicular to each other (at a 90-degree angle) at the center point of the countertop.

4 **PICK UP TWO OR THREE** tiles at a time, leaving the others undisturbed. Using a caulking gun, apply squiggles of clear silicone caulk to the plywood in a close, regular pattern. Immediately set the tile in place and move quickly to the next one. Press down so the surface is uniform. After tiles have set, have the exposed edges of top front tiles buffed. (Your tile dealer can probably recommend a professional who does this.) Alternately, polish them with a rubbing stone and brush on several coats of clear lacquer. Finish with a granite sealer (see pages 180-181 for information about sealing countertops).

Adding a stainless steel backsplash

Stainless steel has long been a favored material for commercial kitchens because of its near indestructibility and easy maintenance. Now homeowners are discovering that it makes for sleek and stylish countertops and backsplashes.

The first step in installing a stainless-steel backsplash is to locate the material. If your local home center or hardware store doesn't stock it, check the phone book under stainless steel or sheet metal. Find a shop that provides sheets of stainless steel cut to precise lengths. Stainless steel often has to be ordered from a specialty supplier, so set your schedule accordingly.

One of the most critical steps in installing a stainless-steel backsplash is providing the correct measurements. You can also provide a template to the shop to ensure you get correctly sized pieces. Although stainless steel is extremely hard, it can be damaged during installation. As you work, support the sheet with your free hand so it doesn't get crimped or scratched. Better yet, have a helper assist you. Stainless steel is expensive.

You can cut the backsplash to make holes for electrical outlets, but doing so is a bit tricky. To make as straight and smooth a cut as possible, use a drill to start the hole, then cut the opening with a saber saw that has a metal-cutting blade designed for cutting stainless steel. The edges of the opening will probably be rough, but they'll also be covered up by the outlet plate.

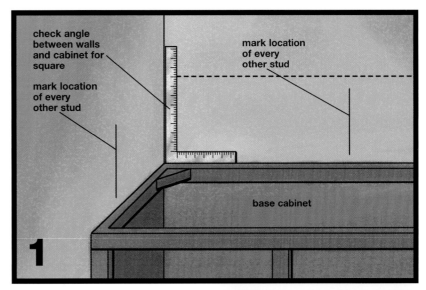

1 **IF POSSIBLE, lay out the back-splash before you install the countertop or wall cabinets. Check the walls for square and measure the lengths you need. Corners are critical areas; any variation along the length of the piece will be covered by the wall cabinet above and the counter-top or backsplash below, but that's not so for corners. If your walls are plumb, you may be able to get away without the corner trim pieces shown in Step 3. If the walls are not plumb, you may be able to compensate by cutting a slot in the corner and sliding a bit of one piece of steel into it.**

2 **SET THE SHEET OF METAL in place and make sure the pieces line up. Drill holes and drive stain-less-steel screws, fitted with trim washers, into the studs. Because stainless steel is rigid and the back-splash will also be anchored by the cabinets, two screws driven into every other stud is adequate.**

3 **IF YOUR CORNER isn't matching up, use a corner mold. Attach it**

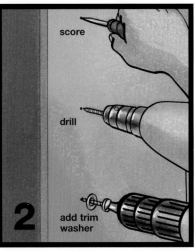

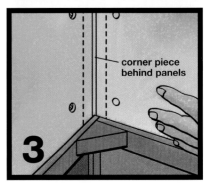

to the wall with clear silicone sealant and butt each panel against it. If one wall is wavy, scribe and curve-cut one of the pieces with a belt sander.

Installing a drop-in sink

Whether they are made of stainless steel, cast iron, or some composite material, most kitchen sinks are installed the same way. With the exception of integrated sinks that are made of natural stone or solid-surfacing material, which usually have to be installed by a professional, standard rimmed sinks are easy to put in place. Because they have a lip that sits on top of the countertop, installing them is usually a simple matter of clamping or adhering them to the countertop, then making the plumbing connections (see page 160).

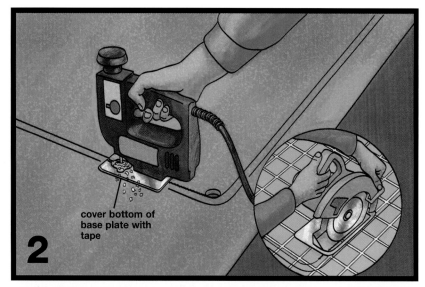

2 cover bottom of base plate with tape

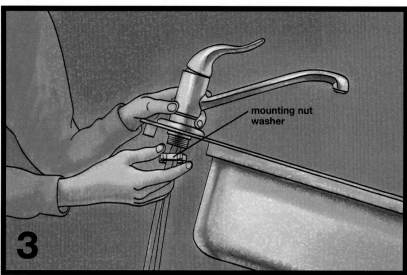

3 mounting nut washer

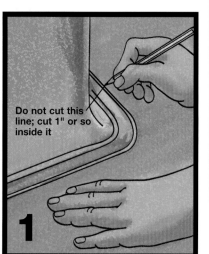

1 Do not cut this line; cut 1" or so inside it

1 FOR A DROP-IN SINK, turn the sink upside down on the countertop. Be sure it is correctly positioned, safely set back from the cabinet underneath with the front edge of the sink lip at least 1¾ inches from the countertop edge. Trace the outline of the sink, then draw a line that is an inch or so inside of that outline. Erase the outside line so you don't acciden-

tally cut it. Make sure the bottom of the sink, sitting upright, fits in the smaller opening.

2 TO CUT INTO LAMINATE countertop, drill 1-inch holes at the corners slightly inside the line to allow for chipping. Cut out the countertop with a saber saw with a fine-tooth blade. Protect the surface from scratches by covering the base plate of the saw with electrical or masking tape. Saw slowly to avoid splintering the laminate.

For a ceramic tile countertop, use a circular saw with a diamond blade. Cut the tiles slowly and carefully. You may have to remove tiles, cut them with a tile cutter, and replace them.

3 BECAUSE WORKING under the sink is cramped and difficult, it makes sense to attach as many things to the sink as possible before installing it in the countertop.

To install a faucet, either apply a rope of plumber's putty around the three faucet holes or use a gasket provided by the faucet maker. Set the unit in place and tighten the mounting nuts and washers, making sure the base of the faucet remains correctly aligned. (For instructions on how to hook up the faucet to the supply lines, see page 160.)

For faucets that have sprayers, secure the hose guide to the sink with a washer and mounting nut. Thread the spray hose through the hole in the guide. Apply pipe-joint compound or Teflon tape to the threaded nipple at the end of the hose and secure the nipple to the faucet's spray outlet. If you're adding an air gap for a dishwasher drain or soap dispenser, install it now as well.

4 ATTACH A BASKET STRAINER to each bowl. A double-bowl sink comes with two basket-strainer assemblies. Lay a bead of putty around the outlet, set the gasket in place, and lower the strainer body into the hole. With your other hand, from underneath, slip the friction ring

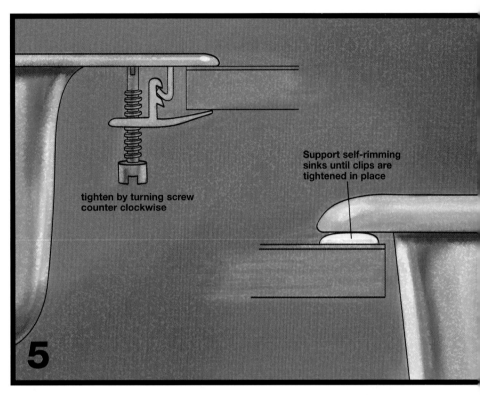

tighten by turning screw counter clockwise

Support self-rimming sinks until clips are tightened in place

5

in place and screw on the locknut. Tighten everything and clean up any plumber's putty that oozes out.

5 TO INSTALL a flush-mounted stainless-steel sink whose lip sits on the countertop, turn the sink upside-down and run a bead of plumber's putty around the rim, including the corners. Turn the sink right-side up and lower it into the opening. Position it so the front lip is parallel to the front of the countertop. For self-rimming sinks (above), putty the counter and sink edge. Support the sink from below and position the rim.

Secure both types of sinks to the countertop with sink clips every 6 to 8 inches, tightening the clips with a screwdriver. Remove excess putty with a putty knife.

For a cast-iron sink, no clips are

required. Turn the sink upside down and run a bead of silicone sealant under the rim. Turn the sink right side up and set it in place. Wipe away excess sealant with a clean rag dipped in paint thinner. Run a bead of caulk along the edge and use your finger to make a smooth line.

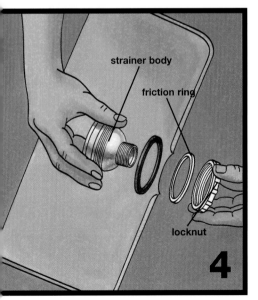

strainer body

friction ring

locknut

4

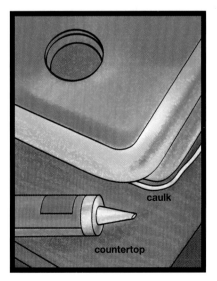

caulk

countertop

Hooking up a faucet

Your kitchen faucets may be one of hundreds of styles to choose from, but the below-the-sink workings of most faucets are pretty much the same—and so is the process of connecting them to the water-supply lines. All kitchen faucets are made to fit the three standard holes (spaced 4 inches apart) found in all kitchen sinks. The fourth hole provides room for a spray unit or other accessory.

Whatever faucet you choose, it will have one of two types of supply connections: flexible copper supply inlets that require compression fittings in the center of the unit, or hand-tightened supply hoses located under the hot and cold handles.

1 AFTER THE FAUCET has been secured to the sink (see pages 158–159), the space below your sink will look something like the diagram, above. (Here, we show a faucet with inlets located under the handles.)

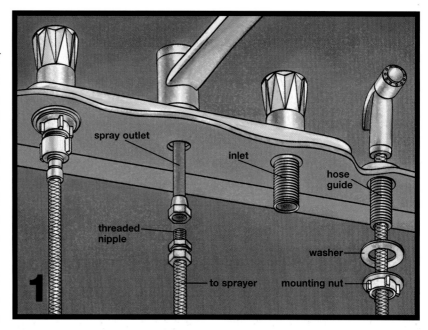

1 spray outlet · inlet · hose guide · threaded nipple · washer · to sprayer · mounting nut

2 IF YOUR LINES ATTACH under the handles, as these do, brush the inlet threads with pipe-joint compound or wrap them with Teflon tape. Twist on the supply-line nut and tighten it by hand. Then use a basin wrench or pliers to tighten it about a half-turn further (not too tight or it might crack). Connect the other end to the shutoff valve the same way.

3 IF YOUR FAUCET uses flexible copper inlets for the water supply, connect the supply lines the same way you would regular inlets, but be very careful not to twist the copper tubes. If they become kinked, the faucet will be ruined. Use two wrenches: one to hold the tubing stationary and the other to tighten the supply-line nut.

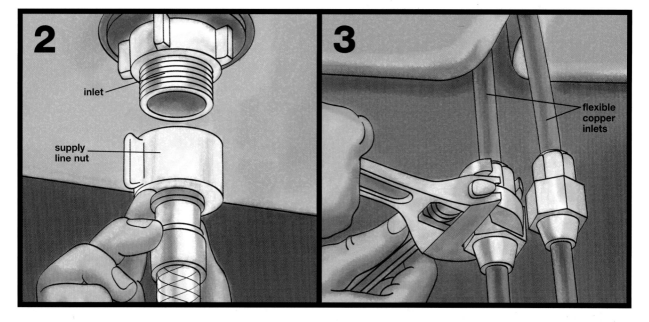

2 inlet · supply line nut

3 flexible copper inlets

installing a tile floor

Laying out a ceramic tile floor

Tile looks best when set in clean, straight lines and when it at least appears to be square and level with adjacent surfaces. Laying out the installation is the most important step for ensuring such an outcome. Floors and walls are never as square and level as you hope, so one of the secrets to a successful layout is learning how to fudge a little so that the fudging isn't obvious. The other secret is to plan for as few cut tiles as possible (and to hide those that are cut along less conspicuous walls and under baseboard trim), which may require you to adjust your layout in a dry run.

Though it may take only a long weekend to actually set and grout a ceramic tile floor in the average-size kitchen, the preparation that's done well in advance can make the actual tiling go as quickly and smoothly as possible.

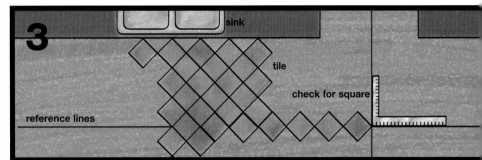

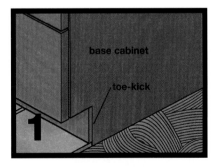

1 **AS A GENERAL RULE,** you don't have to install tile where cabinet bases or permanent fixtures will cover it. Use a thin pry bar and a stiff putty knife to remove the toe-kick and any other baseboard or molding along the floor. You can set the tile up to the cabinet or wall. After the tile is installed and grouted, trim the upper edge of the toe-kick to fit (it won't show under the overhang of the cabinet) and reinstall it and the baseboard or molding along the walls.

2 **ONE OF THE DECISIONS** you will have to make is whether to install tile underneath appliances. Freestanding appliances, such as most refrigerators, ranges, and dishwashers, must be removed in order to install tile underneath them. It's also best to tile beneath built-in appliances, even though the work is trickier. Tiling under a built-in dishwasher, for example, raises the floor level enough that the dishwasher no longer fits under the countertop. To make amends, you can raise or notch out the countertop a bit to accommodate the appliance. Adjustments may also have to be made to existing plumbing connections. If you are struggling with whether or not to tile underneath an appliance—and you know that you may want to take it with you if you move—consider how your kitchen would look if it were empty. Untiled spaces where appliances once sat are not so attractive.

3 **AT THE CENTER** of the kitchen floor, mark perpendicular reference lines with a chalk line. (In odd-shape rooms, you may want to center the layout on the most visible section of the floor, rather than in the center of the room.) Check the lines for square by setting a framing square in all of the corners. Check the floor for level along each wall using a 2- or 4-foot level. To check for level over a longer span, place the level on the edge of a straight 6- or 8-foot board. If the floor is slightly out of level and you are not planning to run tile up the wall, don't worry. Using tile spacers, if tiles don't have them built-in, dry set tiles along the reference lines to check the layout. Adjust the layout to minimize the number of cut tiles and to avoid creating extremely small pieces (see page 154 for instructions on cutting tiles).

Preparing the surface
• Remove the original flooring if: it is not firmly stuck to the subfloor; it is uneven; the thinset mortar will not adhere to it.
• Make sure the subfloor is at least 1⅛ thick and composed of suitable materials (usually a combination of plywood, backer board, or concrete).
• Fill low spots in the subfloor, then smooth the surface and clean it thoroughly.

Setting a ceramic tile floor

Once you have perfected your layout, it's time to set the tiles into the adhesive. Work in sections small enough so you can set the tiles before the adhesive begins to dry out. Start by spreading adhesive in a 2- to 3-square-foot area. When the adhesive has been combed to the right thickness with a notched trowel, immediately set the tiles in that area.

The most important tile is the first one you set; make sure it's perfectly aligned in your layout so the rest of the tiles fall into place. The time spent getting the layout just right will pay off now. The reference lines you made will help guide you through the entire process. Be careful not to cover them with adhesive.

As you set the tiles, remove the excess adhesive before moving on to the next section. With practice, you may be able to work in larger sections. If the adhesive has begun to develop a skin, don't set tiles into it; scoop it up and apply a fresh layer.

If you can, set all the full tiles first, then cut and set the partial tiles. You'll want to avoid kneeling on top of just-set tiles in order to lay the cut ones. In a large kitchen, you may want to set all of the full tiles on one day and then do the cut ones the next day.

Just as you don't want to paint yourself into a corner, you don't want to tile yourself into a corner, either. Be sure to set the tiles in an order that allows you to leave the room without walking on them. Don't disturb the floor tiles until the adhesive has cured for several hours—preferably overnight.

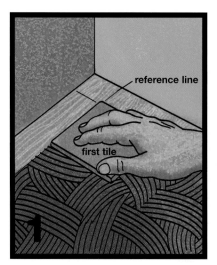

1 WITH THE ADHESIVE SPREAD and combed, place the first tile at the intersection of the reference lines. Press and twist it slightly into place, aligning the tile with both lines. Do not slide the tile through the adhesive.

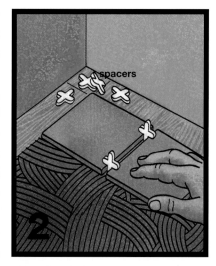

2 UNLESS YOUR TILES are self-spacing, use spacers to place another tile next to the first. Press and twist the tile to ensure it fully embeds in the adhesive. The accurate placement of the first few tiles is critical to keeping the remainder of the tiles in straight lines.

3 CONTINUE SETTING TILES along the layout lines. Then set the tiles in the field, working out from a corner. Insert spacers as shown. (Spacers also can be laid flat at the intersection of the grout lines but must be removed before grouting.) If the tiles are self-spacing, keep an eye on the gaps between tiles to make sure they remain uniform. Don't slide tiles once they've been set in the adhesive.

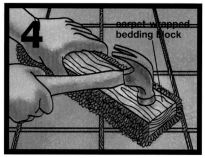

4 AFTER SETTING TILES in one section, use a bedding block (see page 155 for tips on making a bedding block) to ensure a level surface and full adhesion of the tiles. Place the bedding block across several tiles, then give it a few light taps with a hammer. Make sure each tile gets tapped.

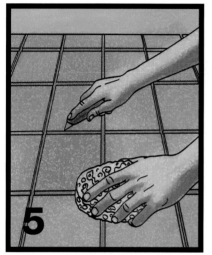

5 IMMEDIATELY AFTER SETTING tiles in a section, go back and remove any excess adhesive that has oozed out onto the tiles before it starts to dry. Clean the tile surfaces with a damp sponge and use a putty knife, utility knife, or margin trowel to remove excess from between tiles.

6 WHEN THE FULL TILES have been set in the field, set the cut tiles around the perimeter (see page 154 for instructions on cutting tile). Since walls are rarely square, it's usually best to cut one tile at a time. The most accurate method is to measure each tile in place. Place the tile that is to be cut directly on top of the adjacent tile. Then set another full tile on top, two grout joints away from the wall. Use the top tile to mark

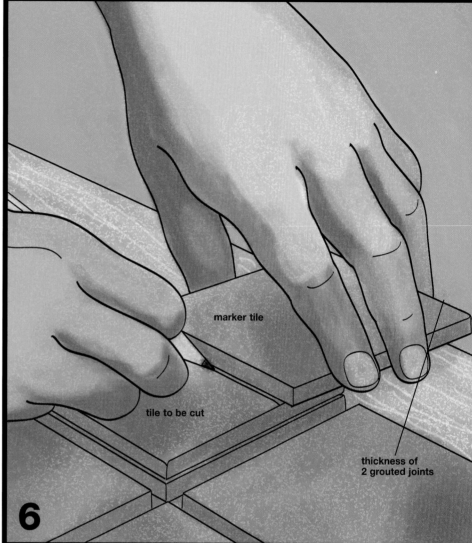

marker tile

tile to be cut

thickness of
2 grouted joints

the cut line.

7 WHEN YOU CAN'T use a trowel to apply the adhesive on the setting surface—as is often the case with tiles that are to be set in tight spaces around the perimeter of a room—you have to do what's called back-buttering individual tiles. Depending on the size of the tile, use a notched trowel or putty knife to spread adhesive on the back. Use enough adhesive so that the tile will be level with the other tiles.

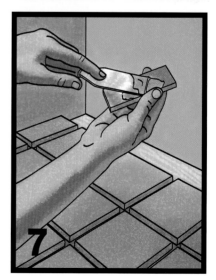

Grouting a tile floor

Grout, a thin mortar mixture used to fill the joints between tiles, protects tile edges from nicks and cracks and helps stop kitchen spills from seeping below the tile surface. The size and color of the grout joints have as much impact on the finished appearance of the floor as the tile itself, so choose and apply grout carefully. Pick a color to complement, match, or contrast the tile. Increase or decrease the joint size to provide a balance based on the room's size.

Grout is usually sold with all the necessary dry ingredients mixed together; you just add the liquid. It is also available, premixed, in caulking-gun and squeeze tubes with wet and dry ingredients already mixed and ready for application.

Apply grout after the adhesive has set, generally 24 hours. For stronger, less permeable, and more stain-resistant grout, mix the powder with latex additive rather than water.

One type of joint you should not grout but should instead caulk is called an expansion joint. Expansion joints allow for movement of the materials beneath the tile and grout due to seasonal and temperature changes. Use expansion joints around the perimeter of all tile installations, especially where tile edges meet a foreign material: i.e., where floors meet walls, countertops meet backsplashes, and where tile meets wood or another material. Also any run of tile that exceeds 24 feet must be interrupted with an expansion

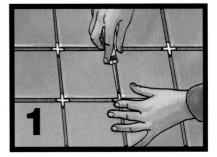

joint.

The most typical method of creating an expansion joint around the perimeter of a floor is to leave a ¼-inch gap between the tile and the wall, then fill the joint with caulk after the grout is dry. Be sure to use silicone—not latex—caulk for this purpose.

1 BEFORE YOU APPLY the grout, remove the spacers between tiles. An awl or other thin tool will make the job easier. Also remove any adhesive that squeezed into the joints between tiles with a razor blade or grout saw. Vacuum the joints and put masking tape over all expansion joints.

2 YOU CAN MIX the dry ingredients with the liquid—whether it's water or latex additive—by hand or with a mortar mixer. To mix grout by hand, measure the liquid and pour it into a large, clean plastic bucket. Add the dry ingredients a little at a time. Stir carefully with a clean trow-

el. Add more dry ingredients as needed. To mix grout with a mortar mixer (when larger amounts are needed), attach the mortar mixer to an electric drill. Set the blade in the mixture, then mix at a slow speed. Don't lift out the blade until it stops turning.

3 PUT ENOUGH GROUT on the tiles to cover about 3 square feet. Hold the grout float at about a 35-degree angle, and spread the grout diagonally across the tiles. Press the grout firmly and completely into the joints. Make two or three passes, working in a different direction for each pass.

Tilt up the float so it is nearly per-

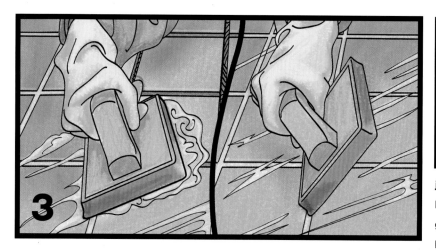

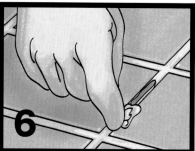

joint, refill it right away. Wearing rubber gloves, press a small amount of grout into the gap, filling it completely. Then shape the joint and remove any excess grout.

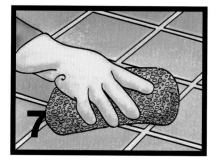

pendicular to the surface, and wipe away excess grout. Move diagonally to the joints to avoid digging into them with the float.

clean out the grout or wait for the grout to dry and cut it out with a grout saw or utility knife. Then let the joint dry completely, and vacuum before caulking.

4 WHEN YOU HAVE FINISHED grouting one area, use a dampened sponge to wipe the tiles in a circular motion. Take care that the joints remain consistent in depth. Rinse the sponge often.

As you work, some grout will invariably seep under the masking tape into the expansion joints. When you have finished grouting the whole floor, either remove the tape and

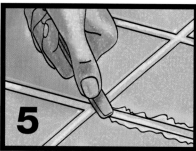

5 AFTER WIPING the tiles with a dampened sponge, clean and shape the joints. Pull a barely dampened sponge along grout lines, removing high spots as you go. Decide whether you like a thick grout line that is nearly flush with the tile surface or one that recedes; either way, make them consistent. Use an adjustable grout shaper, a toothbrush handle, or a wood dowel. The shaper should be a bit wider than the joint.

6 IF YOU NOTICE A GAP or inadvertently pull grout out from a

7 AFTER YOU'VE CLEANED the tile surfaces and shaped the joints, let the grout set up for another 15 to 20 minutes. Then, wearing gloves, clean the tiles thoroughly with the sponge and a bucket of clean water. Timing is critical: The grout must be dry enough not to be affected by the sponge, but the haze on the tile surface must not be so dry that it's difficult to remove. Rinse the sponge and wring it out. Pass the sponge slowly over a line of tiles. Flip the sponge over and make another straight run. Rinse the sponge and repeat until you've wiped every tile. After another 15 minutes, polish the tiles with a soft clean rag. (See pages 180–181 for information about sealing tile floors.)

Installing case molding

Case molding—the trim that goes around doors and windows—gives a room an elegant finished look. This highly satisfying task is fairly easy to do but, admittedly, takes a little practice. Start installing the molding in the area of the room that's least visible. Before long, you'll be moving fast and making tidy joinery. The most common mistake is to cut a miter in the wrong direction. Whenever possible, mark the trim pieces carefully for length and for the direction of the cut.

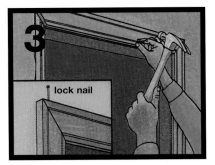

lock nail

3 AFTER YOU'VE CUT the first piece, drill pilot holes and tack of your mark. Hold the molding against the back of the miter box. Grasp it tightly so it will not slide as you cut it. As an alternative, use a power miter saw or radial-arm saw.

the piece in place (don't countersink the nails yet). Then work on the top piece: Cut a piece of trim with a miter at one end to fit against the vertical piece you installed first. Fit the miters together, mark and miter the other end, and tack the top molding in place. Measure and miter the second vertical piece of trim and fit it to the top piece. It might be necessary to use a block plane to make this second miter fit perfectly. Around a window, measure and miter the bottom piece, and tack it into place. When you're satisfied with the fit of the miters, face-nail the last piece.

jamb

¼" reveal on edge

1 WHEN INSTALLING molding around a door or window, work in a clockwise fashion. Cut the bottom of the first vertical piece off straight, set it in place, and mark the top for a miter cut. It's best to hold the piece in place and mark it with a knife, rather than using a tape measure. For window and door casings, take into account the ¼-inch reveal on the edge of the jamb. As a guide, use a compass set to ¼ inch to mark the reveal on the jamb.

2 TO CUT THE MITER, sight down the blade of the saw and slide the molding until the saw will cut only a millimeter or two to the scrap side

In the market for molding?

The cost of molding adds up, so determine ahead of time exactly how many pieces of each size you'll need. On a piece of paper, make a column for each size—8 feet, 10 feet, 12 feet, and so on. As you measure for individual pieces, tally how many you need under each column. If you have an old house, you may want to match moldings that are not available at your local home center. A lumberyard with a mill or a millwork company may make replicas, or you can make a reasonable facsimile with a router, tablesaw, radial-arm saw, and a belt sander.

Molding style

Molding, also called trim or casing, comes in many different styles. The molding you choose helps define the look of a room, whether it's minimalist or decorative. Molding is available in lengths from 6 to 16 feet. Most is made from softwood, such as pine. Some popular styles are available in oak too.

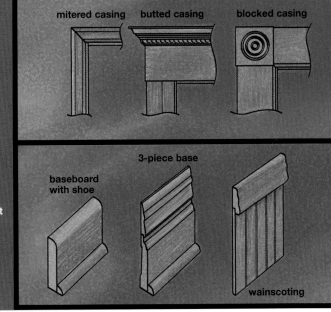

mitered casing   butted casing   blocked casing

baseboard with shoe   3-piece base   wainscoting

Drill pilot holes through the top edge of each corner into the ends of the verticals and lock-nail the joints. Then countersink the nails and fill the nail holes.

Installing base molding

Install all door and window casing before you begin installing base molding around the bottom perimeter of the walls.

The three basic types of base molding include ranch and colonial, which are the most common, and a three-piece base that's more formal and traditional. After the base molding is in, the quarter-round, or base shoe, which bends easily with variations in the flooring and protects the base from vacuum-cleaner scuffs, is installed.

Note: Don't be tempted simply to miter-cut molding for the inside corners. Imperfect miters lead to unsightly gaps and misaligned joints because the corners are nearly never true 90-degree angles. Instead cut the first piece to length with a regular 90-degree cut and cope-cut the second piece.

To do this, cut the first piece of molding at a 90-degree angle so it butts against the adjacent wall. To cope the overlapping piece, make an inside 45-degree miter cut. Use a coping saw to cut away the excess wood along the molding profile. Back-cut slightly (cut a little more off the back of the piece than the front) to ensure a neat fit. If possible, make the cut on the coped end first, hold the piece in place, then mark the cut on the other piece.

Top-notch trim

THIN STOCK, which is often used for baseboard molding, splits and cracks easily. When you need to drive a nail within 3 inches of the edge of a piece, drill a pilot hole first. Attach short pieces of molding with construction adhesive. DRIVE IN only as many nails as you need to hold the molding firmly against the wall. IF YOU ARE staining your molding, do it before you install it. If you are painting it, install the molding first, then paint.

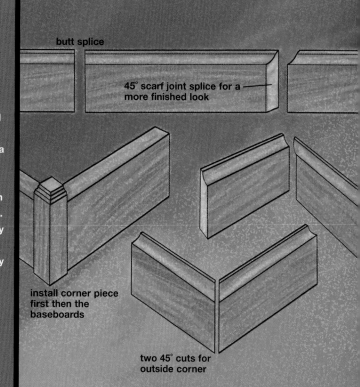

butt splice

45° scarf joint splice for a more finished look

install corner piece first then the baseboards

two 45° cuts for outside corner

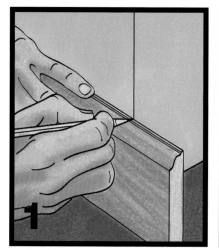

bow slightly for a tight fit

1 **FOR THE GREATEST ACCURACY** in the fit of the molding, hold and mark the pieces in place wherever possible. For an outside corner, butt one end of the molding in place, letting the other end extend past the corner of the wall. Make the mark exactly even with the corner.

2 **MARK AND CUT** the piece about $1/16$ inch longer than the space. Make sure any casing is well secured, so it doesn't move when you press against it. Push the baseboard in place by bending it into position to create a tight fit on both sides. Nail molding into place and fill the holes.

Installing crown molding

Crown molding is literally the crown at the top of a room, and, like a jeweled crown, it can transform an ordinary space into an elegant, aesthetically pleasing one. Home centers, lumberyards, and millworks offer many molding profiles, so you have a multitude of options for adding this attractive topper to your kitchen.

Crown molding installation takes patience, and a few tricks of the trade don't hurt, either. If you're comfortable with basic carpentry tools and know how to cope molding miters, you'll have few problems. Careful fitting and refitting are the keys to getting a close fit between sections of molding. (Tip: Arrange to have your saw professionally sharpened before you begin this job. A sharpened saw provides better control and a cleaner cut, which undoubtedly makes your work more pleasant.)

Because you will be working over your head, a solid working platform makes all the difference in both your comfort and the success of the installation. Don't attempt the careful fitting and nailing that crown molding requires while standing on a stepladder. The job will be much easier if you find a plank and two sturdy sawhorses to make a platform to stand on while installing the molding. You'll also need another set of hands. Get a helper to hold the lengths of molding while you measure, position, and fasten them.

Before you begin this challenging project, review the following:

MEASURING AND MARKING: Use a steel measuring tape to get the most accurate measurements. Note that on the first few inches of most tapes, each inch is divided into ⅟₃₂-inch increments for extra-fine measurements. When you're making a mark for cutting, make a V mark, not a line, with an extra-sharp pencil. When you cut material, the saw blade reduces some of it to sawdust. When measuring, allow for the opening left in the blade's wake, called the kerf, usually about ⅛ inch wide. If you're making just one cut, account for the kerf by marking the waste side of the cutoff line with an X, so there's no confusion when it comes to which side to cut.

HOW TO USE A MITER BOX: A miter box is essentially a jig for holding the saw at the proper angle to the work as you cut. Before placing the piece of molding in the miter box, support it on a scrap of lumber or other material. This allows you to saw completely through the work without marring the bottom of the miter box. Place the molding against the far side of the miter box, positioned as it will be when in use, and make the cut with a backsaw. Hold the work firmly against the back of the box with your free hand.

NAILING TECHNIQUES: Drive the heads of finishing or casing nails below the surface. Fill the hole with wood putty later. Hold a nail set against the nail head and tap it in.

1 TO GET A PERFECTLY MITERED look in corners that are seldom perfectly square, run the first piece of crown molding tightly into the cor-

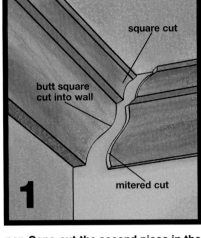

ner. Cope-cut the second piece in the shape of the profile of the molding, so it butts neatly against the face of the first piece (see "Installing base molding" on page 167).

2 USE A DEEP MITER BOX and a fine-toothed backsaw to make a cut that reveals the profile of the molding. Think upside down as you make miter cuts on crown molding: Position the molding so that it's upside down in the miter box. Double-check which edge of the molding belongs at the top; the difference can be quite subtle. Place the face of the molding that goes against the ceiling on the bottom of the miter box. Remember, for inside corners, the bottom of the crown molding will be the longest edge. (Tip: Use plenty of clamps to hold the molding while you cut it. The less you have to rely on your own holding power, the more easily and accurately you'll make the saw cuts.)

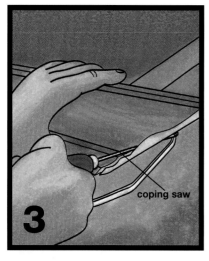

3 IF YOUR MITERED CUT is correct, you'll be able to see the profile of the molding. Cut away the excess wood along the back side of the molding with a coping saw. Err on the side of removing too much rather than too little; only the outermost edge of the coped molding will be seen. (Tool tip: Buy new saw blades before you start this project. They break easily, so have a half-dozen on hand.)

4 TO FINE-TUNE YOUR CUT use a utility knife to remove any excess material you missed with the coping saw. Be careful that you don't cut into the exposed face of the molding. Hold the piece in place to

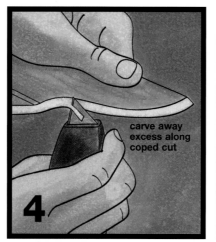

test the fit. Take it down and carve it further, if necessary.

5 MAP OUT THE JOB so one end of each piece of molding will be cut straight and one end will be mitered and coped. Use butt joints (see page 167) for long runs. Save the most visible areas of the kitchen for last. By then you will have honed your coping skills.

6 IF THE MOLDING RUNS perpendicular to the ceiling joists, determine the location of the joists—before you begin nailing the molding in place—so that you can nail into

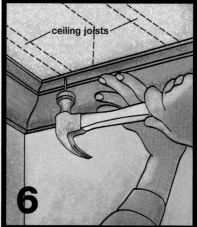

them. Drill pilot holes to keep the molding from splitting, then tack the molding in place with a few nails. Stand back and take a good look at its positioning before you complete the nailing.

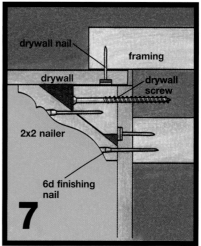

7 IF THE MOLDING RUNS parallel to the ceiling joists, you'll need to provide a solid nailing area. Cut a beveled face of 2×2, as shown above. Cut the 2×2 to length and screw it into the wall in the corner of the ceiling and the wall. The 2×2 provides a solid surface to which you can nail the molding.

installing a range hood

The difficulty of installing a range hood varies greatly, depending on what your house is made of. If you have an older house with double-brick construction, cutting a hole for the vent most likely will be a major job; if you have a wood-frame house, on the other hand, it may take just an hour or two. Running the vent duct is a pretty straightforward job: Simply connect the vent pieces with screws and seal each joint with duct tape.

While each house may require a slightly different path of ductwork, every path winds up in the same place: outside. Don't vent a range hood into an attic or crawlspace; the grease it emits creates a fire hazard. If venting your range outside isn't practical, purchase a ductless hood that captures grease in washable filters. A major disadvantage to the ductless hood, however, is that it doesn't get rid of heat, moisture, or odor.

Be sure to purchase the right size fan for your range. Vent fans are rated according to how many cubic feet of air per minute (CFM) they can move. Many variables come into account when figuring out how powerful a fan you need. The average cook with a residential-type range fares well with a vent rated at 150 CFM. If you have a commercial-style range, you'll need something with more power.

In addition, know that the greater the vent length, the stronger your fan needs to be, and a flexible duct is less efficient than a smooth duct. The larger the fan, the larger diameter the vent duct should be.

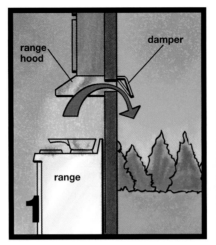

1 VENTING OUT OF THE WALL is the easiest and most common way to vent a range hood. Use the template provided by the manufacturer to locate the hole. If you have a wood-frame house, cut the hole with a saber saw; use a drill with a masonry bit and a cold chisel if you have to pass through brick. A damper keeps drafts from entering the house.

2 IF YOU CAN'T GO through a wall, venting through the roof is the next best option. For the most efficiency, choose the shortest route to the outside. Run the duct through the cabinet above the range, then cut holes in the attic and the roof. Install a roof jack and be sure to use flashing so the roof doesn't leak.

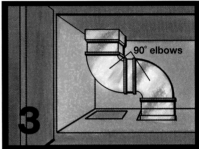

3 IF A DUCT already exists but it's not in the right place, you may be able to tap into it by using elbows. Cover the old hole so the cabinet will be usable. Take extra care in sealing the ductwork at this point so grease doesn't leak into the cabinet later on.

4 IF YOUR ISLAND HAS A COOKTOP or range, you can buy a large vent that comes down from the ceiling, or you can get a cooktop with a built-in downdraft vent. The ductwork for a downdraft vent runs through the floor to the outside.

Running cable for ceiling fixtures

Every kitchen needs some kind of overhead lighting. If there's no cable in the walls for a switch-controlled ceiling fixture, running some is an afternoon's work. First determine the location and direction of the wall studs and ceiling joists. If you can, run the wires parallel to the framing members to save time-consuming work patching and painting. When you cut notches in the drywall, make clean cuts and save the pieces for reinstallment, if possible. When you're done running the cable, all you'll have to do is glue them back in place with construction adhesive and patch the wall with drywall tape and compound. Notches in plaster require more repair work; fill the hole with nonshrinking patching plaster.

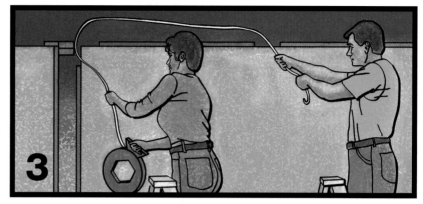

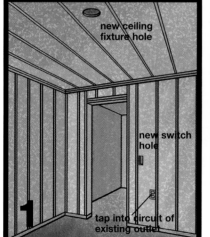

new ceiling fixture hole

new switch hole

tap into circuit of existing outlet

1 DECIDE WHERE you want to hang the fixture. If a framing member is in the way, move the location of the switch or fixture a few inches to one side. If you have to run cable across framing members, make notches at each joist or stud: Cut openings in the drywall that span each of the studs. Save the cutouts for patching later. Chisel a notch in the stud. Install a nail plate to protect the cable, and patch the wall. Then cut the holes for the switch and fixture (see pages 123–125).

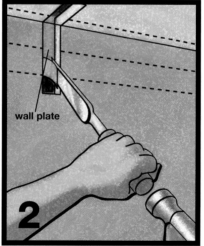

wall plate

2 AT THE POINT WHERE the wall and the ceiling meet, make a 1-inch-wide opening. Extend the opening at least 1 inch below the wall plate and 2 inches at the ceiling. Chisel a channel just deep enough to make room for the cable into the framing.

3 SLOWLY FEED FISH TAPE into the opening. If the tape meets resistance, pull back a few feet, shake the tape, and try again. For longer runs, use two tapes, feeding in one from each end and snagging them together.

4 USUALLY THE WALL CAVITY provides a clear enough path to push the cable down through the wall to the switch opening. If not, work a fish tape up, and pull the cable to the switch box opening. Staple the cable into the notches before patching the wall and ceiling.

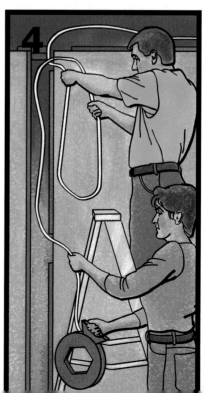

Installing overhead lighting

When it comes to overhead kitchen light fixtures, options are myriad, but only a couple of methods for attaching them to electrical boxes prevail. If you are simply replacing an existing fixture, you can probably install the new one right on the old box. Simply make sure the hardware on the old and new fixtures match up. Closely inspect the old wires for cracked and discolored insula-tion. If any looks worn, strip it back to where it is sound (see page 126).

If you are adding an overhead fixture where there wasn't one before, refer to pages 124–125 and page 171 for how to install the boxes and cable you'll need. As always, shut off the power before doing any electrical work.

1 IF THE SCREW OR BOLT HOLES in your fixture's canopy match those in the electrical box, choose from the three mounting systems shown below at left. For fixtures with side mount-ing bolts, adapt by fastening a strap to the box. Some straps have several screw-in holes to choose from. For center-mounted fixtures, screw a nip-ple into the center hole of a strap and secure it in place with a locknut. If your box has a center stud, attaching a hickey is another way you can adapt the box to fit the new fixture.

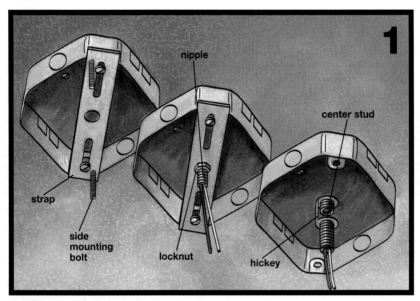

nipple

center stud

strap

side mounting bolt

locknut

hickey

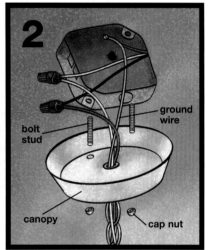

bolt stud

ground wire

canopy

cap nut

2 TO INSTALL A HANGING fixture, attach the canopy with a pair of bolt studs screwed directly into the box. Connect the wires and coil them up inside the box. Push the canopy into place so the studs poke through the holes. Secure the canopy with cap nuts.

3 TO INSTALL TRACK LIGHTING, attach the canopy using one of the mounting systems shown in Step 1. Connect the wires from the fixture box to the connector unit (see page 127). Install the connector unit to the canopy. Measure from the wall that is visually most important and draw

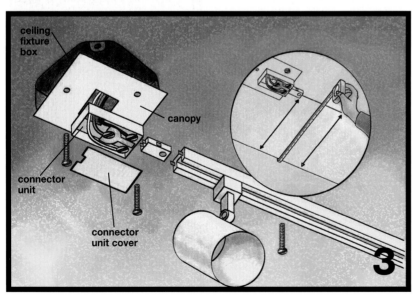

ceiling fixture box

canopy

connector unit

connector unit cover

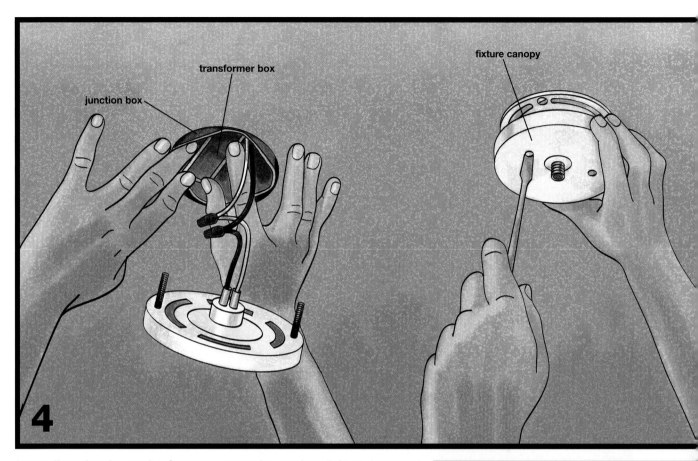

junction box

transformer box

fixture canopy

4

layout lines for the tracks. Connect the track to the connector unit, then fasten the track firmly to the ceiling. Snap on the connector covers. Twist each light into place on the track. Be sure to follow the manufacturer's installation instructions specific to your fixture.

4 TO INSTALL a low-voltage hanging light fixture, use an electrical junction box at the site of the light fixture. Connect the wires as you would for a hanging fixture (see Step 2 on page 172). Mount the transformer inside the box using the adhesive patches that are provided.

5 INSTALL THE FIXTURE CANOPY as you would install a standard fixture. Decide how far down you

want the pendant light to hang and add 1¼ inches. Cut the coaxial cable and strip off 1¼ inches of the outer wrap. Strip ½ inch of plastic insulation from the inner wires of the coaxial cable (see page 126). Feed the coaxial cable into the bottom of the conical connector.

6 WITH AN ALLEN WRENCH, fasten the strain relief on the cable, overlapping the stripped end of the outer wrap. Follow the manufacturer's instructions to be sure the cable is seated. Tighten the allen screw that grips the strain relief inside the conical connector. Screw the conical connector into the canopy. Insert the light bulb.

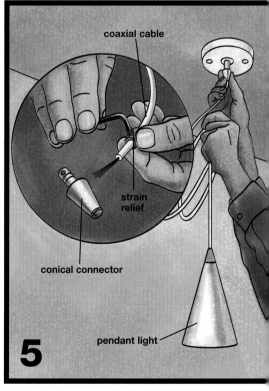

coaxial cable

strain relief

conical connector

pendant light

5

Installing recessed lighting

Recessed ceiling lights have gained popularity for several good reasons: They're inexpensive and unobtrusive, and they provide soft, pleasant general lighting minus the shadows cast by other types of ceiling fixtures (especially when connected to a dimmer switch). What is perhaps most appealing to do-it-yourselfers, though, is their ease of installation: If you don't have a fixture box already in place, don't worry. They come with one attached.

Buy units with silver or white reflectors for the most brightness, or black reflectors for more subdued lighting. Recessed lighting fixtures come in a variety of sizes. Be sure the ones you buy will fit in your ceiling space. If your ceiling joists are smaller than 2×10, for instance, you will need to buy a fixture with a side-mounted box.

1 **RECESSED FIXTURES** are designed for installation where there's no access from above—a common problem when you want to add recessed lighting in a first-floor kitchen ceiling of a two-story house. Recessed units sit on top of drywall or plaster and can be installed from below. The mounting frame spreads out the weight of the unit.

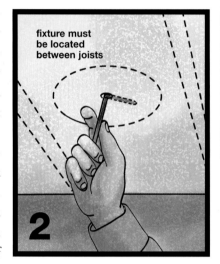

2 **DETERMINE THE GENERAL** location of the light fixture, then drill an exploratory hole in the ceiling. To be sure a joist is not in the way of the intended location, insert a bent wire into the hole and spin it around in a circumference that follows that of the fixture. If the site is clear, carefully mark and cut an opening with a keyhole saw.

fixture must be located between joists

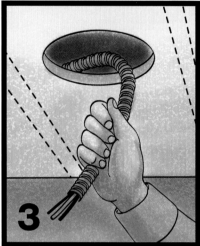

3 **FOR THE ROUGH WIRING,** simply run cable to the hole where the fixture will go. Leave a foot or so of extra cable hanging out of the hole.

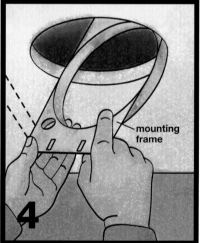

4 **SLIP THE MOUNTING** frame through the hole—it should just fit—and place it so the flange sits in the hole. Pull the cable through the mounting frame. Strip about 6 inches of sheathing from the cable and about ¾ inch of insulation from each wire (see page 126).

mounting frame

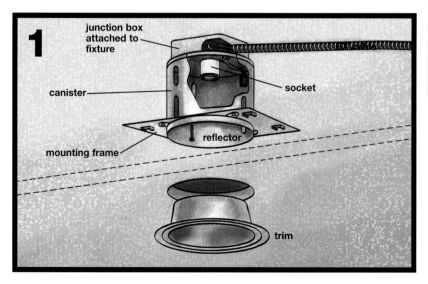

junction box attached to fixture

canister

socket

mounting frame

reflector

trim

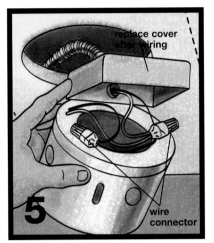

5 **REMOVE THE COVER PLATE** from the fixture's electrical box. Secure the cable to the box and connect the wires in the box. Follow the same procedures as if you were wiring a regular box (see pages 128 and 131). Push the wires into the box, and replace the cover plate.

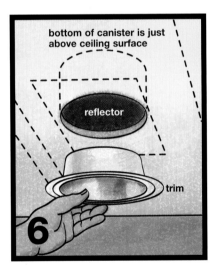

6 **FINISH IT OFF** by sliding the canister up through the mounting plate until it is slightly recessed above the ceiling. Secure it to the mounting plate by tightening the screws. Attach the reflector. Screw in a lightbulb and attach the trim.

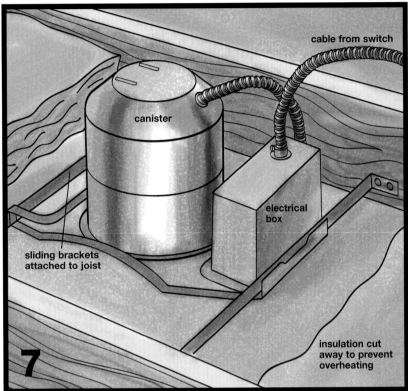

7 **SEVERAL TYPES** of recessed lights are available, all with their own ways of connecting to the ceiling. The type shown here works well if you do have access to the space above your kitchen ceiling. Once the fixture is positioned over the hole, sliding brackets attached to the canister extend out to reach joists on either side. With brackets secured to the joists, the unit is more firmly attached than most other recessed fixtures. As with all recessed fixtures, this style comes with its own electrical box.

To install, pound a nail through the ceiling in the place you want to install the light. Go into the space above, find the nail, cut back the insulation, and cut a hole for the cannister. Install the reflector in the canister. Set the canister in the hole, slide out the brackets, and attach it to the joists with nails or general purpose screws. Wire the box, screw in a bulb, and attach the trim.

Stay cool!

It's necessary to take precautions with recessed lighting fixtures to prevent them from building up a lot of heat, which can damage your ceiling, melt wire insulation, or even cause a fire. First, give the fixture room to breathe: Keep ceiling insulation at least 3 inches clear of it, and don't place it in a cramped space. Be sure to use the bulbs of the recommended type and wattage, and don't leave flammable materials, such as scraps of insulation paper, near the fixture.

Adding under-cabinet lighting

Illuminated countertops go far in creating a cheery, user-friendly kitchen. Undercabinet lighting makes for a sparkling decorative effect, especially on pretty stone countertops, while providing excellent task lighting at the same time. When your kitchen isn't in demand, undercabinet lighting connected to a dimmer switch can be turned down to create a soft, quiet mood.

The low-voltage halogen lighting shown here is simple to install, especially if your cabinets are already in place. If you're in the process of installing cabinets, or if you don't like

halogen lights, you can install thin (1- to 1½-inch thick) fluorescent units that connect to electrical cable behind the walls. If you're installing undercabinet fluorescent lighting, plan on one 20-watt unit per 3 running feet of countertop. For halogens, use one 12-watt unit per 3 feet. For incandescent lighting, use one 75-watt unit for every 3 feet of countertop.

In addition to the method of installation, halogen and fluorescent lights differ in another way too. Halogen lighting is bright, clear-white light. Fluorescent light tends to be more blue-green.

If your wall cabinets hang at the

standard 54 inches above the floor and 18 inches above the countertop, the lights will rest below eye level.

Halogen systems usually come in a kit, with the number of lights and the length of the wires predetermined. Plan your job well before you purchase lights—and shut off the power before you begin installing them.

1 **DETERMINE A LOCATION for each light fixture, keeping in mind two considerations: You don't want the lights to shine in your eyes as you work at the counter, and lights can not be installed near combustible materials, such as paper plates or**

light fixture base

light fixture with trim ring and lens

power block

transformer

120-volt receptacle

Cove lighting

If your wall cabinets don't bump up against the ceiling, consider adding a dramatic lighting effect to your kitchen by placing fluorescent fixtures on top of the cabinets. The light, directed upward, will create a halo effect around your kitchen. Installing cove lighting is easy because there is little wiring to hide. Simply run exposed cables and place the fixtures toward the rear of the top of the cabinets. A piece of cove molding hides the bulbs from view.

napkins (halogen lamps get quite hot). Remove the trim ring and lens from each light fixture and attach them with screws to the underside of the cabinet. Select screws of the right length, so they don't poke up through the cabinet.

Drill small holes to allow the wires to pass into the cabinet. Plug the ends of the wires into the power block, which is mounted inside the cabinet. Run another wire to the transformer. Because the wires cannot be cut, you will have to hide excess wire inside the cabinet. Drill a hole and run a wire from a receptacle to the transformer.

2 TO ASSEMBLE THE LIGHTS, plug the halogen bulb into the socket. Install the lens cover. Most halogen kits come with a CAUTION label warning of the bulb's heat. For safety's sake, put it in a place where guests in your kitchen can see it.

3 THE SWITCH OPERATES on battery power, so it can be installed anywhere in the kitchen without further wiring. Put it wherever it is most convenient for you. Attach the switch housing by screwing it into the wall. If you can't find a stud to attach it to, use plastic anchors. Screw the cover plate to the switch housing.

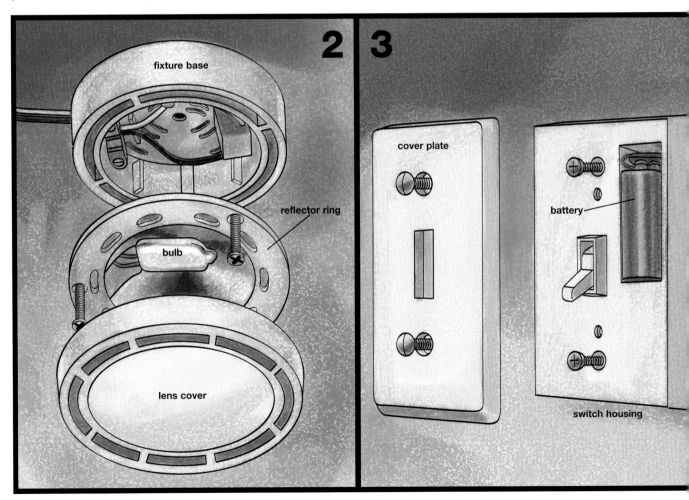

2 fixture base

reflector ring

bulb

lens cover

3 cover plate

battery

switch housing

10

finishing touches

YOU'VE REACHED THE HOME STRETCH. At this point in the process, you can cook up a five-course gourmet meal, a Sunday dinner, or simply pour yourself a cup of coffee and enjoy the scenery. But would you have a place to sit? Your kitchen may be fully functional at this point, but it may not be furnished. Or painted or wallpapered or personalized with your collection of pottery, oil paintings, or cookbooks. Ironically it's the last few details that may be the most difficult to get to, when your house is in decidedly less chaos than it was when the refrigerator was in the living room and there was drywall dust in your eyebrows. But those details are the very things that make your new kitchen look finished and feel truly your own. You may have some ideas about the color scheme you'd like to use or the seating arrangement that would be most comfortable, but those ideas are still forming. With a little interior design guidance and a few pointers on products, these pages will help you refine your vision.

A funky 1960s-style print fabric window treatment gives this contemporary-cum-retro lime green kitchen, *opposite,* a fun twist. What to hang in the windows is just one of the design decisions you'll have to make in putting the proverbial icing on the cake. Color is clearly the dominant design element in this kitchen.

Cover me

This countertop's unglazed hexagon tiles were thoroughly and carefully sealed to prevent stains and to simplify cleanup.

If you've installed a ceramic tile, concrete, or stone (such as granite, marble, slate, or limestone) countertop or floor, you have one more step to take to ensure that they wear well and look great for years to come: sealing the surface.

Tile and grout sealers

The sealers used to protect unglazed tile, stone, and concrete products after they have cured are also applied to grout. Three basic types of sealer are used.

PENETRATING SEALERS, as their name implies, are absorbed beneath the surface of the tile and grout. They reduce the absorbency of the surface without adding a sheen. They're an ideal choice for a terra-cotta tile you want to keep rustic-looking but also want to resist staining.

COATING SEALERS remain on the surface of the tile and lend a glossy or semigloss sheen.

GROUT SEALER, painted on only the grout lines between glazed tiles, keeps grout watertight and makes it easier to clean. Normally it's necessary to wait two weeks after tile installation before applying grout sealer.

Sealing stone

Natural materials vary in hardness, durability, and resistance to staining. All stone has some level of porosity, which varies from slab to slab. The densest stone is often the most expensive, so check with a stone dealer in your area to find the least porous stone you can afford.

After your countertop or floor is installed and polished with the sheen or texture you desire, it must be sealed to protect it from greasy spills, which can soak into the material and stain the surface. To keep your stone countertops or floors in top condition, reseal them annually. If you choose stone tiles instead of slab, you'll need to seal the grout to make cleaning easier.

Marble is especially porous, so it's best to limit its use in the kitchen. Because it stays cool to the touch, marble is ideal for rolling out pastry or cookie dough. Many cooks have a marble insert in the countertop located in the baking area of their kitchen.

Among all of the stone types available for countertop use, porosity varies most widely with slate. Domestic slate is the densest; if you are considering buying slate from Italy, India, or another country, find out how porous it is before you agree to buy.

An ounce of prevention

Sealing your tile, stone, or concrete floors and countertops isn't a guarantee that they'll remain mark-free forever. You can, however, take steps to keep them looking their best.

USE COASTERS to prevent water rings.

AVOID PLACING hot pots or pans, which can damage the glossy finish of some stone (as can hard plates or silverware), directly on the countertop surface.

LIGHTLY SAND SLATE, soapstone, or limestone to remove surface nicks and marks.

CLEAN STONE WITH stone soap (available at hardware stores or stone dealers) or mild dishwashing liquid added to warm water. Rinse well to remove excess cleanser, as the residue leaves a film and causes streaks.

DON'T LET FOODS or products that contain lemon, vinegar, or other acids sit on the countertop for any length of time; they can mar or dull the surface.

Seal every surface

The majority of the surface area in this kitchen, *above*, requires sealing. The granite countertop had to be sealed immediately after it was installed. Experts recommend that you reseal your granite (and other stone) surfaces annually to keep them in the best shape. Although the ceramic tile floor in this kitchen is glazed, the grout lines must be sealed to prevent stains from spilled liquids and food, and soil from foot traffic. The cement countertop and slate backsplash, *left*, also require sealing. Cement is sealed after it has cured (curing greatly increases its strength), usually a period of about 7 days after it's poured. Slate must be sealed immediately after installation. Of all types of stone used for countertops, backsplashes, and flooring, slate varies most widely in terms of porosity. Domestic slate is the densest and therefore the most stain-resistant. Slate from Italy or India is less porous and requires even more careful sealing and maintenance.

Begin the process of choosing a color for your kitchen by asking yourself whether or not you can live with your choice day in and day out, for years to come, through many meals, homework sessions, and parties. The kitchen is perhaps the most used room in the house, so the color you choose for it should be highly livable.

Although colors come and go with the winds of fashion, some classic kitchen color schemes have stood the test of time. Perhaps the most basic scheme for the kitchen is white. White—often accented with one color, such as blue—is a popular choice for the kitchen because it looks clean and helps to visually soften the clutter a kitchen is prone to. Kitchens are also a tremendous financial investment, and white never goes out of style.

If you do choose a mostly white scheme for your kitchen, you can keep it from looking sterile and cold by accenting it with natural materials that have easy-to-live-with tones of their own. Wood floors add a warm element to kitchens, as do natural-finish or stained wood cabinets, stone countertops and floors, and ceramic tile in colors other than white. Remember, too, that there are multitudes of whites, both cool and warm.

Brighten your day with color
Although the color scheme in this kitchen is very bold and vibrant, clean lines and solid swaths of color without a lot of pattern keep the room looking simple and fresh.

Color determines the mood of the room. Soft, cool tones such as green, blue, and violet—as well as neutrals such as white, gray, and tan—set a mood of tranquility and ease; deeper tones of green, blue, and violet have a dramatic effect. Warm tones such as red, yellow, and orange envelop and energize. Just as the all-white kitchen remains a classic for a reason, so, too, does the red dining room. Studies have shown that exposure to red increases the appetite.

Whether you have a penchant for pastels or a yearning for bold, vibrant color combinations, ensure the success of your kitchen's color scheme—and your satisfaction with it—simply by following a few guidelines:

PICK ONE COLOR as an overall base color, then one or two (at the most) accent colors. Complementary colors—those located across from one another on the color wheel—intensify each other and inject energy into a space. Colors that sit next to each other on the color wheel, called analogous colors, visually soften an area and make it seem more serene. Easy-to-live-with neutrals, such as taupe, tan, black, white, and cream, are easily combined. These hues are timeless classics; they make great choices for kitchens of many design styles.

Beyond color
Color isn't the only thing to consider when putting the finishing touches on your kitchen. Texture and pattern come into play too. Because the kitchen has a lot going on both visually and literally, it's a good idea to use pattern sparingly and to keep what pattern is used pretty simple. Geometrics, such as checks, stripes, and plaids work well, as do airy florals and classic fabrics, such as toile and Provençal-style prints.

Texture reflects or absorbs light and helps define style. Smooth surfaces reflect more light than dimensional surfaces, thereby making a room brighter. The smooth surfaces in a kitchen not only promote easy cleanup, they also have a design aspect. If you prefer a sleek, contemporary look (think stainless steel), use more smooth surfaces. If you like a touch of rusticity, consider using some surfaces that have texture. That may be a section of stuccoed wall in the dining area or nubby chenille chair pads. Even an old pine table with dents and knots adds texture to a kitchen.

Color and mood

A fresco-style paint treatment in a shade of pumpkin, *left*, recalls the colors and textures of the hill towns of Italy. Using warm colors such as orange, yellow, and red makes a room feel inviting and embracing and increases the energy of the space as well. Cool colors such as blue, violet, and green have less energy but are calming and serene. They also make a space look fresh and airy. Even a cool color, however, can have warm overtones. Note that the shade of green in this 1930s-era kitchen, *below,* leans toward yellow rather than blue. It may look like a bold and adventuresome color choice but is actually fairly authentic to the period.

PAINT IS A GREAT cost-effective way to bring color to a kitchen. You can paint your kitchen a color you love and, if you no longer love it in a few years, you can change it without great expense or hassle.

LOOK FOR COLOR-SCHEME CUES in your closet. You probably wear colors you love and can live with every day. Look also to a favorite painting or the dishes you inherited from your grandmother, or even to fond recollections you have of places you've been in your travels. Perhaps you love the serene gray granite of the mountains, the salmon pink of a villa in Italy, or the vibrant colors of Mexico. If you select a color scheme based on something you love, walking into your kitchen will be a pleasant experience each day.

Paint aplenty

Rich colors and decorative scrolls painted on cabinets and chairs give this kitchen a distinctly Tyrolean look. Even the floor is painted. Specially formulated floor paint will wear far better than standard paint. A gloss finish is easiest to clean.

A visit to a paint store or to your local home center's paint aisle boggles the mind, given the types, brands, and colors of paint that stock the shelves. Knowing the attributes and typical uses of different types of paint will help you choose the right one for your walls.

Oil or water?

Latex paint has a water base. Compared with oil-base paint, it is less likely to fade, chalk, or crack. Recent advances have made latex as adhesive as and longer-lasting than oil-base. It cleans up with soap and water and dries in one to six hours.

Most of the liquid in oil-base or alkyd paint is made of petroleum solvent. It has excellent adhesion and durability but is more likely than latex to harden, become brittle, and yellow over time. It has a strong odor and must be cleaned up with mineral spirits. Drying time is 8 to 24 hours.

You can paint latex over oil-base as long as you are painting over fewer than four layers of old oil-base. Avoid painting oil-base over latex, however, because the latex will expand and contract, causing an oil-base top coat to crack. To identify the paint type on a wall, rub mineral spirits on the surface. Oil-base will dissolve; latex will be unaffected.

Prime condition

Priming is necessary when working with new or weathered wood, raw surfaces such as new drywall, and on uneven or deteriorated painted surfaces or stripped surfaces. Primers and sealers come in latex or oil. Choose a primer that has the same base as your paint. Some primers are formulated for special circumstances, such as stain-blocking, drywall, wall-paper, or metal primers.

Keep the mildew out

Mildewcide is a chemical additive that prevents mildew growth on paint—it does not kill existing mildew. Usually in liquid form, it can be added to the paint at a paint store. While a kitchen is a higher-moisture room than the living room, adding mildewcide to your kitchen paint is not a necessity.

Custom colors

A custom color has to be tinted and mixed, whether it's a color-chip shade or one mixed to your specifications. For the

Texturizing with paint
The simple but eye-catching swirling effect on these cabinets was achieved by a technique called combing.

Paint techniques

Once you've decided on a paint color and sheen, you're not necessarily finished making decisions about your paint job. You may decide simply to cover your walls in one solid color, or you may opt for a special effect. Paint effects can be as simple as sponging or ragging, or more complicated, such as fresco, color wash, combing, or even trompe l'oeil.

Here's how to achieve the two simplest and most popular paint effects in your kitchen. You can use two or more colors—just be sure they are of the same intensity to achieve a balanced look that is not jarring to the eye. Two or three closely related shades of the same color give a soft, luminous effect to the walls.

SPONGING: Paint walls with a base coat. When base is dry, moisten a clean sponge in water and wring it out well. Dip the sponge into paint, then blot on paper. Stamp the wall lightly with the sponge, changing position slightly each time to vary the pattern.

RAGGING: Paint walls with a base coat and let dry. Loosely bunch up a damp, clean, absorbent rag and dip it into the paint. Blot the rag on paper, then lightly press it to the wall. Rebunch and rotate the rag to vary the pattern. When the rag begins to dry out, repeat the process, beginning with dipping it into the paint.

closest match, most retail outlets of major paint manufacturers have a colorimeter, a machine that electronically scans an item, then reproduces the color in paint.

Sheen

Of the four paint sheens, flat paint is the least reflective type. It hides imperfections, so it's best for ceilings.

Eggshell, satin, or low-luster are basically synonymous. They're best used in places where you want an easy-to-clean surface—such as a kitchen.

Semigloss is more reflective than eggshell paint. It appears a shade lighter on the wall than it does on the paint strip.

Gloss is the most durable and stain-resistant sheen. It is also more likely than other types to highlight imperfections. Use gloss or semigloss on trim, doors, and cabinets.

choosing wallpaper

The full range of styles, colors, and finishes available makes choosing the perfect wallpaper a real challenge. Use the following information to select patterns with success.

1. COLOR. Like paint, the color of your paper sets the mood of the room. To make your kitchen appear larger and the ceiling higher, choose patterns with cool-color backgrounds, such as green, blue, or violet. To the eye, these hues seem to recede. Soft cool colors set a mood of tranquility, while intense cool colors set a mood that's fresh and dramatic. Warm colors such as reds, yellows, and oranges live up to their "warm" label and actually make people feel warmer. Warm tones are a popular choice in colder climates and work especially well if your kitchen faces north. The more intense the color, the more excitement it brings to a kitchen.

2. SCALE. Small-scale patterns make a room feel spacious, while large-scale designs make a room feel more intimate. To give flat walls depth, consider a large, open dimensional pattern, which gives the sense of looking beyond the walls.

3. STYLE. For a more formal look, choose a large-scale pattern in a dramatic color. For a fun, bright style, pick a small motif that's open and regularly spaced, such as polka dots. Don't forget the decorative impact of borders. Available in multitudes of motifs and styles appropriate for the kitchen, borders quickly establish the theme of your room.

4. LIGHT. If your kitchen faces north or is short on windows, look for wallcoverings that reflect light, such as patterns with light colors and those with metallic or iridescent inks. Also consider patterns with smooth surfaces, simply because they reflect the most light. Dark colors absorb light, making walls appear closer together and, in turn, the room smaller. Textured surfaces tend to make walls look darker.

5. PATTERN. A room devoid of pattern can be dull, but a room with too much pattern will give you the jitters. If you're mixing stripes, florals, or plaids in the kitchen, or between adjacent areas, such as a breakfast room or family room, pick patterns that repeat the same color or values of

that color. Wallcovering books usually group designs by color to make coordinating easy.

6. ACCENTS. Stripes and other vertical patterns, which emphasize height, suggest dignity, vitality, and formality. Vertical patterns, including florals where the motif's shape suggests a V or a U, will make a ceiling appear higher. Horizontal patterns accent width, suggest quietness and repose, and make narrow rooms appear wider.

7. TEXTURE. Patterns with real or perceived texture can effectively hide, or camouflage, imperfections in the drywall or plaster or architectural elements that are an eyesore to the homeowner. Patterns with actual tactile surfaces include grass and string cloth, burlap, foil, expanded vinyl, and fabric. Simulated textures include marble, wood, leather, fabric, and animal skins. A pattern with a layered design also creates a perception of texture even where it does not exist in reality (such as a monochromatic damask design behind a floral pattern).

How much wallpaper do you need?

After you've found the perfect pattern, it's time to determine how many rolls of wallcovering you'll need. Here's how:

CALCULATE THE WALL SPACE to be covered in square feet. Measure a wall from ceiling to floor, then horizontally from corner to corner. Multiply the two figures. Repeat for remaining walls. Add the totals.

IF YOU'RE COVERING a ceiling, calculate square footage by multiplying the width of the floor by the length.

DIVIDE EACH FIGURE by 25 (the average square footage in a standard single roll of wallpaper).

SUBTRACT FROM THE TOTAL one-half single roll for each window and door. This figure is the final number of single rolls needed. Always round fractions to the next-highest whole number. If your wallpaper comes in double rolls, divide this figure by two.

Pretty papers

The strawberry motif on the walls of this banquette, *opposite*, is a fine match for the modified plaid fabric used for the seat cushions and window treatment because a strong, warm color—red—ties the two together. Patterns add interest to a room, but beware of using too much: Overdoing it can make you want to flee the area. A soft, colorwashed blue and white paper, *left*, is reminiscent of the decorative painting on the china. To keep things clean-looking, white was chosen for the cabinets and trim. Simple patterns such as this one work well in the cooking area of the kitchen. With its pots, pans, dirty dishes, and everyday activity, less really is more.

Sit back and enjoy the view

Don't limit yourself to a matching dinette set for the eat-in area of your kitchen. The table, *above*, seats more than four, thanks to the addition of an antique pew on one side. Furnishing your kitchen includes personalizing it with your favorite collections, such as this rustic pottery, *below*.

Given the modern kitchen's many roles, it's not surprising that furnishing it has gone beyond buying cabinets for the walls and a dining set for the eating area. As a gathering spot, the kitchen begs for comfortable seating; as the communication nerve center of the home, it calls for a desk, bookshelves, and filing cabinet.

The first function of the kitchen, however, remains the preparation of food and, if there's dining space, the enjoyment of meals. If you have the space, a kitchen table outfitted with dining chairs is the most comfortable seating arrangement for eating.

Use the style you've chosen for your kitchen as a guide for selecting an appropriate dining set. Maybe you're drawn to the 1950s-style laminate and chrome table you dined on as a child, the one with easy-to-clean vinyl-padded chairs, or perhaps you've always longed for the generosity of a long pine farm table surrounded by ladder-back chairs with rushed seats. Don't assume you have to go out and buy a matching table and chairs the minute you drive in the last nail. Pairing a family heirloom table with an eclectic collection of chairs found at a tag sale or antiques store offers both tradition and character. Remember, the dining arrangement has aspects of both form and function.

If your kitchen doesn't include room for a full table and chairs but does have a peninsula or island for casual meals, you still have several decisions to make about what kind of seating to choose: barstools that are round or square, with backs or not, fitted with seat cushions or sleek and bare, made of chrome or wood, and painted or stained.

If space is limited, but you'd still like to have a dining table in the kitchen, consider a round table. Round tables fit better in small spaces than do square or rectangular ones. A round table about 4 feet in diameter comfortably seats four.

Beyond the table

Kitchen seating isn't limited to the chairs that gather around the kitchen table or the stools that pull up to the eating bar. If you have the room, having a comfortable chair (or two) in the kitchen for visitors who just want to sit down and have a chat with the cook is a plus too. Simply keep one thing in mind: Because the kitchen is a place where grease, steam, drips, and spills are an everyday occurrence, upholstered furniture doesn't work well here as a general rule. Any fabrics used in the kitchen should be stain-resistant and easy to clean. If you have small children, consider machine-washable slipcovers for chairs used in the kitchen. That way, when spaghetti sauce or chocolate pudding gets splattered, your evening won't be ruined.

If you have the space and like the unfitted, furnished look so many people are choosing for their kitchens today, consider installing just a few built-in base and wall cabinets and using freestanding pieces such as an antique armoire or buffet for storing dishes, appliances, and foodstuffs. If the efficiency of such pieces is a concern, have them retrofitted with stationary or pullout shelves.

A word about window dressings

Window treatments serve several functions in a kitchen. They provide privacy, soften the many hard lines and angles inherent in the space, and filter harsh light that comes through the window glass.

When choosing a fabric for your window dressings, consider what else is going on in the room visually. If you have elaborately patterned granite or solid-surfacing countertops, you might consider a solid. If you have a solid laminate countertop, a pattern might perk things up a bit.

Consider, too, whether the fabric you like is appropriate for the kitchen. If there's a sink below the window, don't go with a fabric that stains easily when it's splashed with water. Silk, for example, is famously easy to stain.

One more consideration for your window dressings is whether they have to do more than soften the windows and filter light. Do you want them to block a view or provide privacy? If not, you can mount the treatment up and out of the way so it is merely decorative while you enjoy an unfettered view of your yard or gardens.

Style it right—for you

Limiting the number of base and wall cabinets and choosing a few freestanding pieces instead, such as the hutch, *above*, gives your kitchen the much-sought-after unfitted look. With this kitchen's classic black and white checkerboard floor, '50s-style chrome-and-vinyl diner stools fit right in.

For more information on kitchen design, remodeling, appliances, or products seen in Better Homes and Gardens Complete Kitchens, contact the following sources:

Organizations

The National Kitchen and Bath Association
877/NKBA-PRO
www.nkba.org

Kitchen Cabinets

KraftMaid Cabinetry
800/654-3008
www.kraftmaid.com

Merillat Industries
www.merillat.com

Plain & Fancy Custom Cabinetry
800/447-9006
www.plainfancycabinetry.com

Rutt Custom Cabinetry, LLC
800/420-7888
www.rutt1.com

SieMatic
Maker of high-end European-style cabinetry
900/765-5266
www.siematic.com

Appliances

Amana Appliances
800/843-0304
www.amana.com

Dacor
High-end cooktops, ranges, and ovens
800/793-0093
www.dacor.com

DCS (Dynamic Cooking Systems, Inc.)
Maker of high-end cooktops, ranges, and ovens
800/433-8466
www.dcsappliances.com

Fisher & Paykel Appliances, Inc.
Maker of high-end dishwashers and dish

drawers
800/863-5384
www.fisherpaykel.com

Frigidaire Home Products
800/444-4944
www.frigidaire.com

GE Appliances
800/626-2000
www.geappliances.com

Jenn-Air
Maker of high-end cooktops, ranges, and ovens
800/536-6247
www.jennair.com

Kenmore, by Sears
888/536-6673
www.kenmore.com

KitchenAid
800/422-1230
www.kitchenaid.com

Sub-Zero
Maker of high-end refrigerators and freezers
800/222-7820
www.subzero.com

Thermador
Maker of high-end cooktops, ranges, and ovens
800/656-9226
www.thermador.com

Viking Range Corp.
Maker of high-end cooktops, ranges, and ovens
888/845-4641
www.vikingrange.com

Sinks and Faucets

Delta Faucet Company
www.deltafaucet.com

Elkay
630/572-3192
www.elkay.com

Kohler
1/800-456-4537
www.kohler.com

Moen
1/800-BUY-MOEN
www.moen.com

Other Better Homes and Gardens Resources

Visit our website at bhg.com, where you'll find an interactive kitchen planner. Or, look on your newsstand for the following publications:
Kitchen & Bath Ideas
Kitchen Planning Guide
Kitchen & Bath Products Guide
Remodeling Ideas
Remodeling Products Guide

INDEX